EXPANSIONISM

EXPANSIONISM

Its Effects on Cuba's Independence

Frank R. Villafaña

Routledge
Taylor & Francis Group

LONDON AND NEW YORK

First published 2012 by Transaction Publishers

2 Park Square, Milton Park, Abingdon, Oxfordshire OX14 4RN
711 Third Avenue, New York, NY 10017

Routledge is an imprint of the Taylor & Francis Group, an informa business

First issued in paperback 2017

Copyright © 2012 Taylor & Francis

Library of Congress Catalog Number: 2011023783

Library of Congress Cataloging-in-Publication Data

Villafaña, Frank, 1941-
  Expansionism : its effects on Cuba's independence / Frank R. Villafaña.
     p. cm.
  Includes bibliographical references and index.
  ISBN 978-1-4128-4308-9 (alk. paper)
1. United States—Territorial expansion. 2. Spain—Colonies—America—Administration—History—19th century. 3. Cuba—History—1810-1899. 4. Cuba—History—Insurrection, 1868–1878. 5. Cuba—History—Revolution, 1895–1898. 6. Cuba—History—Autonomy and independence movements. 7. Spanish-American War, 1898. 8. United States—Foreign relations—Cuba. 9. Cuba—Foreign relations—United States. I. Title.
  E179.5.V45 2012
  973.5—dc23
                    2011023783

ISBN 13: 978-1-4128-4308-9 (hbk)
ISBN 13: 978-1-138-50993-1 (pbk)

Contents

List of Figures

Acknowledgments

This book is about a subject which is very close to my heart. My original intention was to conduct some research in an attempt to clarify, for my own edification, some controversial chapters in Cuban, American, and Spanish history. Writing a book was far from my mind, but eventually the research came together, the material flowed, and the manuscript started to look like a book.

Many people and institutions helped this project come to fruition.

I am grateful to Dr. Irving Louis Horowitz, Chairman of the Board and Editorial Director of Transaction Publishers, for his in-depth analysis of my manuscript and the trust he has placed in my ability to produce historical research. My thanks also to the able team of Transaction for making the idea of this book become a physical reality.

Jaime Suchlicki, Director of the Institute for Cuban and Cuban American Studies at the University of Miami, has been particularly helpful. Jaime introduced me to Transaction Publishers, which, in addition to this book, published my *Cold War in the Congo*. Jaime has also assisted in promoting and marketing this book in Miami as well as with the many people in the academic community interested in Cuban studies, and I thank him for his help and support.

Jean-Paul Deschamps, my friend from Belgium, patiently read two versions of this work. He provided invaluable advice on the arrangement of the chapters, pointed out some interesting facts about Napoleon's takeover of Spain, and asked many questions which led me to provide better explanations and more clarity for the reader. I am grateful for Jean-Paul's assistance and encouragement.

Many thanks to my friend Armando González, columnist from Miami's *El Nuevo Herald*, who read a late version of my manuscript and made insightful suggestions as to how to improve reader comprehension. Armando has also provided inestimable aid in promoting this book.

My personal thanks also go to Doug Williams, Roger Presas, Pat Moxley Jones, my brother David Villafaña, sister-in-law Patricia F. Villafaña, and Dr. Anita Buckley. Each of them read different versions of the manuscript, providing important suggestions on ways to improve the content, flow, and organization of the material.

I am grateful to the Library of Congress for allowing me to reproduce maps 2.1, 2.2, 2.3, and 5.1 in this text. Many thanks go to my son David Martin Villafaña, geographic information systems extraordinaire, for producing maps 8.1, 8.2, 12.1, and 14.1.

My thanks go to Carlos Alberto Montaner (international syndicated columnist), Ramón Barquín (President, Barquín International), Eusebio Mujal-León (Georgetown University), and Javier Figueroa (University of Puerto Rico) for taking time from their busy schedules to read the final version of the manuscript. They, along with Jaime Suchlicki and Armando González, provided advance comments to Transaction.

The helpful staff of the Polk County (Florida) Library ordered many books for me and I am grateful for their assistance.

And finally, my special thanks go to my wife Karen G. Villafaña, who offered grammatical advice throughout the evolving versions of the manuscript and encouraged me to continue writing.

Frank R. Villafaña
Lakeland, Florida
April 2011

Introduction

I was born in Cuba and lived there through high school. History was one of my favorite subjects, and I particularly enjoyed reading about Cuba's many struggles for its independence. When I went to college in the United States, I found out that many of the facts I had learned about Cuban history were taught quite differently in American high schools and colleges. The thought crossed my mind to go to original documents to determine how these events actually occurred. But I did not, rationalizing at the time that some day historians would eventually get to the bottom of these events.

Many years later, while living in Spain, I learned that Spain had yet a third version of Cuban history, particularly in regards to the Cuban wars of independence, and the war referred to in American textbooks as the Spanish American War and in Spanish textbooks as *La Guerra de Cuba*, or Cuba's War. As a further dissimilarity, Cuban history textbooks call this war the Cuban Spanish American War.

Discrepancies were not limited to the name of the war. Authors disagree on Cubans' efforts for independence, the participation of Cuban rebels in the Cuban Spanish American War, and the impact of the Platt Amendment coupled with the American military occupation on Cuba's independence. The purpose of my research was to bridge these areas of differences and attempt to postulate how the actions of American administrations, starting with McKinley's, affected Cuba's independence.

I started my research by examining all documented U.S. attempts to acquire Cuba by nonmilitary means. I then looked at possible common threads in the United States' territorial expansion.

Starting with President Thomas Jefferson, the United States publicly declared its desire to own Cuba. From the early days of the American nation, successive administrations embraced expansionism, starting with the purchases of Louisiana and Florida, but with Cuba ever present on their minds.

Manifest Destiny appeared in 1845 as an instrument to legitimize expansionism, and it stated that the United States would eventually absorb its neighbors. Presumably, this meant Canada, Mexico, and perhaps Central America, but John L. O'Sullivan, the man who coined the phrase, managed to include Cuba as a neighbor, somehow forgetting about the existence of the Florida Straits.

Expansionism continued with the Mexican-American War, with a hiatus for the U.S. Civil War. The purchase of Alaska met strong popular opposition, particularly from the Anti-Imperialist League, but it was carried out. The two strongest arguments in favor were that Alaska is part of the North American continent, and that if Manifest Destiny were to run its course, Canada would join the Union and Alaska would then become a neighbor.

President McKinley was not an expansionist, but was well aware that the American public was clamoring for Cuba's liberation from Spain. After a last ditch effort to purchase Cuba from Spain failed, and with the sinking of the *Maine* on his mind, McKinley acquiesced that war was the only answer, and with the assistance of the media, convinced the American people that war against Spain was necessary to end the suffering of the Cuban people. The liberation of Cuba was not monopolizing the U.S. political scene; expansionists were demanding the immediate annexation of Hawaii.

The annexation of Hawaii was controversial. The United States was on the verge of declaring war on Spain, ostensibly to liberate Cuba. The well-organized anti-expansionists argued that the location of Hawaii in the middle of the Pacific Ocean would be logistically difficult to protect.

The McKinley administration had left their options open for the possible annexation of Cuba, by not acknowledging the existence of a Cuban rebel government or a Cuban rebel army. McKinley, influenced by a small group of powerful empire-builders, became convinced that if the United States would wage an expanded war against Spain, under the pretense of liberating Cuba, the United States could gain control of the remaining Spanish colonies: Philippines, Cuba, Puerto Rico, and the Mariana Islands. If the United States owned the Philippines and the Mariana Islands, Hawaii could be defended more easily. Under that scenario, the annexation of Hawaii would make sense.

The benefits of defeating Spain in an all-out war would be significant. Spain would be out of the Western Hemisphere, and with Hawaii, the Philippines, and Guam, the United States would have a powerful presence in the Asia-Pacific region. With U.S. troops stationed in Cuba and Puerto Rico, the defense of the southern coast of the United States would be enhanced. Also, Cuba and Puerto Rico would help to protect the proposed Central America canal, which once completed would be a vital artery for the defense and increased commerce of the expanding American nation.

While the United States had been gaining territory and becoming more powerful, Spain had lost most of the colonies in the Americas and had become weaker. Spain was broke, both financially and politically; nevertheless, Spain insisted in continuing to defend Cuba against internal as well as external forces who were demanding freedom for Cubans.

Cubans were not sitting idle waiting for outsiders to liberate them from Spanish oppression. Thus, my next area of research was to study the significant Cuban efforts to liberate their island from Spanish domination. Cuba had been struggling for independence from Spain since the 1830s, followed by the Ten Year War which started in 1868. During the 1895–1898 War of Independence, Cuba had come close to defeating Spain, but a merciless Spanish Captain-General had converted Cuba into a series of concentration camps.

When I started researching the Cuban Spanish American War, I was fortunate that one of the first books I read was *United States in War with Spain and the History of Cuba* written in 1898 by war correspondent Trumbull White. This was no second-hand account of history. The author was there, in the thick of the action, and he saw the Cuban patriots fighting alongside American soldiers. Yet, as time went by, a number of U.S. history books stated that there were no Cubans present in the battlefields, or alternatively, if they admitted that Cubans were there, they would state that Cubans refused to fight.

It appears that the McKinley administration had been led to believe that a significant percentage of Cubans wanted annexation to the United States, and the strategy for the war effort was possibly developed accordingly. As the war progressed, U.S. troops distanced themselves from the Cuban rebels. And whenever possible, U.S. military commanders blamed Cubans for any setbacks in the war effort. Were these actions part of the American strategy?

Spain surrendered quickly after decisive naval defeats at Manila Bay and Santiago de Cuba and following a lackluster ground campaign in eastern Cuba. After the United States occupied Cuba militarily, it promptly realized that it was only a small minority of Cubans who were annexationists. It was then that War Secretary Elihu Root developed the Platt Amendment as a substitute to annexation.

The Platt Amendment, under the guise of protecting American lives and investments, was used as a tool to manipulate Cuban politics and commerce. Cuban governments were weak by design and after a half century of constrained independence, the way was paved for a Fidel Castro to emerge and take control of the Cuban governments.

Castro communism has ruled Cuba since 1959, and examining the results of this type of government, most Cubans would agree that independence constrained by the United States was infinitely better than the current enslavement by the Castro brothers.

Cubans living in Cuba as well as abroad, still wait for the day that Cuba will be truly free and independent.

Part 1

Expanding the U.S. Nation

1

U.S. Attempts to Acquire Cuba

Starting in the early part of the nineteenth century, American administrations openly expressed a desire to own Cuba. A rationale for adding Cuba to the territory of the United States could be built based on Cuba's sugar and tobacco industries, as well as for Cuba's mineral deposits. But economics was not the primary reason. American presidents were knowledgeable in military history and they knew that in the event of war, the nation occupying Cuba would have a distinct advantage over the United States.

Early American presidents feared European powers in general, and Great Britain in particular. And this fear was well founded, for in mid-1762 a British fleet under the command of Lord Albemarle had attacked and occupied Havana and the western part of Cuba. The British had seized the opportunity that Spain had entered the Seven Years' War on the side of Austria and France against Britain to attack Havana. The British held on to Cuba for less than one year, since the Treaty of Paris (February 1763) stipulated that Britain would return Cuba to Spain, while Spain ceded Florida to London. France compensated Spain for the loss of Florida by giving Spain the Louisiana Territory.

While American administrations craved Cuba for its strategic location, early Cuban patriots were equally concerned about holding on to a free Cuba for the same reason. The Coat of Arms of the Republic of Cuba, Figure 1.1, as drawn by Miguel Teurbe Tolón in 1849, expresses this combination of pride and fear. The rectangle in the upper part of the Coat of Arms contains two points of land on either extreme. These represent North and South America. The golden key represents Cuba, as the key to the Gulf of Mexico. And this key is precisely the reason why for 150 years, the Unites States wanted to own Cuba.

A number of U.S. administrations openly expressed a desire to absorb Cuba. Thomas Jefferson (1801–1809) was the first U.S. President

Figure 1.1 Republic of Cuba Coat of Arms

to publicly discuss the obtainment of Cuba, as well as the first to actually attempt to acquire the island. Jefferson's idea was the outright purchase of Cuba from Spain, following the model of the Louisiana Purchase.

In 1808, President Jefferson asked General James Wilkinson, the man who had taken possession of Louisiana from the Spanish, to meet with Cuba's Captain-General Salvador Muro, Marqués de Someruelos, to explain that the United States would prefer for Cuba to remain in Spain's hands rather than Britain's or France's and that the United States was prepared to purchase the island if Spain felt that they could not maintain control of the island. The negotiations failed as the Spanish showed no interest in the transaction.[1]

However, Jefferson's strategy would later be formalized by President James Monroe (1817–1825), into what would be known as the *no transfer policy*. The central premise of this policy is that Cuba would remain outside the North American Union as long as it belonged to the Spanish Empire. There are two corollaries to this policy. The first one is that eventually the United States would replace Spain in Cuba. This would later be termed colonial succession. The second, and most troubling, corollary is that a threat to Spanish sovereignty from within Cuba would also be a challenge to the United States.[2]

After the United States acquired Spanish Florida in 1819, successive U.S. administrations realized that Cuba was now much closer to the U.S. border. Proponents of the acquisition of Cuba cited national security and rising wealth as reasons for the United States to annex Cuba, but the issue of slavery took center stage in extinguishing the U.S.' desire to own Cuba. On the other side of the Straits of Florida, wealthy Cuban planters and some influential Cuban writers and businessmen wished for the annexation of Cuba by the United States for motives related to either the abolition of, or the perpetuation of slavery on the island.

The western portion of La Hispaniola island was a profitable French colony called *Saint Domingue* (now Haiti), with a predominantly black slave population. In 1791 the slaves rebelled and by 1795 the colony had fallen to black rebels. Some French refugees returned to France, but the vast majority moved to the eastern part of Cuba. French settlers brought to Cuba their knowledge of agriculture, foreign trade, as well as horrible stories of rape and murder during the slave revolt. Wealthy Cubans, particularly plantation owners, worried that a similar rebellion could take place in Cuba.

Not all black and mulatto people in Cuba were slaves, but at the time it was generally believed that non-white residents were a clear majority. This belief only became a certainty after the census of 1841 "...revealed that the slaves and 'free people of color' formed a substantial and verifiable majority, 58 per cent."[3]

White Cubans felt they needed protection, and they believed that a militarily weakened Spain could not provide this protection. If the powerful Napoleon army could not save the *Saint Domingue* settlers, how could they expect protection from a Spain which had just lost the vast majority of its colonies in the Americas?

These white Cubans lived in the shadow of the Haitian slave rebellion, but wanting to maintain slavery, they felt confident that the United States could provide the protection they needed. This relative small but rather powerful group became annexationists and their preference was annexation by the southern states, for they felt that their economies were much alike, in addition to the common denominator of slavery.

The political situation appeared straightforward: the United States wanted to purchase Cuba and a number of important Cubans were in favor of annexation. What was preventing the annexation from being consummated? In the first place, Spain had a special love for Cuba and it would have been a highly unpopular act to sell Cuba. There were many enlightened Cubans who viewed the United States as an empire-building nation and thought that Cubans were perfectly capable of determining the destiny of Cuba. Also, several American politicians were not sure if expanding outside the lower part of the North American continent was an intelligent move.

John Quincy Adams was Secretary of State during the presidency of James Monroe. On April 23, 1823, Adams, who would become president (1825–1829), wrote to Hugh Nelson, U.S. Ambassador to Spain, a letter that summarized U.S. feelings vis-à-vis Cuba during the nineteenth century. Excerpts of this letter[4] follow:

> These islands are natural appendages of the North American continent, and one of them-almost in sight of our shores-from a multitude of considerations has become an object of transcendent importance to the commercial and political interests of our Union. Its commanding position with reference to the Gulf of Mexico and the West Indian seas, its situation midway between our southern coast and the island of San Domingo, its safe and capacious harbour of the Havana, fronting a long line of our shores destitute of the same advantages, the nature of its production and of its wants, furnishing the supplies and needing the returns of a commerce immensely profitable and mutually beneficial, give it an importance in the sum of our national interests with which that of no other foreign territory can be compared, and little inferior to that which binds the different members of the Union together...it is scarcely possible to resist the conviction that the annexation of Cuba to our Federal Republic will be indispensable to the continuance and integrity of the Union itself...There are laws of political as well as physical gravitation. And if an apple severed by the tempest from its native tree, cannot choose but to fall to the ground, Cuba, forcibly disjointed from its unnatural connection to Spain, and incapable of self-support, can gravitate only towards the North American Union, which, by the same law of nature, cannot cast her off from her bosom.

President Thomas Jefferson continued to be influential in American foreign policy several years after his presidency. Jefferson wrote a letter to President Monroe in October 1823 stating that, inasmuch as Cuba would be a significant addition to the Union, he would not fight England to obtain Cuba. His preference was that Cuba should be independent of any European power.

Possibly inspired by Jefferson's letter, on December 2, 1823, President Monroe asked John Quincy Adams to draft a message to Congress which would later be known as the Monroe Doctrine. During the negotiations with Russia regarding the future of the northwest coast of North America, Americans had stated that European powers should stay out of the Western Hemisphere. Russia had agreed. This was the seed of the doctrine which the United States followed during the nineteenth century but would abandon in the middle of the twentieth century when the USSR ruled the destiny of Cuba.

As the American Civil War approached, the freedom of Cuba from Spain started to be viewed by Washington as a potential liability. In 1839, President Martin van Buren (1837–1841) wrote: "Other considerations connected with a certain class of our population make it the interest of the Southern section of the Union that no attempts should be made in the island to throw off the yoke of Spanish dependence, the first effect of which would be the sudden emancipation of a numerous slave population, the result of which could not but be very sensibly felt upon the adjacent shores of the United States."[5]

Manifest Destiny, which signifies many different things to many people, first appeared in American historiography in 1839. In its most general form, it can be defined as a belief that the United States was destined and divinely ordained by the God of Christianity to rule its neighbors. This included Canada, Mexico, and Central America. Cuba was included as a neighbor, somehow forgetting about the Florida Straits. Over the years, some people have believed that Manifest Destiny is inevitable, and would just naturally happen, as countries would ask to become a part of the United States, while others have argued that the United States should purchase these countries or take them over by military action.

The concept of Manifest Destiny, although known by other terms, was first utilized around 1812 when President James Madison (1809–1817), tried to develop a strategy to take over the Oregon Territory to facilitate commerce with Asia. Madison stated that as American and European settlers moved west, a *flourishing empire* would be created. It is generally believed that at that time, the term empire had a meaning similar to what we would define today as a sovereign nation.

The first known use of the term Manifest Destiny was by John L. O'Sullivan in his July 1845 issue of the periodical *United States Magazine and Democratic Review*.[6] The O'Sullivan article also contains possibly the first publicly written expression of support for the forcible seizure of Cuba from Spain and its annexation to the United States. O'Sullivan was a friend of President James K. Polk (1845–1849) and had provided invaluable assistance during Polk's presidential campaign.

O'Sullivan's sister Mary was married to Cristóbal Madán, a wealthy Cuban planter who kept a residence in New York and had become a naturalized American citizen, presumably to avoid Spanish taxes. Madán was the self-appointed leader of the Cuban annexationist movement in New York. In 1847, O'Sullivan and Moses Yale Beach, the editor of the *New York Sun,* traveled to Havana and met with Madán's Cuban colleagues. Upon their return, they launched a campaign for the United States to buy Cuba.

On July 6, 1847, O'Sullivan wrote to the-then Secretary of State James Buchanan, who would later become president (1857–1861), telling him that many rich Cubans would rather join the Union than be independent from Spain. Furthermore, O'Sullivan stated that these Cubans were willing to contribute financially to the purchase of Cuba by the United States.[7]

During the middle of the nineteenth century, Cuban bourgeoisie viewed annexation as the only logical way to be patriotic and republican. They did not believe in independence because they were aware of the chaos reigning in Latin America after becoming independent from Spain. They believed in becoming a part of a great republic which would allow them self-government and their own constitution. They thought that if the French from Louisiana and the Mexicans from Texas were happy to be a part of the United States, then, why not Cuba?

Regardless, the timing of O'Sullivan's proposal was poor, for Polk and Buchanan were busy with the Mexican-American War. In 1848, after the conclusion of this war, U.S. public opinion once again picked up the issue of expansionism. Senator Jefferson Davis, a hero of the Mexican-American War, became an advocate for the annexation of Cuba.

President James K. Polk proposed the purchase of Cuba to his cabinet on May 30, 1848, with somewhat mixed results. Since Cuba had slavery, members from the South accepted the idea; however, the idea was unwelcome in the North. Buchanan instructed Romulus Sanders, U.S. Ambassador to Spain, to offer $100 million for Cuba. Information on this sensitive matter was leaked to United States and

Spanish newspapers, and as a result of this indiscretion, Spain rejected Sanders' proposal.

It is generally believed that O'Sullivan became obsessed with the annexation of Cuba by the United States. When Polk's initiative failed, O'Sullivan commenced to conspire with leading southern politicians and became involved in filibustering invasions aimed at annexing Cuba to the Confederacy. Madán had introduced O'Sullivan to Narciso López, and O'Sullivan actively assisted in planning and financing López's expeditions.

On May 18, 1848, General Robert Campbell, U.S. Consul in Havana, wrote to Secretary of State James Buchanan that a charismatic former Spanish General was preparing to lead a revolt in Cuba and that the next step would be Cuba's annexation to the United States. The Spanish General was Narciso López. In June 1848, Buchanan betrayed to the Spanish Minister in Washington that López planned a revolution against Spanish rule in Cuba. Buchanan's motivation for this betrayal in not known. It is possible that Buchanan found out about López's ties to the Confederacy. It is also possible that President Polk ordered Buchanan to betray López in order to prove to Spain that the United States wanted to acquire Cuba by honest means, and thus move Spain to accept the $100 million offer. Spain's reply was negative, adding that they would rather sink Cuba in the ocean than sell it to the United States.[8] López and some of his co-conspirators, including famed Cuban novelist Cirilo Villaverde, were able to flee. López settled in New Orleans. The remaining conspirators were caught and sent to prison in Spain.

Narciso López was born in Venezuela to Spanish parents. He fought on the Spanish side against Bolívar and withdrew to Cuba after Venezuela's independence. He was married for a short time to the sister of U.S.-educated, wealthy Cuban Count of Pozos Dulces. López moved to Spain where he fought against the Carlists and was rewarded with the rank of General and important civil service posts. López returned to Cuba in 1841 when his good friend Gerónimo Valdés was appointed Captain-General of the island.

The López conspiracy and his two expeditions to Cuba do not belong in a chapter on attempts for Cuba's independence. Rather, they belong in a chapter on annexationist movements. He was a salaried agent of annexation, at first to the Union, and finally to the South. In fact, Professor Tom Chaffin subtitles his book *Fatal Glory* in such a way that there is no doubt that López was a U.S. agent: *Narciso López and the First Clandestine U.S. War against Cuba.*[9]

Professor George C. Herring goes beyond Professor Chaffin inasmuch as he refers to López as a *filibuster*[10] a term which specifically refers to an American engaged in fomenting insurrections in Latin America during the mid-nineteenth century. The term filibuster entered the English language directly from the Dutch word *vrijbuiter*, or literally freebooter. Filibusters were considered updated versions of pirates, buccaneers, and corsairs. In any event, Cuban historians ignore available historiography and continue to consider Narciso López as a patriot and one of the first men to fight for Cuba's independence from Spain. López was not interested in Cuba's freedom; rather, his only interest was Cuba's annexation to the United States. He should be remembered as a filibuster, if at all.

López's first expedition sailed from New Orleans in May 1850, on the steamer *Creole*. The manifest for the *Creole* stated that she was sailing to California by way of the Chagres River. Before the Panama Canal was constructed, it was quite difficult but possible to cross from the Caribbean Sea to the Pacific Ocean via the Chagres River in Panama. A low-draft vessel was required, as well as a full knowledge of the tides on both bodies of water. Pirate Henry Morgan successfully conquered Panama City in 1671 by using this route. When the gold fever broke out in California in 1849, many prospectors took the Chagres route to California to avoid the treacherous cross-country crossing. It was therefore not unusual, at the time, to have a vessel depart New Orleans to travel to California via the Chagres River. By writing the manifest in this manner, López hoped to evade the Neutrality Law of 1818, which forbids military operations against powers at peace with the United States from being launched from the United States.

His 600-man troop was comprised mostly of young men from Alabama, Louisiana, and Mississippi who had fought in the Mexican-American War and had since become unemployed. In fact, out of the 600 members of the expedition only five were Cuban. López attempted to recruit Jefferson Davis to lead the expedition, but Davis declined and proposed Colonel Robert E. Lee who also refused. López then decided to lead the expedition himself.

The expedition landed in Cárdenas, Cuba's north coast about 160 kilometers east of Havana, on May 19, 1850, and the current Cuban flag flew for the first time on Cuban soil. López's troops overpowered the small Spanish garrison, but the population fled believing that it was an American or British invasion force since obviously the troops were primarily speaking English. López withdrew and made it to a hero's welcome in Key West after being closely pursued by Spanish war ships. López was tried in New Orleans for violating the U.S. Neutrality Law. After three hung juries, the charges were dismissed.[11]

A number of American citizens, including O'Sullivan, were also charged in New Orleans in 1850 and in New York in 1851 with violation of the Neutrality Law. After successive hung juries, the first trial ended in *nolle prosequi*. O'Sullivan was acquitted in a second trial in March 1852.

After the failure of López's first expedition, the Cuban annexationist group broke up. López then aligned himself with more violent Southern politicians. Mississippi governor and Mexican-American War hero John Quitman was a strong supporter of López's second expedition. This time he had some 400 men, mostly Hungarian exiles and a few Cubans. They landed in the north coast of Pinar del Río, westernmost portion of Cuba, where the invaders were defeated by Spanish forces. López and most of his men were captured and summarily executed by garrote. The garrote was a tightening iron collar designed to strangle or break the neck of the condemned person.

The U.S. government as well as wealthy U.S. industrialists still wanted to acquire Cuba by peaceful means. Nevertheless, conspiracies continued in 1851 through 1853. On April 3, 1854, President Pierce offered Spain $130 million for Cuba. Spain refused.

During the presidencies of Zachary Taylor (1849–1850) and Millard Fillmore (1850–1853), the constant bickering between pro and antislaving members of Congress prevented any action on the Cuba issue. In 1854, during the presidency of Franklin Pierce (1853–1857) a most controversial document about Cuba was prepared at the suggestion of Secretary of State William L. Marcy.

Marcy asked three key American diplomats stationed in Europe to hold a secret meeting and develop a U.S. policy toward Cuba. Pierre Soulé, Minister to Spain, James Buchanan, Minister to Great Britain, and John Mason, Minister to France, met at Ostend, Belgium. The resulting document was drafted at Aachen, Germany, and sent to Marcy in October 1854.

The chief author of the document, which would later be known as the *Ostend Manifesto*, was Soulé, an outspoken advocate of Cuban annexation. The basic theme of the Manifesto is that the purchase of Cuba by the United States would be beneficial to all parties, and would further prevent Cuba to pass to a stronger power such as France or Great Britain. The controversial part of the Ostend Manifesto is that it stated that if Spain refused to sell, the United States would be justified in "wrestling" the island from Spanish hands. The document was widely distributed and soon denounced by Northern states as well as Madrid, Paris, and London. Soulé was ordered to keep silent on Cuba matters, and he quickly resigned. President Pierce was blamed for the fiasco, and any possibility to consider Cuba's independence was deferred until after the U.S. Civil War.[12]

In December 1857, President James Buchanan began the third attempt to purchase Cuba, but Congress failed to approve the necessary funds.

By 1860 the United States was sliding into Civil War. Jefferson Davis suggested that if a Republican were to be elected in November, the South would secede and that the South would certainly acquire Cuba. Presidential candidate Lincoln had announced that the United States would not purchase Cuba as long as it was a slaving colony.[13]

During the four-year U.S. Civil War (1861–1865), the thoughts of expansionism lay dormant in the minds of Americans as well as U.S. politicians.

During the presidency of Ulysses S. Grant (1869–1877), a fourth attempt at purchasing Cuba took place.

Spain was fighting Cuban rebels during the 1868–1878 war. Mexico's President Benito Juárez and the administrations of some Latin American countries had recognized that a state of belligerency existed in Cuba. Diplomatically, this was as far as they could go short of recognizing the rebel government as the legitimate ruler of the destiny of Cuba.

The Grant administration was being pressured to accept that Cuba was in a state of belligerency. Secretary of State Hamilton Fish was opposed, ostensibly on the grounds that it would be tantamount to accepting that the Cuban issue could only be settled by war. The pro-Cuban Congress was threatening to unilaterally declare Cuban belligerence. In reality, accepting that a state of belligerence existed in Cuba would have implied that Cuban forces were fighting against Spain as well as acknowledging that some sort of a Cuban government existed. This would have been in contravention to the *no transfer* policy. Instead, Fish's proposal was to make a cash payment to Spain of $100 million for Spain to exit the island. Said payment would be in the form of a loan to Cuban patriots fighting for independence, who would then be expected to pay this money back to the United States from Cuban Customs revenues. Side conditions were the abolition of slavery and an armistice during the negotiations. The Spanish government of General Prim was reportedly ready to negotiate and Grant appointed General Daniel Sickles to head the U.S. team. Sickles arrived in Madrid on July 21, 1869, but the Spanish Parliament had just closed for the summer. Grant's fifth attempt of purchasing Cuba died of natural causes when Prim's enemies leaked news to the press that the "ever faithful" island of Cuba was being sold.[14]

In addition to political considerations, economics stood in the way of President Grant's public admission that a state of belligerence existed in Cuba, although his Secretary of War, John Rawlins, urged Grant to recognize Cuban belligerence. The economics factor was the settlement of the complex *Alabama* reparations case against Great Britain. The *Alabama* was a Confederate cruiser purchased illegally from England, proving the absence of British neutrality during the American Civil War. Senator Charles Sumner, chairman of the Foreign Relations Committee, postulated that Great Britain's actions had prolonged the war for two years, at a cost to the United States of $2 billion plus many lives. Sumner went as far as to suggest annexing Canada to settle the claim. Fish placed the negotiations with Britain on hold. Meanwhile, Sumner, the leader of the pro-Cuba movement, died in September 1869. Sumner's death, coupled with the fact that Cuban insurgents were not having much military success, and Fish's threat to resign, finally convinced Grant to send a message to Congress thwarting the recognition of Cuban belligerence. The *Alabama* Claim was settled with a British payment of $15.5 million to the United States. Had Grant sided with the Cubans, his claim against Britain would have been jeopardized. Economics trumped Cuban independence during the Ten Year War.

A halfhearted sixth attempt at purchasing Cuba took place during the Cuban War of Independence, not by the U.S. government, but by a syndicate of U.S. bankers led by Samuel Janney and Colonel John McCook. There was an agreement with the Cuban rebel junta in August 1897, whereby the Cuban debt to Spain would be paid off by a fifty-year lien on Cuban customs. This proposal was not taken seriously by Spain and wilted on the vine.[15]

President William McKinley (1897–1901) made the seventh and final attempt to purchase Cuba by sending a private message to Christina of Austria, Spain's Queen Regent, offering to pay $300 million for Cuba. Christina was unable to find anyone in her government willing to take the responsibility for accepting McKinley's offer. Spain therefore refused this seventh and last official U.S. government diplomatic effort for either the independence of Cuba or its incorporation into the Union.

War correspondent Trumbull White, in his revealing book published in 1898 states that Spain went to war because of a lack of leadership in the country. "It was recognized in all quarters that the [Spanish] Queen Regent would have been willing to let the Cuban insurrectionists have their island without further protest, had it not been for the fact that giving up probably would have incited an insurrection at home, resulting in a loss of the crown to her son before he should have a chance to wear it."[16]

Americans and Spaniards were clamoring for war. Spain and most U.S. citizens thought the war would be limited to a fight for possession of Cuba. The McKinley administration was visualizing a larger conflict. "Assistant Secretary of the Navy, Theodore Roosevelt dispatched Commodore George Dewey to the Asiatic Squadron in Hong Kong with orders to attack Manila if war came."[17]

One of the most respected of all Cuban thinkers, José Martí was sharply opposed to following any path that would lead to Cuba's annexation to the United States. Martí's writings reveal that he believed that the United States represented the greatest threat to Cuba's complete independence. Martí further clearly understood the dominant relationship between economics and politics. "Martí warned in 1890 'economic union means political union.' In 1891 Martí warned 'the nation that buys, commands - the nation that sells, serves.' Martí concluded 'the first step taken by a nation to dominate another one is to separate it from other nations.'"[18]

In a May 1886 letter to his friend Ricardo Rodríguez Otero, Martí wrote "Never, except as an idea hidden away in the depths of some generous souls, was Cuba anything more to the United States than a desirable possession, whose only inconvenience is its population, which it considers to be unruly, lazy and worthy of scorn."[19]

With Cuba ever present in the minds of most U.S. administrations, the young American nation quickly embarked in projects to increase its territory. The thirteen colonies started moving west and south, taking land from France and Spain. To a larger extent, territories to the north were respected, for a new war with England was not wise at that time.

The Louisiana Purchase and the acquisition of West and East Florida would follow. The U.S.-Mexico War would further increase the size of the United States, and after the Civil War, the Purchase of Alaska became the first expansion into noncontiguous territories, but still in the North American continent.

The annexation of Hawaii marked the start of global expansion, west and south, and once again Cuba was sighted on the crosshair of the United States.

Notes

1. Hugh Thomas, *Cuba or the Pursuit of Freedom* (New York: Da Capo Press, 1971), 88.
2. Louis Pérez, *Cuba and the United States: Ties of Singular Intimacy* (Athens: University of Georgia Press, 1997), 40–42.
3. Ibid., 12.
4. Quoted in Willis Fletcher Johnson, *The History of Cuba*, vol. 2 (New York: B. F. Buck Publisher, 1920), 261–62.
5. Quoted by Pérez, *Cuba and the United States*, 9.
6. John L. O'Sullivan, "Annexation," *The United States Magazine and Democratic Review* 17 (July 1845): 5–10.
7. Thomas, *Cuba or the Pursuit of Freedom*, 211.
8. Robert L. Scheina, *Latin America's Wars, Volume 1: The Age of the Caudillo, 1791-1899* (Washington, DC: Brassey's, 2003).
9. Tom Chaffin, *Fatal Glory: Narciso López and the First Clandestine U.S. War against Cuba* (Charlottesville: University Press of Virginia, 1996).
10. George C. Herring, *From Colony to Superpower: U.S. Foreign Relations since 1776* (New York: Oxford University Press, 2008), 214–19.
11. Antón Alex and Roger E. Hernández, *Cubans in America* (Miami: Kensington Books, 2003), 42.
12. David M. Potter, *The Impending Crisis 1848-1861* (New York: Harper & Row, 1967), 190–95.
13. Thomas, *Cuba or the Pursuit of Freedom*, 228–32.
14. Ibid., 245–53.
15. Ibid., 351, 356, 359, and 376.
16. Trumbull White, *United States in War with Spain and the History of Cuba* (Chicago, IL: International Publishing, 1898), 395.
17. J. A. Greenville, "American Naval Preparations for War with Spain," *Journal of American Studies* 2 (1968): Appendix III, 33–47.
18. Quoted by Pérez, *Cuba and the United States*, 77–81.
19. Peter Turton, *José Martí: Architect of Cuba's Freedom* (London: Zed Books, 1986), 17.

2

Louisiana Purchase (1803)

The territory we now know as the forty-eight contiguous states of the United States was loosely divided among Great Britain, France, and Spain during the sixteenth and seventeenth centuries. The vast majority of this large expanse of land was unexplored and with the exception of European settlements on the Atlantic coast, the Gulf of Mexico and the Pacific coast, the inhabitants were Native Americans.

The American cartographer H. C. Robertson authored an extremely interesting atlas entitled *Geographic-Historical Series Illustrating the History of America and the Unites States from 1492 to the Present Time*. Robertson's work was published by R. O. Evans and Company of Chicago in early 1898. Figures 2.1 through 2.3 and 5.1 in this text are from Robertson's atlas and are reproduced with permission from The Library of Congress.

Figure 2.1 depicts the English, French, and Spanish possessions in today's continental United States during the early 1600s. The borders were variable, and since the decisions on land ownership were taken in London, Paris, and Madrid, settlers did not bother to steak their land claims.

The American Revolutionary War started in 1775 and ended in 1783, although American colonists were discontent with British rule long before 1775. The First Continental Congress met in 1774, and the thirteen self-governing colonies petitioned King George III to allow American representation in the British Parliament. The American petition was ignored.

The Second Continental Congress, convened in Philadelphia in mid-May 1775, placed the colonies in a state of defense and appointed George Washington as general and commander-in-chief of the newly formed Continental Army. The British Parliament reacted by declaring that the members of Congress were traitors and the thirteen colonies to be in rebellion.

Figure 2.1 English, French, and Spanish North America Possessions

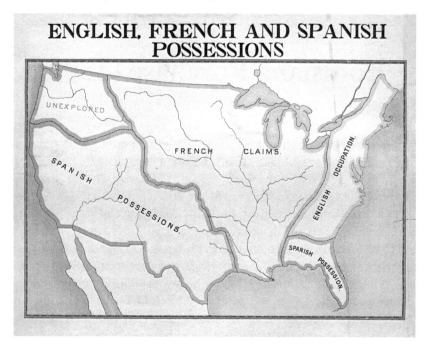

The reaction of the Continental Congress was to proclaim the United States of America an independent nation on July 4, 1776, and to reject any allegiance to the British crown. The war that started with the Kingdom of Britain attempting to suffocate a rebellion of thirteen colonies on the eastern seaboard of North America ended as a global war when a coalition of France, Spain, and the Dutch Republic joined the Americans against Britain.

With battlefields in Europe, the Americas, and the Indian subcontinent, Britain was able to hold its own, until the French Navy won a decisive battle at Yorktown in 1781, which caused the British army to surrender. The war ended with the Treaty of Paris, signed in 1783. Britain recognized the sovereignty of the United States over a territory with boundaries of East and West Florida to the south, Canada to the north, and the Mississippi River to the west.

Figures 2.2 and 2.3 portray the U.S. territory after the Treaty of Paris. Figure 2.3 defines the boundaries of the first thirteen states. Figure 2.2 shows the northern borders of East and West Florida to be a straight line, while Figure 2.3 shows West Florida's northern border

Figure 2.2 United States after September 3, 1783

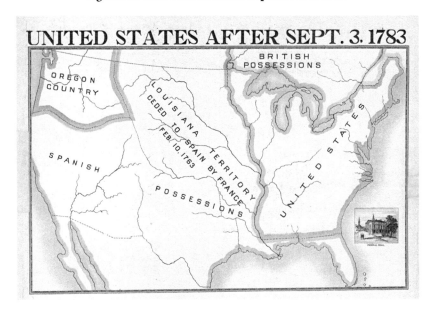

higher than that of East Florida. In fact, the northern border of West Florida occupied about the lower one-third of the current states of Alabama and Mississippi.

It did not take very long for the young nation to develop an appetite for increasing the size of its territory, which some politely called expansionism while others chose the term empire building. Initially, the strategy was limited to pushing Native Americans west and south of the boundaries of the original thirteen colonies, but soon the idea of major expansion surfaced. The first such venture was the purchase of the Louisiana Territory from Napoleon's France in 1808. The efforts to acquire Cuba, as detailed in Chapter 1, would not begin until five years later.

Around 1800, the territory of the sixteen states (Vermont, Kentucky, and Tennessee had joined the original Union) of the young United States of America included the land east of the Mississippi River with the exception of today's state of Florida east from the Apalachicola River (then known as East Florida), the extreme southern portions of the states of Alabama and Mississippi, the current Florida panhandle west from the Apalachicola River, and the portion of today's Louisiana east of the Mississippi River (then known as West Florida). East and

Figure 2.3 The Thirteen Original States

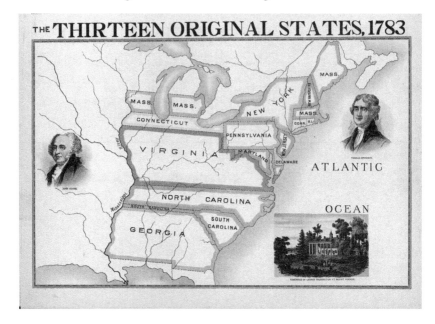

West Florida were Spanish possessions which Spain had recovered from Great Britain in 1783 by virtue of the Treaty of Versailles. The city of New Orleans, at the time mostly on the west bank of the Mississippi, was part of the Louisiana Territory which was a French colony.

How large was the Louisiana Territory? It was almost as large as the United States at the time. The Louisiana Territory had an area of 828,000 square miles, or 2,145,000 square kilometers. Before the Louisiana Purchase, the area of the United States was less than one million square miles, with a mostly rural population of 5.3 million.[1]

Since a large portion of the territory purchased by the United States was unexplored, the exact boundaries were not clearly defined until several years after the execution of the Purchase Agreement. We now know that the United States purchased from France all or part of fifteen current U.S. states and two Canadian Provinces.

The territory purchased contained all of the following current states: Arkansas, Iowa, Kansas, Missouri, and Nebraska. It also included the portion of Minnesota south of the Mississippi River, all of Oklahoma minus the panhandle, most of North Dakota, practically all of South Dakota, northern Texas, northeast New Mexico, the portions of

Colorado, Montana, and Wyoming that are east of the Continental Divide, and Louisiana west of the Mississippi, including the city of New Orleans. The Louisiana land purchased also contained small portions of the Canadian Provinces of Alberta and Saskatchewan, which the United States later ceded to Great Britain in the Anglo-American Convention of 1818. Based on today's territorial extension, the Louisiana Purchase included 23 percent of the United States.

Louisiana had been a Spanish colony since 1762, but was returned to France in 1800 under the terms of a secret treaty. In fact, Spain continued administering Louisiana until a few weeks before the territory was turned over to the United States by France.

The driving force behind the Louisiana Purchase was President Thomas Jefferson, who was born to wealthy parents in Virginia in 1743 and studied law. Jefferson, in addition to possessing a brilliant legal mind, was a man of many talents as he was also an architect, a linguist, and an inventor. The Second Continental Congress elected Jefferson to head a committee of five to prepare the Declaration of Independence. Jefferson was stationed in France from 1784 to 1789, first as a commercial envoy, and later as the successor of Benjamin Franklin in the position of Minister to France. In 1789, Jefferson was appointed Secretary of State in the first administration of President George Washington (1789–1797). In 1792, Jefferson steered the United States into adopting a decimal monetary system based on the dollar, rather than the pound. Jefferson reluctantly ran for the presidency in 1796, but lost to John Adams (1797–1801), by a narrow margin. Under the system in effect at the time, Jefferson became vice president. Jefferson won the 1800 presidential election, starting his first term on March 4, 1801.

Thomas Pinckney, the U.S. Minister to Britain, had negotiated a *right of deposit* treaty with Manuel de Godoy, Spain's first Minister of State, whereby the United States could navigate the lower Mississippi and store and transport goods in and out of the Port of New Orleans free of duty.[2] This treaty, known alternatively as the Treaty of San Lorenzo or Pinckney's Treaty was executed on October 27, 1795. On October 16, 1802, Juan Ventura Morales, the Spanish administrator of New Orleans, revoked the Pinckney Treaty and closed the port to American trade. American businessmen affected by the port closing were threatening to unilaterally declare war on Spain. In 1803, with the help of Manuel de Godoy, who had recently been promoted to serve as Spain's Prime Minister, the new Spanish Governor of New Orleans, Juan Manuel de Salcedo restored the Pinckney Treaty.[3]

President Jefferson was concerned that U.S. access to the Port of New Orleans and the Mississippi River waterway could once again be blocked by either France or Spain. He appointed a negotiating team consisting of Robert R. Livingston, the American ambassador to France, and James Monroe, who would later become a U.S. President.

Monroe, born in Virginia in 1758, had been stationed in Paris (1794–1796) as U.S. minister to France during the Washington presidency, but was recalled when France accused the United States of being pro-British. Monroe was sympathetic to the French Revolution, but sternly maintained the strict policy of neutrality between France and Britain which had been espoused by President Washington.

The first attempt at purchasing Louisiana was in 1801, when President Jefferson sent Livingston to Paris to negotiate for the purchase of the City of New Orleans and for the right to use the Mississippi River for transportation. These negotiations failed.

At Jefferson's request, Pierre du Pont de Nemours, a well-connected Frenchman living in the United States, and a personal friend of President Jefferson, traveled to France in 1802 to hold discussions with Napoleon regarding the purchase of land in the Louisiana Territory. It is believed that du Pont was the one who conceived the idea of purchasing the entire Louisiana Territory as a way to avoid a potential showdown between Napoleon and the United States over France's colonial ambitions in North America.[4]

President Jefferson had mixed feelings about the Louisiana Purchase. In the first place, the U.S. constitution is silent as to whether a U.S. president has the authority to purchase land to be annexed to the U.S. territory. Clearly, a constitutional amendment would have been required in order to consummate the purchase. Furthermore, the treaty had to be approved by two-thirds of the Senate, and afterwards both the House of Representatives and the Senate had to approve an appropriation for a payment to be made.

Jefferson was also concerned about what the Louisiana Purchase might do to state rights vis-à-vis federal executive power. Finally, Jefferson worried that if France turned the purchase down, the fact that the United States had approached France to purchase the territory, would be an admission that France owned Louisiana and had the right to be in North America. Du Pont reported to Jefferson that the deal had a fair chance to go through, even though Napoleon's foreign minister, Charles Maurice de Talleyrand-Périgord, was opposed to the deal, fearing that the sale of the Louisiana Territory would preclude the future presence of France in North America.

In 1803, after the advantages and disadvantages were weighed by Jefferson, he decided to send Monroe to Paris to meet Livingston and commence negotiations, without authorization by constitutional amendment. Congress had granted $2 million to be offered for the City of New Orleans and the right to use the Mississippi River waterway. President Jefferson instructed Monroe that they could go as high as $10 million, including West Florida, which he believed may have been a French possession based, perhaps, on the secret treaty of San Ildefonso, signed by Spain and France on October 1, 1800.

President Jefferson had a Plan B for the acquisition of Louisiana. He instructed Monroe that if the negotiations in Paris should fail, he was to travel to London to discuss an alliance with Britain to take Louisiana from France forcibly.

This was long before the age of telecommunications, and it must have come as a large shock when Napoleon's Minister of the Treasury, Marquis François Barbé de Marbois told Livingston and Monroe that France did not own East and West Florida, but that France was prepared to sell the entire Louisiana Territory for $15 million.[5] Marquis Barbé de Marbois was a trusted Napoleon executive and was later appointed to the important post of *Président de la Cour des Comptes*, or President of the Court of Auditors, an office which is still powerful in today's France.

Napoleon's precise motives for selling the Louisiana Territory may never be known. President Jefferson had strategically dropped hints in key European capitals that if U.S. merchants would continue to be denied the right to navigate the lower Mississippi, he might be compelled to form an alliance with Britain to take Louisiana by force. Having lost its colony of *Saint-Domingue* (now Haiti), and no longer able to use East and West Florida (which had been ceded to Britain) for war logistics, Napoleon rightly considered Louisiana to be indefensible from a British–American force. Additionally, Napoleon was in desperate need of money to fight Spain, and Jefferson's threat probably made an impression.[6]

It would have taken about two months to get a message to Jefferson and then obtain his reply. Considering the time constraints, and believing this was a fantastic deal for the United States, Livingston and Monroe accepted the deal and went to work on the terms of the agreement before Napoleon could change his mind.

Barbé-Marbois, Livingston, and Monroe executed the Louisiana Purchase Agreement on May 2, 1803. Napoleon signed the Agreement, acting for France, on May 22, 1803. U.S. ratification of the Agreement was a complex process, but the Senate approved the Louisiana Purchase on October 20, 1803, by a vote of twenty-four to seven. There were seventeen states at the time the Louisiana Purchase Treaty was signed. Ohio had joined the Union on March 1, 1803.

On November 20, 1803, the Spanish governor of the Territory officially handed Louisiana over to the French. Louisiana became a part of the United States with a ceremony at the Old Cabildo of New Orleans on December 20, 1803, with General James Wilkinson taking physical possession of Louisiana for the United States. An additional ceremony was held in St. Louis on March 10, 1804, to officially transfer the lands west of the Mississippi River from France to the United States.

To administer this newly acquired territory, in March of 1804, Congress divided the acquired Louisiana territory into two districts. The southern part, which comprised today's State of Louisiana minus the portion east of Lake Pontchartrain, which still belonged to Spain's West Florida, became the Territory of Orleans. The vast northern part became the District of Louisiana, later the Territory of Missouri, with its administrative site in St. Louis.

The easy part of the Louisiana Purchase ended with the ceremony at St. Louis. The United States still had to deal with two formidable obstacles to the implementation of the Agreement: Native Americans who occupied the land, and Spain, which believed that France had no right to sell Louisiana and was further convinced, with good reason, that the United States was trying to take over Spanish land in Western North America, as well as West and East Florida.

France and the United States neither consulted with nor informed Native Americans that their land was being sold and purchased. The United States slowly acquired the land from Native Americans, sometimes purchasing it or trading it for other property, other times seizing it by force through bloody wars.[7]

Spain showed its displeasure with the Louisiana Purchase by publicly complaining that under the terms of the San Ildefonso Treaty, France could not sell the Louisiana Territory. After being ignored by both France and the United States, Spain adopted the posture that all the United States had purchased were the cities of New Orleans and St. Louis and the right to navigate the Lower Mississippi River. Eventually, Spain accepted the Rocky Mountains as the western limit of U.S.

territory. The southern limit along today's California, Arizona, New Mexico, and Texas would continue to be disputed until after Mexico's independence and the conclusion of the U.S.-Mexico War.

Since the United States did not know what they had bought, and France was quite uncertain as to what they had sold, shortly after the ratification of the Purchase Agreement, Jefferson commissioned the Corps of Discovery as a scientific expedition to explore the newly purchased territory. Jefferson chose Meriwether Lewis, his personal secretary, to lead the expedition. Lewis secured the help of William Clark, a well-known cartographer and frontiersman. The expedition, named after the two men, left from near St. Louis in the summer of 1804, and returned to St. Louis in September 1806 to deliver their report to President Jefferson. The knowledge generated by the Corps of Discovery expedition paved the way for U.S. expansion to the west and the Pacific Ocean.

President Jefferson's vision in executing the Louisiana Purchase is unquestionable. It was a good business deal and also eliminated France, a major European power, from playing a role in the North American territory. He did, however, set a constitutional precedent for expansionism which would be employed by future U.S. administrations.

Notes

1. Henry Adams, *History of the United States of America during the Administrations of Thomas Jefferson* (New York: The Library of America, 1986), 241.
2. Alexander De Conde, *This Affair of Louisiana* (New York: Charles Scribner's, 1976), 59–63.
3. Susan Dudley Gold, *Land Pacts* (New York: Twenty-First Century Books, 1997), 20–22.
4. Marc Duke, *The du Ponts: Portrait of a Dynasty* (New York: Saturday Review Press, 1976), 77–83.
5. Michael P. Malone, Richard B. Roeder, and William L. Lang, *Montana-a History of Two Centuries* (Seattle: University of Washington Press, 1991), 29–33.
6. George C. Herring, *From Colony to Superpower: U.S. Foreign Relations since 1776* (Oxford: Oxford University Press, 2008), 104–6.
7. Robert J. Miller, *Native America, Discovered and Conquered: Thomas Jefferson, Lewis & Clark, and Manifest Destiny* (Portsmouth, NH: Greenwood Publishing, 2007), 71–72.

3

Florida Purchase (1819)

When Christopher Columbus arrived in the tiny cay of Guanahani in the Bahamas, he conducted a ceremony and took possession of the newly "discovered" lands in the name of the sponsors of his voyage, the Spanish Catholic Monarchs, Ferdinand and Isabella. Columbus' ritual of possession was not a random act. He was following accepted Christian principles which were the only available legal guarantees to Spain's ownership of the newly discovered lands.

In the-then predominantly Catholic Europe, the Pope was the recognized Supreme Court of Western civilization. The Vatican mediated disputes among European monarchies, particularly the ones involving land ownership. In fact, as early as 1452, at the request of King Afonso V of Portugal, Pope Nicholas V issued the bull *Romanus Pontifex*, declaring war against any non-Christian nation and giving Portugal the right to "...capture, vanquish and subdue the ...enemies of Christ, put them in perpetual slavery and to take all their possessions and properties."[1]

The Spanish monarchs, wishing a more official guarantee of ownership than Columbus' ceremony, approached Pope Alexander VI, who on May 4, 1493, by means of the bull *Inter Caetera*, granted to Spain the possession of lands (presumably yet to be discovered) one hundred leagues west and south of any of the islands of the Azores or the Cape Verde Islands.

A league was an ancient and somewhat variable unit of distance, equivalent to somewhere between 3.9 and 7.4 kilometers. *Inter Caetera* is clearly explained in the revealing book *International Law in Historical Perspective*[2] by Professors Verzijl, Heere, and Offerhaus from Utrecht University in The Netherlands, by drawing two partial meridians, one north from a point one hundred leagues west of the Azores Islands and one south from a point one hundred leagues south of the Cape Verde Islands. The Vatican, not known for its knowledge of geography, was essentially giving Portugal rights to a small portion (easternmost corner) of the continent of South America, while Spain was getting the rest of the Western hemisphere. This Papal decision only aggravated the already delicate relationship between Spain and Portugal. Portugal and Spain had been arguing for many years about their rights to land along the African coast.

The King of Portugal contended that the land they had discovered on the easternmost tip of Brazil, site of the current city of Recife, and all lands west of that point were Portuguese possessions. The King of Portugal further alleged that the bull *Romanus Pontifex* was still in effect and that since the Pope was a Spaniard, born in Valencia, and a good friend of King Ferdinand, he was biased in favor of Spain. After difficult negotiations between Spain and Portugal, the Treaty of Tordesillas, an amendment to the bull *Inter Caetera*, was signed on June 7, 1494. Said treaty confirmed the division of the New World into two hemispheres: the oriental belonging to Portugal and the occidental belonging to Spain. The line of demarcation between the two hemispheres was set as an imaginary line 370 leagues west of the Cape Verde Islands, which explains why Portugal was granted Brazil and Spain the rest of the Western Hemisphere. Portugal began colonies in east as well as in west Africa. This was the first known application of the Doctrine of Discovery.[3]

The Doctrine of Discovery is an international legal principle which was created and justified by ideas of Christianity and European ethnic superiority over other religions and ethnic groups in the world. The Doctrine grants automatic property rights over native lands without the consent of the original inhabitants.

During the sixteenth century, as Protestantism took root in Europe, the authority of the Pope diminished. But Protestants were still Christians and therefore European monarchs amplified and gave new interpretation to the Doctrine of Discovery to suit their needs, to wit that any Christian nation had the divine right to claim title to the land and authority over the non-Christian inhabitants of any land discovered. The Doctrine of Discovery was used by the Christian nations of England, France, Holland, Portugal, and Spain as recently as the late nineteenth century.

Following the Louisiana Purchase, U.S. administrations vacillated as to how to interpret not only the Constitution, but also the existing legal framework to actually take possession of the territory purchased. In 1823, the Christian Doctrine of Discovery was incorporated into the U.S. legal system by the *Johnson v. McIntosh*[4] case. Since no challenges have been made to this ruling, presumably the Doctrine of Discovery is still a part of the U.S. jurisprudence.

Supreme Court Chief Justice John Marshall wrote the opinion of a unanimous court in this 1823 landmark decision, observing that Christian European nations had assumed dominion over the lands of America during the Age of Discovery, and that Native Americans only retained the right of occupancy in their lands. Marshall further elucidated that when the United States won its independence from Great Britain in 1776, it became a successor nation to Britain's Rights of Discovery and the Power of Dominion over the territories.[5]

Professor Robert J. Miller of Lewis and Clark Law School in Portland, Oregon, explains in his revealing book[6] how the Doctrine of Discovery was applied to implement the Louisiana Purchase and further territorial expansions of the United States. Professor Miller provides evidence that President Jefferson utilized the legal principles of the Doctrine of Discovery in planning and implementing the Lewis and Clark expedition in 1804, long before the 1823 Supreme Court ruling. Professor Miller further explicates that Manifest Destiny evolved from the principles of the Doctrine of Discovery.

West Florida had unofficially decreased in size since the Louisiana Purchase. The east boundary had been moved west from the Apalachicola and Chattahoochee rivers to the Perdido River, east of Mobile Bay. In other words, East Florida was defined by the boundaries of today's state of Florida. The 1764 northern border of West Florida, as defined by the British, consisted of approximately the lower third of the present states of Mississippi and Alabama. Since the Louisiana Purchase, the northern border had de facto moved south to about the level of today's Florida panhandle. The western border had continued to be the Mississippi River.

Following the Louisiana Purchase, the United States and Spain held many fruitless negotiations on the status of West Florida. This territory had been settled mainly by Americans and British, all obviously Anglophones who resented Spanish rule and anxiously waited for a resolution, their preference being annexation to the United States.

On September 23, 1810, tired of waiting, West Florida settlers rebelled, took the Spanish fort at Baton Rouge and established the Republic of West Florida with its capital at St. Francisville. They adopted a constitution based on that of the United States and elected Fulwar Skipwith as their first and only governor.

President Madison felt that this act of insurgency had created a dangerous situation for the United States. Spain could consider this an act of war instigated by the United States, and Spain had a significant military presence in Cuba, just a couple of days sailing time to Mobile or Pensacola. Madison also feared that Britain might seize the opportunity and attempt to retake West Florida.

Considering that he was running out of time and options, on October 27, 1810, President Madison annexed West Florida from the Mississippi to the Perdido Rivers to the United States by proclamation, using the pretext that this region was a part of the original Louisiana Purchase. The U.S. Constitution does not grant power to the President to seize territory by proclamation, and clearly Madison had no right to proceed as he did. It might have been an acceptable action had he obtained prior Congressional approval, but he failed to do so.

Spain complained, but did not send in troop reinforcements to West Florida. The United States did not attempt to attack either Mobile or Pensacola and allowed both cities to temporarily remain in Spanish hands. President Madison sent his envoy William C. C. Claiborne to negotiate with Skipwith and the rebellious West Floridians.

To Madison's surprise, Skipwith and the West Florida government were opposed to his presidential proclamation. But Claiborne refused to recognize the legitimacy of the Republic of West Florida, and after a few tense days Skipwith and his legislature backed down and accepted Madison's proclamation. The U.S. flag was raised in St. Francisville on December 6, 1810, and in Baton Rouge on December 10, 1810. The Republic of West Florida lasted for seventy-four days.

The area of West Florida in today's state of Louisiana was incorporated into the Territory of Orleans. To this day, this portion of the state of Louisiana is referred to as the "Florida Parishes." The land in today's states of Alabama and Mississippi was annexed to the Mississippi Territory. The State of Louisiana was admitted to the Union on April 30, 1812, and it includes land from the Louisiana Purchase as well as from the purchase of West Florida.

Spain would have had many valid reasons to declare war on the United States. The United States had unilaterally taken over West Florida and the United States was attempting to take a large portion of Texas away from Spain by interpreting boundaries in the Louisiana Purchase which were not clarified by France.

President Madison had encouraged his Secretary of State, James Monroe, to engage Spain in negotiations aimed at the Purchase of

East Florida. Negotiations started in 1815 during a visit to Washington by Spanish foreign minister, Luis de Onís. These negotiations continued after Monroe became president, under the direction of his Secretary of State, John Quincy Adams. This was a difficult time for U.S.–Spanish relations, since Spain suspected that the United States was supporting the independence efforts of Spain's colonies in Central and South America.

John Quincy Adams, perhaps the most brilliant American diplomat of all times, was born in Massachusetts in 1767. The son of President John Adams, he accompanied his father overseas, while he served as American envoy to France (1778–1779) and the Netherlands (1780–1782). During this time, John Quincy Adams studied in the most prestigious European institutions, including Leiden University. He later served as secretary to Francis Dana at the American mission in St. Petersburg, Russia.

Francis Dana was an American statesman who served as a delegate to the Continental Congress in 1777, 1778, and 1784. In 1780, Dana left the Congress to take the post of minister to Russia. Even though Catherine II never gave the American legation official recognition, Dana and Adams remained in St. Petersburg until 1783.

Adams, an accomplished linguist, was appointed by President Washington as minister to the Netherlands in 1794 (at age twenty-six), to Portugal in 1796, and to Berlin in 1797. President Madison appointed Adams as the U.S. Minister to Russia in 1809. In 1814, Adams was the chief negotiator for the Treaty of Ghent, which ended the 1812 War between the United States and Great Britain. From 1815 until 1817, he was Minister to the Court of St. James. From 1817 until 1825, Adams, while serving as Secretary of State to President Monroe, was instrumental in the acquisition of Florida and wrote the Monroe Doctrine.

The purchase of East Florida from Spain was possibly the first act of gunboat diplomacy in the American political scene. While Adams and Onís were negotiating, President Monroe authorized General Andrew "Old Hickory" Jackson to pursue warring Seminole Indians, but supposedly instructed him not to attack any Spanish installations. Jackson assembled a large force consisting of 800 U.S. Army Regulars, about 2,000 volunteers and militiamen from Tennessee and Georgia, respectively, and approximately 1,400 Lower Creek Native American warriors.

Jackson entered Florida south along the Apalachicola River. Contrary to orders, he seized the Spanish fort at St. Marks and headed to

Pensacola. The population left town, and the 175-man Spanish garrison retreated to Fort Barrancas. After two days of sporadic fighting, mostly involving exchanges of cannon fire, the Spanish surrendered Fort Barrancas on May 28, 1818. President Monroe came close to dismissing General Jackson, but Secretary of State John Quincy Adams convinced Monroe that Jackson's actions might have given the United States the upper hand to negotiate the purchase of Spanish East Florida.[7] Jackson went on to become the President (1829–1837).

Spain was losing its grip on its colonial empire and wisely decided to sell East Florida to the United States, before the United States decided to take it forcibly. The treaty was negotiated by Adams and Spanish foreign minister Luis de Onís. The United States agreed to pay $5 million in claims against Spain by U.S. citizens of both East and West Florida. "The claims had been filed by merchants whose business had suffered during the closure of New Orleans and by ship owners whose ships had been plundered during hostilities in 1799."[8]

As a part of the deal, Spain would also sell to the United States its claim to the Oregon Country north of the forty-second parallel. In return, the United States would cease claiming Spain's territory west of Louisiana from Texas to California. The new boundary was the Sabine River north from the Gulf of Mexico to the thirty-second parallel north, then due north to the Red River, west along the Red River to the one-hundred meridian, due north to the Arkansas River, west to its source, north to the forty-second parallel north, and finally west along the parallel to the Pacific Ocean.

In terms of today's states, in addition to Florida, the United States gained Washington, Oregon, and Idaho. Great Britain still claimed ownership of these three western states. It would be June 15, 1846, before Great Britain would sign a treaty accepting that these three states were a part of U.S. territory. Additionally, Spain recognized U.S. ownership of other states, or portions thereof, which were contested by Spain after the Louisiana Purchase. These were Montana, the southwest portion of Wyoming, the Dakotas, and a portion of Nebraska. The United States had previously established ownership of Arkansas, most of Missouri, and most of Iowa.

Again in terms of today's states, Spain kept California, Nevada, Utah, Arizona, a small portion of Wyoming, about half of Colorado, all of New Mexico and Texas, and the Oklahoma panhandle as a part of its Mexican colony.

The Adams-Onís Treaty of 1819 is alternatively known as the Transcontinental Treaty of 1819, or as the Florida Treaty. The Treaty was executed in Washington, DC, on February 22, 1819. After all the required approvals and ratifications from Spain and the United States were obtained, the Treaty was proclaimed on February 22, 1821. The inevitable war between the United States and Spain was delayed by seventy-seven years by the Adams-Onís Treaty.

Manifest Destiny was becoming a self-fulfilling prophecy for the United States, while Spain's territory was shrinking exponentially due to the loss of South and Central American colonies. After the Florida Treaty, the United States owned all the land east of the Mississippi River plus a large northern passageway to the Pacific Ocean. But the work was not yet completed.

Notes

1. Frances Gardiner Davenport, *European Treaties Bearing on the History of the United States and its Dependencies to 1648*, vol. 1 (Washington, DC: Carnegie Institution, 1917), 20–26.
2. J. H. W. Verzijl, W. P. Heere, and J. P. S. Offerhaus, *International Law in Historical Perspective* (Leiden, The Netherlands: Martinus Nijhoff, 1979), 230–34.
3. Ibid., 237.
4. *Johnson and Graham's Lessee V McIntosh* 21 U.S. (8 Wheat.) 543, 5 L.Ed. 681 (1823).
5. Steve Newcomb, "Five Hundred Years of Injustice," *Shaman's Drum* (Fall 1992): 18–20.
6. Robert J. Miller, *Native America, Discovered and Conquered: Thomas Jefferson, Lewis & Clark, and Manifest Destiny* (Portland: Lewis & Clark College Press, 2007).
7. Michael Gannon, ed., *The New History of Florida* (Gainesville: University Press of Florida, 1996), 191–96.
8. Susan Dudley Gold, *Land Pacts* (New York: Twenty-First Century Books, 1997), 50.

4

Mexican-American War (1846–1848)

The Mexican-American War was the result of a number of issues, the most visible one being the annexation of Texas by the United States in 1845. Additionally, Britain's public expressions of establishing colonies in California and the U.S.' wish of territorial expansion to the Pacific Ocean, in keeping with Manifest Destiny were influencing factors.

The British minister in Mexico, Richard Pakenham, openly lobbied for the establishment of British colonies in California. He further advocated that once Mexico ceased to own California, Britain should move in, before the United States did so.[1]

One of the goals of President James K. Polk was territorial expansion to the Pacific coast, and southward to Cuba. The issue of slavery stopped Polk from taking action to seize these territories from Mexico, a country without political stability. In fact, during 1846, the presidency of Mexico changed hands four times.[2]

At the time of its independence, Mexico was much larger than the United States. In addition to today's Mexico, Mexican territory included the current U.S. states of Arizona, California, Nevada, New Mexico, and Utah, as well as parts of Colorado, Kansas, Wyoming, and Oklahoma. At least one-half of today's Texas was Mexican, while the other half was claimed both by Mexico and the United States as a part of the Louisiana Purchase.

The Mexican legislature, perhaps thinking that American settlers would make the Texas land more valuable, encouraged Americans to settle in Texas. In 1810, Moses Austin, a Missouri banker, was given a grant by the Mexican government to arrange for American families, preferably of the Catholic faith, to settle in Texas. The American settlers were required to take an oath of loyalty to Mexico. Austin died before he could implement this plan.

Stephen F. Austin, Moses' son, continued his father's unfinished work and was able to bring more than 300 families to Texas. The majority of the American settlers in Texas were coming from southern states and many were bringing slaves with them, even though slavery had been abolished in Mexico in 1829. Mexican authorities looked the other way.

By 1830, American settlers greatly outnumbered Mexicans living in Texas. Most Americans were Protestant, not Catholic as Mexico had requested. In 1830, the new Mexican dictator, General Antonio López de Santa Anna arranged for the Mexican legislature to pass a law that would stop any further Americans from settling in Texas.

Angered Texas settlers attempted to negotiate some form of autonomy with Mexican authorities, but all efforts failed. In 1833, Stephen Austin and other Texas leaders drew up a constitution and asked to meet with General Santa Anna. Some of the requests by the Americans were granted, but a few days later Austin was apprehended and jailed for treason by Mexican authorities.

In September 1835, Austin was released from prison and immediately stated that Texas must become a part of the United States and declared war against Mexico.[3] The Mexican army was not too eager to fight and did not engage the Texans during a brief encounter on September 30, 1835. Emboldened by this apparent victory, the Texans attacked and captured a Mexican fort at the town of Goliad. The Texans then moved north on to San Antonio, where they scored an easy victory over the Mexican defenders of the mission-turned-fort named the Alamo. General Santa Anna was furious and commenced assembling a large military force.

Santa Anna and his troops arrived in San Antonio on February 23, 1836. There were less than 200 Texans defending the Alamo. Santa Anna forces slowly commenced to surround the Alamo. Meanwhile, Sam Houston was heading a convention in central Texas where a new constitution was adopted, creating the Republic of Texas.

William Travis, the senior officer at the Alamo, aware that they did not have a chance against Santa Anna's large force, sent a message to Santa Anna agreeing to surrender if their lives would be spared. Santa Anna turned Travis down.[4]

There were a total of 1,900 men in Santa Anna's force.[5] They attacked at dawn on Sunday, March 6, 1836. It took the Mexicans only four hours to overrun the Alamo. All the defenders, including the men who surrendered, were killed with bayonets. It is estimated that

182 Texans were killed. Women, children, and Travis' black slave were spared. There were 600 Mexican casualties.

Santa Anna then marched to Goliad and executed an estimated 400 Texan prisoners. Inspired by the slogan "Remember the Alamo," Sam Houston raised an army of some 700 men intent on seeking revenge for the slaughters at the Alamo and Goliad. Santa Anna's force consisted of 750 of his best men. The battle took place on April 21, 1836, at San Jacinto, east of the city of Houston. The Texans attacked in the early afternoon, while the Mexicans took their siesta. The Mexicans surrendered and begged for their lives after an eighteen-minute fight.[6] The Texans did remember Goliad and the Alamo and shot and clubbed the Mexican soldiers to death. Hiding in the brush, the mighty General Santa Anna pleaded to have his life spared.

Sam Houston, in spite of a painful bullet wound on his ankle, drove a hard bargain. Santa Anna would have to sign the Treaties of Velasco whereby Mexico would give up claim to Texas and would recognize the Republic of Texas as an independent country, and Santa Anna would additionally have to withdraw all Mexican troops south of the border. At the time, the southern border of Texas with Mexico was the Nueces River, and not the Rio Grande, which in Mexico is called *Río Bravo del Norte*. In exchange, Santa Anna's life would be spared. Santa Anna signed.

Upon learning of the Treaties of Velasco, Santa Anna was deposed as president and sent into exile to Cuba. The replacement Mexican government declared the treaties signed by Santa Anna null and void and promised the Mexican people that they would get Texas back. However, saddled with a huge debt and facing an unstable internal situation, Mexican authorities postponed going to war over the Republic of Texas.

Texas asked to be admitted to the United States, but President Andrew Jackson was not prepared to make such a controversial decision, since the 1837 presidential election was approaching, and he did not want to hurt the chances of his hand-picked candidate, Martin van Buren.[7] There were two main reasons why the annexation of Texas would create problems for the United States. The first one was that Texas would be a slaving state, which would strengthen Southern power. The second was that it would mean a certain war with Mexico and wars, particularly those fought within your own borders, are generally unpopular. There was a possibility that Mexican forces would attack inside U.S. territory. Martin van Buren did win the presidential election.

The Mexican government had repeatedly warned the United States that annexation of Texas would mean war. France and Britain had recognized Texas' independence and tried to persuade Mexico not to declare war, as they sensed that annexation of Texas by the United States was imminent. Mexico viewed Texas as a runaway province, much the same way the People's Republic of China views Taiwan in today's political scene.

President Martin van Buren continued delaying the annexation of Texas. In fact, van Buren managed to skirt the issue of Texas statehood during his four-year term. William Henry Harrison (1841) defeated van Buren and became president, but died after only one month in office. President John Tyler (1841–1845) continued to delay any action regarding the annexation of Texas.

The President of the Republic of Texas, Sam Houston, started rumors that Texas was considering annexation with England or France. This worried President Tyler and in June 1844 a Texas annexation treaty was presented to the Senate, but failed to pass. During the country's national election, surprisingly, the Democratic Party nominee, James K. Polk, was elected as president. Tyler, not wanting to be remembered as a president who did nothing, rushed to obtain approval for the annexation of Texas before Polk took office. Tyler personally walked the annexation resolution through the House and Senate, and obtained approval three days before he was to leave office. Tyler received the credit for the annexation of Texas and Polk suffered all the after-the-fact headaches. Texans were happy with the resolution and overwhelmingly voted in favor of accepting the annexation. Texas became the twenty-eighth state on December 29, 1845.

As soon as Mexico learned about the annexation of Texas, the Mexican government broke diplomatic relations with the United States and started positioning troops along the border. President Polk sent his envoy, Louisianan John Slidell, to Mexico with an offer of $30 million for its northern territory, upper (presently the state of) California, Arizona, and New Mexico. Mexican leaders refused to meet with Slidell since they felt that selling the territories to the United States would represent a black mark on Mexico's national honor.

Polk was aware that if Slidell's mission was to fail, it would lead directly to war. After learning of Slidell's return to the United States, Polk instructed General Zachary Taylor to take his army of 3,500 men to southern Texas and wait. Polk did not want the United States to fire the first shot. Taylor positioned his troops on the north shore of the

Rio Grande. Mexico considered its border with Texas to be the Nueces River, much farther north than the Rio Grande. Understandably, Mexican troops shot and killed some U.S. soldiers on April 24, 1846.

Polk could now claim that Mexicans had killed U.S. soldiers on American soil. On May 13, 1846, the U.S. Congress declared war on Mexico.

Fortunately for U.S. civilians, the Mexican War was fought entirely on Mexican soil. General Taylor won a number of battles in northern Mexico and in a few months had captured the capital cities of three northern Mexican provinces.

President Polk ordered Colonel Stephen W. Kearny to move along the Santa Fe Trail to southern California. Since most Mexican troops were busy battling against General Taylor, freelance opportunists decided to take over California. U.S. Army Captain John C. Frémont, a surveyor, topographer, and explorer, organized a group of recently arrived American settlers to take California away from the Mexicans.

Frémont designed the Bear Flag and proclaimed the Bear Republic. They took Sonoma and later claimed the city of San Francisco for the United States. When Frémont and his band arrived in Monterey, California, they met with U.S. Commodore John Sloat from the American Pacific Fleet, who had taken over the Monterey Custom House. Frémont and Sloat joined forces and marched to and occupied San Francisco. The ailing Sloat was replaced by Commodore Robert Stockton, who appointed Frémont as Military Governor of California. Stockton and Frémont captured San Diego and then moved north to prepare an assault on Los Angeles. Frémont dictated the terms of Mexican surrender, accepted capitulation by the Mexican forces, and officially annexed all of California on August 17, 1846.[8]

Some historians believe that Frémont had secret orders from President Polk to find a way to take California away from Mexico. Evidence of these orders has never been found.

When Colonel Kearny arrived in Santa Fe, the Mexican governor simply ran away. In August 1846, Kearny claimed New Mexico for the United States. After an eight-month campaign, the United States controlled the Mexican provinces north of the Rio Grande.

Clearly, the war was not going well for Mexico and President Paredes was deposed.

The new President was no other than the infamous General Santa Anna, well remembered by Americans for the massacres at Goliad and the Alamo.

Once President Polk learned of the annexation of California and New Mexico, he attempted to put a quick end to the war. In this connection, Polk instructed his general-in-chief Winfield Scott to make plans to take Mexico City. General Scott commenced to assemble his troops, weapons, and supplies at New Orleans.

General Winfield Scott served as the U.S.' general-in-chief for two decades. Scott is possibly the best known American military figure of the time, with the exception of George Washington. Scott, a hero of the War of 1812 and the U.S.-Mexican War, would later become an unsuccessful presidential candidate.

In the meantime, General Taylor had taken over Monterrey, Mexico, on September 23, 1846, after a ferocious three-day battle. Taylor was ordered by President Polk to send the bulk of his army to New Orleans to join Scott's forces. Taylor partially obeyed Polk's orders. He did send about half of his forces to New Orleans, but joined forces with the Center Division commanded by General John E. Wool. Together, they took the town of Saltillo and marched on to the town of Buena Vista, south of Monterrey, where they set camp. The American force totaled about 4,500 men. General Santa Anna, once again in charge of Mexico, had assembled an army of 20,000 men at San Luis Potosí and headed to Buena Vista.

General Wool prepared the defense and organized the troops for the upcoming battle. Upon arrival in the Buena Vista area, Santa Anna's forces totaled about 15,000 men, diminished by desertions and the exhaustive march from San Luis Potosí. Santa Anna, aware of his 3 to 1 numerical superiority, sent a letter to Taylor warning him "... to surrender or your army will be cut to pieces."[9] Taylor declined to surrender. The battle started on February 22, 1847, and ended the following day with a retreat by the Mexican forces. The battle ended with 723 Americans killed or wounded and 1,633 Mexicans killed or wounded and 294 captured.

After the American victory at the Battle of Buena Vista, General Taylor left General Wool in charge and returned to the United States to pursue a political career. General Zachary Taylor would become president, but would only serve sixteen months. He died of a stomach ailment on July 9, 1850.

General Winfield Scott decided that it was necessary to occupy the port city of Veracruz before marching inland to Mexico City. At the time, Veracruz was considered the most heavily fortified port city in the western hemisphere. It was defended by Brigadier General Juan

Morales who commanded a force of 4,390 men in three major forts with significant heavy artillery.

The American forces landed at a beach some five kilometers south of Veracruz on March 9, 1847. The city was slowly surrounded and its water supply cut off. Following orders from Captain Robert E. Lee, a battery emplacement was constructed 700 meters from the city wall. The U.S. Navy ships also had their guns trained on the city.

Morales refused to surrender and the American batteries opened fire. Mexican gunners responded with great accuracy. The Mexicans asked for a cease fire to allow women and children to leave the city, but American troops thought this was a trick and continued firing. The Mexicans finally surrendered on March 25, 1847, which opened the east coast of Mexico to U.S. forces. The United States had only 18 casualties, while the Mexicans had 180.

General Scott left some forces guarding Veracruz and started marching a force of 10,000 soldiers in the direction of Mexico City.

General Santa Anna wanted to avoid the destruction of Mexico City and attempted to defeat the American army before they arrived at the capital. The mountain pass of Cerro Gordo was an ideal place for Santa Anna and his 12,000 soldiers to ambush the Americans. General Scott waited since a frontal attack would have resulted in heavy American casualties.

On April 17, 1847, Captain Robert E. Lee discovered a mountain pass which he assumed that Santa Anna probably considered impassable and had left essentially undefended.

By using the pass found by Lee, the American forces were able to encircle the Mexicans and capture their camps. Mexican forces retreated, leaving behind 1,000 casualties, some 3,000 prisoners, and all their artillery and supplies. American forces had approximately 400 casualties.

As General Scott approached Mexico City with his 10,000 troops, he was convinced that Santa Anna would surrender. The Americans reached Puebla on May 15, 1847. Many of Scott's soldiers had signed up for one year. Their time was up and they returned to the United States. Scott had to wait at Puebla for replacement troops. Finally, in early August, General Franklin Pierce, who would later become U.S. president number fourteen, and his soldiers joined Scott.

The battle for Mexico City took place from September 8 to 15, 1847 and was comprised of a series of engagements. The two key battles were Molino del Rey and the Castle of Chapultepec. U.S. forces numbered

7,200 men, while Santa Anna had at least 16,000 soldiers. The American forces soundly defeated the Mexicans at both engagements. Santa Anna resigned as President on September 16, 1847, followed by the surrender of the city by the Mexican Junta on September 17, 1847. Americans had about 1,000 casualties while the Mexicans had 4,000 plus 3,000 captured. It was time to negotiate.

President Polk had sent State Department chief clerk Nicholas P. Trist along with General Scott's army to negotiate the purchase of Mexico's northern provinces for $25 million. Polk had assumed that the United States would win the war, but after hearing of the magnitude of American victories, Polk ordered Trist to return to the United States in order to be instructed to seek better terms. General Scott, aware of the unstable Mexican political situation, suggested to Trist that he stay and finish the negotiations before a new Mexican administration took power. Trist agreed, stayed, and continued his work.

The people of Mexico were so impressed with General Winfield Scott that they sent a delegation to his camp to inquire as to what he would require to lead the Mexican government. Scott politely refused, as he had his eye on the presidency of the United States. He was indeed nominated for the presidency by the Whig Party for the 1852 election. His rival was Franklin Pierce, also a hero of the Mexican-American War. Scott's antislavery pronouncements cost the election, and Pierce won by a landslide.

The Treaty of Guadalupe Hidalgo was signed on February 2, 1848, by Nicholas Trist representing the United States and Luis Cuevas, Bernardo Couto, and Miguel Atristain as duly empowered representatives of Mexico. The United States paid Mexico $15 million for all the lands north of the Rio Grande and agreed to pay $3.25 million in claims U.S. citizens had filed against the Mexican government.[10] Mexico was allowed to keep Lower (Baja) California and a strip of land joining it to Mexico. In hindsight, Mexico would have been much better off if they had accepted Slidell's offer of $30 million.

Polk was so angry with Trist for ignoring his order to return to Washington that he had him arrested. The Senate ratified the Treaty on March 10, 1848.

The U.S.' need to build a coast to coast rail system resulted in another land purchase from Mexico. James Gadsden, American Minister to Mexico, negotiated the purchase of about 76,800 square kilometers in what is now southern Arizona and the southwestern-most portion of New Mexico. The Treaty was signed by President Pierce on

June 24, 1853, and is named the Gadsden Treaty in honor of its American negotiator.

The forty-eight contiguous states had taken shape. Soon Americans would be fighting one another in an effort to preserve differing ways of life. After the Civil War, land expansion would continue, with the acquisition of Alaska and Hawaii.

Notes

1. George L. Rives, *The United States and Mexico, 1821-1848*, vol. 2 (New York: Charles Scribner's Sons, 1913), 48–49.
2. Ibid., 658.
3. Jeffery Long, *Duel of Eagles: The Mexican and the U.S. Fight for the Alamo* (New York: William Morrow, 1990), 59.
4. Susan Dudley Gold, *Land Pacts* (New York: Twenty-First Century Books, 1997), 58.
5. Carrie Nichols Cantor, *The Mexican War: How the United States Gained Its Western Lands* (Chanhassen, NM: The Child's World, 2003), 19.
6. Long, *Duel of Eagles*, 312.
7. Gold, *Land Pacts*, 62.
8. Ibid., 70.
9. Glenn W. Price, *Origins of the War with Mexico: The Polk-Stockton Intrigue* (Austin: The University of Texas Press, 1967), 265.
10. Gold, *Land Pacts*, 75.

5

Alaska Purchase (1867)

The purchase of Alaska by the United States exemplified a significant magnification of expansionism, since American politicians were looking to expand beyond the natural borders of the nation. In April 1869, Cuban annexationists, encouraged by the bold action of President Andrew Johnson (1865–1869), proposed a meeting between the cabinet of the newly elected President Grant and José Morales Lemus, representing the Cuban rebels. Secretary of State Hamilton Fish informed Morales that the cabinet would not meet with a rebel representative since the United States wanted to keep faith with Spain.[1]

Alaska had been a Russian colony since its "discovery" by Captain Vitus Bering, on October 9, 1741. Bering was a Danish captain serving in the Russian Navy at the time of Czar Peter the Great. The territory had abundant seals and sea otters and large fortunes were made dealing in the animals' pelts.

What prompted Russia to sell and the United States to purchase such a vast and apparently inhospitable territory? The Russian leaders only had a vague idea of the territorial extension of the territory they called Russia America. Starting in the early 1800s, the development of the area was limited to fur trading operations conducted by the Russian-American Company. The brain behind this company was Aleksandr Baranov, a Siberian fur trader who became its aggressive administrator in 1790. Under his able leadership, the Russian-American Company provided handsome profits for the Russians coffers.

Baranov ran the territory most effectively and any way that he saw appropriate. He used to say: "God is in heaven and St. Petersburg is a long way off."[2] At the time, the capital of the Russian Empire was St. Petersburg. Baranov died in 1819.

In 1821, Russia issued a proclamation banning foreign traders from Russia America and issued a twenty-year control of the colony to the Russian-American Company. The United States negotiated a treaty with Russia in 1824 which allowed Americans to trade, under restricted conditions, in Alaskan waters. Great Britain negotiated a similar treaty in 1825.

New York Senator William Seward and his friend, California Senator William Gwin, became interested in Alaska when they learned of the huge profits being obtained by Western American hunters and trappers. In 1853, they secured federal funds to explore and map the area.[3]

The Crimean War started in October 1853 when the Ottoman Empire declared war on Russia. The ostensible reason for the conflict was a trivial disagreement over the Christian shrines in Jerusalem. The real reason was Russia's encroachment over territory controlled by a weakening Ottoman Empire. European powers were concerned about Russia expanding south and their controlling of the Black Sea ports, although trade through these ports was not significant at the time.

In January 1854, the Anglo-French fleet sailed into the Black Sea, and on March 28, 1854, Britain and France declared war on Russia. Sardinia-Piedmont joined the Ottoman-Franco-British alliance in January 1855. The Russian Army offered strong resistance, but when Austria threatened to join the alliance and Russia lost Sevastopol, Russia agreed to peace negotiations which resulted in the March 1856 Treaty of Paris.

When the Russian merchants who ruled Alaska learned that Great Britain had entered the Crimean War on the Ottoman side, they worried that Great Britain would take over the Russian-American Company trading routes. Not knowing how long the conflict could last, and in order to protect their property, the Russians attempted to transfer all their "property and franchises," for a three-year term, to a San Francisco-based firm.[4] The U.S. Secretary of State, William Marcy, determined that Great Britain would not believe the validity of the transfer and did not accept the plan. The Russian-American Company instead worked out a deal with the British-owned Hudson Bay Company and the Russian territory was not attacked by Britain. A more likely scenario is that there was nothing in Alaska that interested Britain at the time.

Somehow, several U.S. newspapers carried reports of the Russian–U.S. conversations and blew the story out of proportion. It was even reported that Russia had already offered to sell the territory to the United States.[5]

At the end of the Crimean War in 1856, Russia was left with a large national debt. Looking for ways to replenish its coffers, Russia considered the matter of selling Alaska to the United States. Russia, aware of the British–American rivalry in North America's northwest, also wanted to complicate American relations with Britain, which had just defeated Russia in the Crimean War.

U.S. Secretary of State William Seward was the driving force behind the Alaska purchase. On the Russian side it was Edouard de Stoeckl, the Russian ambassador to the United States. Stoeckl came to the United States in 1841 and stayed for over twenty-five years. He had an American wife, spoke excellent English, and was well accustomed to U.S. business and diplomatic practices.

There were some conversations between Senator Gwin and Ambassador Stoeckl in 1858 and 1859, but both parties were noncommittal. Stoeckl wanted the United States to make an offer, but Gwin indicated that President James Buchanan (1857–1861), even though interested, could not make an offer as it would upset the balance between free and slave states.[6] It is believed that Stoeckl contacted Russia and indicated that the United States was definitely interested in purchasing the Russia America Territory.

The issue of slavery had continued to polarize Americans for decades. The election of President Abraham Lincoln (1861–1865), in 1860 further divided the American nation. Eleven southern states seceded from the Union, the first shots were fired at Fort Sumter on April 12, 1861, and the U.S. Civil War thus commenced.

The four-year Civil War took center stage during the Lincoln administration. Secretary of State William Seward did not have time to think about purchasing Alaska from Russia. England and France encouraged European powers to mediate the North–South dispute, but Russia chose to stay out of any mediation efforts. The Union was thankful of Russia's attitude and their bonds of friendship strengthened.

In 1863, Polish nationalists demanded independence from Russia and hostilities broke out. Russia became concerned that Great Britain would join Poland in the fighting and sent several warships to the safety of U.S. northern ports. Northerners were convinced that the Russians were there to support their cause against the South. This perceived act of friendship by Russia would later help in the negotiations for the Alaska Purchase.

Confederate General Robert E. Lee surrendered to Union General Ulysses S. Grant at Appomattox on April 9, 1865. The Civil War had ended with a Union victory and it was time to heal the wounds of a divided America.

Five days later President Lincoln was assassinated by John Wilkes Booth at Ford's Theatre. The conspiracy had a wider scope, as three simultaneous assassinations were to have taken place. George Atzerodt was supposed to assassinate Vice President Andrew Johnson but lost his nerve and got drunk instead. Lewis Powell's target was Secretary of State William Seward.

Seward was at home with a badly injured leg. Powell pretended to be the employee of a pharmacy delivering medicine for Seward in order to gain access to the house. Seward's eldest son Frederick tried to stop him, but Powell knocked him unconscious. Powell jumped Seward's male nurse and slit his throat with a bowie knife. Powell then stabbed Seward in the throat and face, but Seward survived the attack. Powell came close to preventing the Alaska Purchase.[7]

Andrew Johnson became president (1865–1869) after Lincoln's assassination. Johnson asked Seward to remain in his post as Secretary of State and Seward accepted.

Seward did not waste time in reviving his Alaska purchase project. He remembered well the costly defeats inflicted by the Confederate Navy to Union shipping at the Aleutian Islands in 1865. Seward considered that Alaska's military strategic significance equaled its commercial value.

Russia was concerned that providing basic human services to Alaska was becoming a logistics nightmare and a drain on its scant resources. Stoeckl was in St. Petersburg during the Christmas of 1866 and attended a meeting on the Alaska situation at the request of Czar Alexander. Alexander instructed Stoeckl to commence negotiations, but to manipulate events such that it would appear that the idea originated with the American administration. Otherwise, it would look as if Russia was too financially weak to hold on to its properties.

On or around March 11, 1867, Stoeckl and Seward met and the subject of Alaska was broached. Seward stated that the United States was interested in purchasing Alaska, to which Stoeckl replied that Russia was interested in selling the territory. The two men agreed to meet again on March 14.

In the meantime, Seward met with President Johnson and the Cabinet to ask for authority to offer $7 million for Alaska and the Aleutian islands. The Cabinet was surprised, but approved Seward's request.

During the March 14, 1867 meeting, Seward made an initial offer of $5 million. The bid was later upped to $5.5 million. Negotiations continued, and by March 23, the offering price had increased to

$6 million and the negotiators had agreed on the key points of the sale. Stoeckl indicated that he would contact St. Petersburg but that if the price were $7 million, the Czar would be more likely to approve the deal.[8]

On March 29, 1867, Stoeckl unexpectedly arrived at Seward's house with the news that Czar Alexander had approved the deal for $7 million. Seward suggested working on the treaty that evening. During this final negotiation, Stoeckl attempted to make some changes to the agreed treaty verbiage. Sewell refused, but did agree to increase the price to $7.2 million. The treaty was signed at 4 a.m. on March 30, 1867. The United States was in the process of acquiring a territory of 1.53 million square kilometers, more than twice the size of Texas, for a little less than 2 cents per acre.

Seward was well aware that the signing of the treaty was the easy part. The next two elements, ratification of the treaty by Congress, and the appropriation of funds to pay the Russians, would be the difficult steps. President Johnson, a southerner, was very unpopular and the Senate was considering impeaching him for abuse of power.

The debate on the purchase of Alaska was not limited to Congress. The press, hungry for controversy, quickly took sides. Thanks to Seward's tireless efforts, the Senate approved the treaty on April 9, 1867. The treaty was then sent to St. Petersburg for Czar Alexander to sign.

On June 20, 1867, Russia and the United States ratified the treaty. The Russians wanted their money, but approval of both houses was required to appropriate the funds to pay for Alaska, and approvals were slow in coming. In order to speed up matters, Seward decided to arrange for the official transfer of control to take place prior to the payment to the Russians. The American flag was raised in Sitka, Alaska, on October 18, 1867. Seward's strategy was that Congress would be too embarrassed to deny funds for a place where the American flag was already flying. In the meantime, the Russians were angrily demanding payment.

The impeachment hearings of President Johnson took precedence over the payment for Alaska. The Alaska matter continued to drag while an army of lobbyists sang the praises of this northwest land. To further complicate and delay matters, the House and the Senate passed different versions of the bill. Finally, a compromise bill was drafted and approved by both Houses on July 23, 1868. President Johnson signed the Alaska Purchase into law on July 27, 1868.

There is no doubt that the Alaska Purchase was a brilliant acquisition on the part of the United States. Unfortunately, to this day there is a cloud over the payment of bribes to secure the approval of the funds by Congress. Stoeckl received $7.2 million for Alaska, but only $7.035 million arrived in Russia. What happened to the missing $165 thousand?

A Congressional investigation accounted for $95 thousand out of the missing $165 thousand. Years later, researchers found handwritten notes by President Johnson where he stated that approximately $70 thousand was divided among Representative Thaddeus Stevens from Pennsylvania and ten unknown Congressmen.[9]

It is unfortunate that William Henry Seward is primarily remembered for *Seward's folly*, or the Alaska Purchase. Seward was a highly intelligent politician, a shrewd negotiator, and a man with an uncanny vision of the future.

Seward was a defender of the Monroe Doctrine and frequently quoted its author, his patron, and guide, John Quincy Adams. Obviously, during the Civil War the United States was unable to enforce the Monroe Doctrine. Nevertheless, Seward made veiled threats of removing by force Maximilian, the French-appointed *emperor* of Mexico. When the Civil War ended, Seward let the European powers know that the temporary suspension of the Monroe Doctrine had ended.

Only two of Seward's expansionist projects came to fruition, both in 1867, Alaska's Purchase, and the taking of Midway Island in the Pacific by the U.S. Navy. Seward nevertheless worked indefatigably on expanding the territory and power of the United States. Some of his projects follow:

- Negotiated treaties for the acquisition of the Virgin Islands and the Danish West Indies.
- Contemplated the acquisition of Cuba, Haiti, Puerto Rico, and Tiger Island off Honduras.
- Negotiated with Colombia a treaty for the right-of-way to build a canal across the isthmus of Panama.
- Eyed the purchase of Iceland and Greenland.
- Looked into acquiring Hawaii and Fiji and building a naval base in Formosa (now Taiwan).

Seward was a crucial link between the early nineteenth-century Manifest Destiny expansionists, Jefferson, Madison, Monroe, and John Quincy Adams, and the late nineteenth-century overseas imperialists,

Figure 5.1 United States Territorial Growth

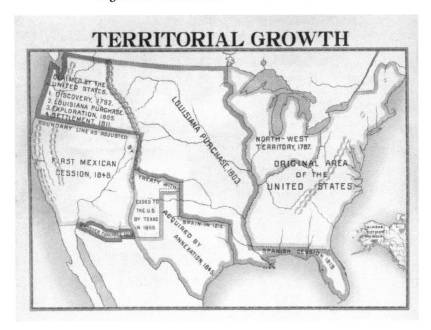

Theodore Roosevelt, Henry Cabot Lodge, Mahan, Dewey, and Wood.[10]

In order to better fulfill his duties as Secretary of State, Seward skillfully cultivated an image of a madman. Many heads of state from world power countries believed that he was reckless and would call for war at the slightest provocation. "Seward now ranks among the nation's best secretaries of state."[11]

Alaska became the forty-ninth state on January 3, 1959.

Figure 5.1, as drawn by H. C. Robertson c1897, provides a representation of U.S. territorial growth, from the founding of the republic until prior to the annexation of Hawaii.

Notes

1. Thomas, *Cuba or the Pursuit of Freedom*, 245–51.
2. Henry W. Clark, *History of Alaska* (New York: McMillan, 1930), 53.
3. Ronald J. Jensen, *The Alaska Purchase and Russian-American Relations* (Seattle: The University of Washington Press, 1975), 9.
4. Ibid., 5.
5. Susan Dudley Gold, *Land Pacts* (New York: Twenty-First Century Books, 1997), 87.

6. Ibid., 89.
7. Susan Clinton, *Cornerstones of Freedom: The Story of Seward's Folly* (Chicago, IL: Children's Press, 1987), 10.
8. Keith Wheeler, ed., *The Alaskans* (Alexandria, VA: Time-Life Books, 1977), 41–43.
9. Jensen, *Alaska Purchase and Russian-American Relations*, 130.
10. George C. Herring, *From Colony to Superpower: U.S. Foreign Relations Since 1776* (New York: Oxford University Press, 2008), 255.
11. Ibid., 227–28.

6

Annexation of Hawaii (1898)

The purchases of Louisiana and Florida as well as the Mexican-American War, were not free of opposition. Several antiexpansionism movements protested against U.S. empire building, citing the fear that continued expansionism would make the United States a target of international power politics. Others held the view that expansionism was antidemocratic and violated the spirit of the U.S. Constitution.

The expansionist President Andrew Johnson's administration was the target of severe criticism during the Alaska Purchase political maneuvering. To a large extent, these antiexpansionists were the same men that had protested during the 1850s against the projects for purchase and/or annexation of Cuba. Ultimately, the American public accepted the Alaska Purchase, partly because Alaska was in the North American continent, but primarily because it was a good business deal.

An attempt by the Ulysses Grant administration to annex Santo Domingo, now the Dominican Republic, met with public disapproval. Even though the expansionists were busy on other pursuits, the anti-imperialists continued to seek public support against the U.S.' deepening involvement in Hawaii and the Caribbean.

The establishment of a German–British–American protectorate over Samoa in 1898, the near U.S. war with Chile in 1891–1892, the first attempt to annex Hawaii in 1893, and the American involvement in the 1895 Britain–Venezuela border dispute in Guiana, put the anti-imperialists on alert. The United States seemed prepared to expand its territory well beyond North America. Two issues would take center stage as the nineteenth century came to a close, war with Spain over Cuba, and the annexation of Hawaii.

Around the middle of the nineteenth century, a number of countries wanted to claim ownership of the Hawaiian Islands, but not one was prepared to wage war for this territory. England claimed rights of discovery since Captain Cook was the first Westerner to visit the archipelago. Japan believed that Hawaii was a de facto colony of the Empire of Japan since approximately 40 percent of the inhabitants of Hawaii were of Japanese ancestry, while France used the argument that they owned most of the South Pacific islands. The United States claimed that it was the closest continental mass to Hawaii, that Americans ran the sugar industry, Hawaii's largest source of income, and that the United States was the biggest market for Hawaii's sugar.

The kingdom of Hawaii signed trade and peace treaties with the United States, England, and other foreign nations, each recognizing Hawaii's independence.[1] A large group of Christian missionaries, mostly Americans, arrived in Hawaii starting in 1820 for the purpose of converting native Hawaiians to Christianity. Many of these missionaries abandoned their intended purpose to seek personal fortune. Soon these men became influential in society and politics. The missionaries-turned-politicians wanted to run the affairs of Hawaii while relegating the King to a figurehead.

Led by the American adventurer Walter M. Gibson, a *coup d'état* took place in Hawaii in 1887. King Kalakaua was forced to sign the 1887 Constitution of the Kingdom of Hawaii which, in addition to removing any administrative authority for the king, eliminated voting rights for Asians. The electorate was thus limited to Americans, Europeans, and a small minority of native Hawaiians who had amassed wealth.

After the death of King Kalakaua in 1891, the throne was passed to his sister, Liliuokalani. The desire to annex Hawaii to the United States was not limited to an isolated group of American and European Hawaii landowners. President Benjamin Harrison (1889–1893), as well as a group of U.S. congressmen, encouraged Hawaii's annexation and actively lobbied for its implementation. "In 1892 a secret Annexation Club was formed in Honolulu, and the American minister to Hawaii worked avidly for the cause."[2]

In 1893, Liliuokalani disclosed plans to establish a new constitution which would return administrative power to the monarch. A group of American and European businessmen, under the leadership of Samuel Dole, formed a Committee of Safety which overthrew Queen Liliuokalani and asked for annexation to the United States. President Harrison encouraged the takeover, and sent sailors from the USS *Boston* to Hawaii with instructions to surround the royal palace.

Dole sent a delegation to Washington in 1894 seeking annexation, but President Grover Cleveland (1893–1897), who had previously served as president (1885–1889) opposed the annexation, and ordered that Liliuokalani be restored to the throne. Dole responded by declaring Hawaii an independent republic and appointed himself president.

Up until the election of President William McKinley in November 1896, the players for the power games in Hawaii were limited to some greedy American and European businessmen and a weakened native monarchy. As the specter of war against Spain was contemplated, a group of unabashed, aggressive American expansionists started meeting at the Metropolitan Club in Washington, DC, and the future of Hawaii became equated with that of the United States becoming a first-tier naval power.

These men were not conspirators. Rather, they were American nationalists who were convinced they were doing the right thing by expanding the Monroe Doctrine to Hawaii, building the most powerful navy in the world, and controlling the sea lanes to Latin America and Asia. Politicians and businessmen were used when necessary, but the brains of the movement were three men, with the assistance of two other men, each necessary in his area of expertise. The three brains of the group were:

- Theodore Roosevelt, originally a writer, adventurer, and conservationist who after developing a political ambition became Police Commissioner of New York, Assistant Secretary of the Navy, second in command to a group of adventurers who would claim to have single-handedly defeated the Spanish, Vice President, and finally President (1901–1909).
- Henry Cabot Lodge, a powerful senator from the sea-faring state of Massachusetts.
- Captain Alfred Thayer Mahan, Head of the Naval War College, the most influential writer of his day, and a man who believed a strong global navy was the key to becoming a world power.

The two specialist-helpers were:

- Admiral George Dewey, who became commander-in-chief of the Asiatic Squadron thanks to the efforts of his friend Theodore Roosevelt.
- Dr. Leonard Wood, an Indian-fighter involved in the capture of Geronimo, personal physician to President McKinley and family, who recruited and commanded Rough Riders during the Cuba campaign, became military governor of Cuba, opposed Harding in the presidential race, and after losing became Governor-General of the Philippines.

Captain Mahan had published *The Influence of Sea Power upon History, 1660-1783* in 1890. The ideas presented in this book made it an instant international best seller. Mahan contended that supremacy of the seas was a requirement for a super power, and this would lead to command of commerce during peace and control of the seas during war. He further contended that any army would capitulate if subjected to a strong naval blockade. Expansionists in the United States utilized Mahan's book as a strategy model to justify growth of U.S. overseas possessions. Some believe that Mahan's book was one of the reasons for the Anglo-German naval rivalry and one of the causes of World War I. "Kaiser Wilhelm ordered a copy placed aboard every ship of the growing Imperial German Navy."[3]

As early as 1895, New York City Police Commissioner Theodore Roosevelt wrote to his close friend Massachusetts Senator Henry Cabot Lodge, "This country needs a war."[4] Senator Cabot Lodge was instrumental in securing Roosevelt's appointment as Assistant Secretary of the Navy on April 19, 1897. Secretary of the Navy, John D. Long, was often sick and absent. In the meantime, Roosevelt prepared the Navy for war.[5]

After less than three weeks as Assistant Secretary of the Navy, it appears that Roosevelt was trying to take over U.S. foreign policy. In a letter to his friend Alfred Thayer Mahan, dated May 3, 1897, Roosevelt wrote "...If I had my way we would annex those [Hawaii] islands tomorrow. If that is impossible I would establish a protectorate over them. I believe we should build the Nicaraguan canal at once, and in the meantime that we should build a dozen new battleships, half of them on the Pacific coast..."[6]

In 1898, Theodore Roosevelt, from his obscure post in the Navy, lobbied for annexation of Hawaii and war with Spain. Secretary of State John Sherman, unaware that a Hawaii annexation treaty was being discussed in the Senate, assured the Japanese minister that no treaty was being negotiated. After the treaty was proclaimed, the Japanese protested. Roosevelt's answer was "The United States is not in a position which requires her to ask Japan or any other foreign power what territory it shall or shall not acquire."[7]

Before his appointment to President McKinley's Cabinet, Secretary Long was a leading figure in the Peace Society and was strongly opposed to the war with Spain. Secretary Long and Roosevelt often argued about the desirability to declare war on Spain. Long usually was successful in calming Roosevelt down. Sometime in early February, 1898, Long's health forced him to take a medical leave which would last for several weeks, and Roosevelt found himself in charge of the Navy immediately prior to the declaration of war.[8]

The vast majority of anti-imperialist leaders were men in their sixties and seventies and their logic was trumped by anti-Spanish patriotism. Men such as Thomas Higginson, William Endicott, Carl Schurz, Charles Francis Adams, Mark Twain, Andrew Carnegie, and Edward Atkinson ranged in age from sixty-three to seventy-five in 1898. These men and their many followers opposed all expansionist projects, but the charisma and media support generated by Roosevelt and Mahan won the test of public opinion.

A large segment of America feared expansion beyond the forty-eight contiguous states. However, it was well known that Germany and Japan were becoming threats to world peace. Led by the politically savvy militarist/expansionist leadership of Theodore Roosevelt, slowly the American public embraced empire building as a way of life.[9]

Perhaps the last stand of the elderly anti-imperialists was the 1900 presidential election. William Jennings Bryan, a Democrat, opposed William McKinley, a Republican. McKinley attempted to interest other men to join his ticket, but being aware of the closeness of the election, finally selected Theodore Roosevelt for the Vice-Presidential post. Roosevelt, a highly popular war hero, had won the hearts of the American electorate, and McKinley achieved a decisive victory. The anti-imperialist movement essentially died of old age after the election, but so did American thirst for further expansion.[10]

As the impending war with Spain approached, an amendment was introduced in the Senate linking the annexation of Hawaii to the War Revenue bill. The sponsor, U.S. Massachusetts senator, Henry Cabot Lodge, said, "Henceforth, the two measures must travel together. Both are equally important, and under the circumstances it would be fool-hardy for us to forgo our advantages in Hawaii."[11] Clearly, Roosevelt, Cabot, and other expansionists knew that it would be difficult to hold the Philippines without controlling Hawaii. A stopping and refueling point for American vessels to/from Manila was needed, and Hawaii was the answer.

The catalyst that ignited visions of America's enlargement across the Pacific was clearly Dewey's victory at Manila Bay. Even before the war with Spain was over, the Hawaiian Islands were declared a U.S. territory after the Newlands Resolution was passed by the House on June 15, 1898, by a vote of 209 to 91 and by the Senate on July 6, 1898, by a vote of 42 to 21. The vote by the Senate was three days after the naval battle of Santiago. War fever and the thought of territorial expansion had caught the interest of public opinion.

McKinley signed the joint resolution to annex the Hawaiian Islands on July 7, 1898. Samuel Dole became the first governor. During the debates, congressmen in favor of the Resolution pointed to the strategic importance of Hawaii and repeatedly stated that the Hawaiians were not capable of self-government.

Hawaii became the fiftieth state of the United States in 1959. The State of Hawaii is composed of eight major islands plus 124 minor islands. Honolulu, the state capital is located 4,118 kilometers from Los Angeles and 6,205 kilometers from Tokyo. In general terms, Hawaii is literally in the middle of the Pacific Ocean, thus possessing significant military strategic value. Hawaii, with a territorial extension of 16,706 square kilometers, is the fourth smallest state in the United States.

The war with Spain became a contentious issue in the Territory of Hawaii. As a newly annexed U.S. territory, Hawaiians were expected to support the American war effort; however, they quickly divided into two factions. One group, fearing an attack by the Spanish Pacific fleet, suggested neutrality, while the other group advocated support of the war effort. The patriotic faction won, Hawaiians refused to declare neutrality, and decided to support the U.S. Navy. In this connection, they bought all the coal in Hawaii and piled it eight feet high on four square blocks next to Honolulu harbor. Hawaii remained a territory for sixty years due to the lobbying of wealthy plantation owners not wanting to be subject to American labor laws and the Chinese Exclusion Act if Hawaii became a State.

Some native Hawaiians claim that their ancestors were never consulted on the annexation of their homeland to the United States. They further claim that a state of war between Hawaii and the United States exist today. On June 27, 1959, a referendum was held in Hawaii asking residents to vote on accepting the statehood bill. Voters accepted the referendum at a ratio of 17 to 1. This referendum is another source of acrimony, since the choices in the referendum were either to accept statehood or to remain a territory. The possibility to become an independent country was never offered.

The territorial expansion that took place from the founding of the United States in 1776 through the Alaska Purchase in 1867 did not follow a plan. The creation of the forty-eight contiguous states was a combination of good luck, intelligent negotiations, and bloody wars by various administrations. The package composed of the annexation of

Hawaii and the war against Spain clearly followed a strategy aimed at taking over Spain's overseas colonies and becoming a first-rate commercial and military power.

In order to implement the expansionist strategy, as will be seen in subsequent chapters, the press was used to convince the American people that the primary purpose of war with Spain was to liberate the oppressed Cuban people. The leaders of the Cuban insurrection, well aware of the principles of marketing and advertising, also helped to generate anti-Spanish sentiments in America through their field offices in New York and Washington, DC.

The strategy was clear. Once Spain would be defeated in the fields of battle, the United States would negotiate taking possession of all the Spanish colonies in Asia, the Philippines and Mariana Islands (which includes Guam), and in the Americas, Cuba and Puerto Rico. Hawaii would be the logical outpost to house a large fleet to defend the Philippines and Marianas. All that would be left to do was to construct a canal across the isthmus of North and South America so that, if necessary, the American navy could simultaneously participate in wars in the Atlantic and the Pacific oceans, as well as to simplify commerce for U.S. products. Historian Louis A. Pérez Jr. determined that "ownership of Cuba by the U.S. was included in the strategy for the construction of a Central American Canal."[12]

Plans worked relatively well. Construction of the Panama Canal commenced during the presidency of William McKinley, the project was personally taken over by Theodore Roosevelt during his presidency, reluctantly continued by President William Taft (1909–1913), with completion of the Canal in 1914, under the presidency of Woodrow Wilson (1913–1921).

Notes

1. Teri Sforza, "Hawaii's Annexation a Story of Betrayal," *The Orange County Register*, November 9, 1996.
2. D. W. Meining, *The Shaping of America*, vol. 3 (New Haven, CT: Yale University Press, 1998), 365–66.
3. Ivan Musicant, *Empire by Default* (New York, NY: Henry Holt and Company, 1998), 10.
4. Henry F. Pringle, *Theodore Roosevelt* (New York, NY: Harcourt, 1931), 167.
5. H. W. Brands, ed., *The Selected Letters of Theodore Roosevelt* (New York, NY: Cooper Square Press, 2001), 62.
6. Ibid., 132.
7. Howard K. Beale, *Theodore Roosevelt and the Rise of America to World Power* (New York, NY: Collier Books, 1962), paperback ed., 66–67.

8.   John Tebbel, *America's Great Patriotic War with Spain: Mixed Motives, Lies and Racism in Cuba and the Philippines, 1898-1915* (Manchester Center, VT: Marshall Jones Company, 1996), 82, 104–6.
9.   Meining, *Shaping of America*, 394.
10.   Robert L. Beisner, *Twelve against Empire: The Anti-Imperialists, 1898-1900* (New York, NY: McGraw-Hill Book, 1968), 9–10, 107–37.
11.   Harvey Rosenfeld, *Diary of a Dirty Little War: The Spanish-American War of 1898* (Westport, CT: Praeger Publishers, 2000), 86.
12.   Louis A. Pérez Jr., *The War of 1898: The United States and Cuba in History and Historiography* (Chapel Hill: The University of North Carolina Press, 1998), 49.

Part 2

The Spanish Empire Disintegrates

7

Madrid Politics (1819–1898)

The destiny of the island of Cuba had been ruled by Spain since its discovery by Christopher Columbus in 1492. Because of its privileged geographic location, Cuba had become Spain's distribution center in the New World and strong bonds had been formed between Cuba and Spain. It would be difficult and quite painful to remove those ties.

As the territorial expansion of the United States was taking place, the opposite was taking effect in the Spanish Empire. Napoleon's invasion of Spain, coupled with Spain's loss of its colonies in the Americas was rendering Spain weak and vulnerable, while the United States was becoming strong and hungrier for additional growth. There was a common variable in the Spain–U.S. system of equations; the United States wanted Cuba even if it meant war and Spain wanted to keep Cuba at any cost.

The decline of the Spanish Empire was far from an expeditious action. Rather, it was a creeping process which significantly accelerated during the early years of the nineteenth century.

The second half of the sixteenth century was the period of Spain's greatest power and prestige. Spain was not only the center of the Holy Roman Empire, but had vast colonies in the Americas, Africa, Asia, and Oceania. The phrase "the sun never sets on the Spanish Empire" has been credited to both Charles V of the Holy Roman Empire, who was also Charles I of Spain, as well as to his son Phillip II. There is no evidence that this phrase, although astronomically correct, can be attributed to either monarch and it may merely be a fabrication of the literature of the time.

In contrast, during the first half of the nineteenth century, specifically during the timeframe from 1808 to 1843, the Spanish Empire suffered a significant transformation as it became a second-rate world power. Two of the great powers of the time, England and France, were involved in a protracted war (1795–1815) which had an important effect on Spain. England was the master of the seas, while France under

Napoleon's rule dominated access to the continent, under the ports blockage known as the *Continental System.*

Napoleon was aware that he could neither carry out a land invasion of the United Kingdom nor defeat the Royal Navy at sea. Instead, he planned to defeat Britain economically by suppressing its ability to trade. To enforce the Continental System, Napoleon issued the Berlin decree forbidding all countries under his rule from trading with Britain. The system failed because Napoleon's land-based enforcers could not stop smugglers, and Britain still had naval dominance and threatened to sink any ship that complied with France's orders.

Charles IV had been crowned King of Spain in 1788, but he was more interested in hunting than in running the government. Charles' wife, Maria Luisa and her alleged lover, Manuel de Godoy filled the power vacuum.

Portugal had refused to join Napoleon in the Continental System, and in November 1806, Godoy negotiated a treaty with France to subjugate Portugal. A French–Spanish army took over Portugal and the Portuguese royal family fled to Brazil. After the war ended, French troops continued to enter Spain and it soon became obvious that France had also occupied Spain as a part of the Continental System.[1]

Godoy continued to support France, while Charles' son Ferdinand lobbied for a closer relationship with the United Kingdom. Charles took Godoy's side and the angry Spanish people revolted on March 17, 1808, in what would be called the *Mutiny of Aranjuez.* Charles abdicated in favor of his son who was crowned Ferdinand VII on March 19, 1808. Napoleon, who had a large army in Spain, did not trust Ferdinand.

Napoleon quickly occupied Madrid and Barcelona and it became clear that he would decide who would rule Spain. Napoleon invited Ferdinand VII to meet him in Bayonne, France. At the same time, French troops were bringing Charles, María Luisa, and Godoy to Bayonne. In a shameful example of lack of integrity of the Spanish royal family, Charles was persuaded to retract his prior abdication in favor of Ferdinand and reabdicate in favor of Joseph Bonaparte, Napoleon's brother. On June 6, 1808, Joseph I was crowned King of Spain.[2]

Napoleon ordered Charles, Ferdinand, María Luisa, and Godoy to be held at four different French chateaux. Incensed Spaniards proclaimed juntas to rule in the name of Ferdinand VII.

The reign of Joseph I did not have an auspicious start, since the Spanish people, led by the middle class, revolted against France and thus the War of Independence (1808–1814) commenced. Additionally, in 1810, Venezuela declared independence from Spain, the first Spanish colony to do so in the Americas.

This revolution of the middle class in Spain would have an international impact in the Western Hemisphere, since the *criollos* (children of European parents born in the Americas) would feel compelled to sever relations with the French authorities ruling Spain. After all, they had sworn allegiance to Spain and not to France. The term criollo has made its way to the English language as Creole, albeit with a broader meaning, as it also encompasses references to dialects of European languages, as well as to highly seasoned cuisine, i.e., shrimp Creole.

Starting around the time of the War of Independence, Spain and Spanish items lost prestige in Europe. This led to the disqualification of Spain as a world power, as Spain had missed the Industrial Revolution, primarily due to the Continental System. The material destruction experienced during the war and the intensity of the conflict created a generation of barbaric Spaniards who only knew how to solve conflicts with violence.

The first half of the nineteenth century was not a time of progress for Spain. The Spanish War of Independence was one of many wars of liberation in Europe, as countries resisted Napoleon's occupation. These wars were fought not only by professional military, but also by common citizens. This general mobilization of Spanish citizens marked the beginning of a lengthy period of belligerence that would last for nearly half a century.

Spanish and Portuguese troops, with the assistance of English forces under the command of Lord Wellington, slowly and painfully pushed Napoleon's army in the direction of the Pyrenees. Joseph I had to flee from Madrid as the French army retreated to the north shore of the Ebro River. The Ebro, located in northeast Spain, parallel to the Pyrenees, is the most important river in the country. Its source is in Cantabria and transits through Logroño and Zaragoza before discharging in the Mediterranean in the province of Tarragona. The French were finally defeated in 1813, at the Battles of Vitoria and San Marcial, and Ferdinand VII was reinstated to the Spanish crown.

Joseph Bonaparte moved to the United States and lived there for fifteen years. To support his lavish lifestyle, he slowly sold the jewels of the Spanish crown which he stole when he departed Spain for France.

To a large extent, Spain had achieved its world power by virtue of the riches of its Western Hemisphere colonies. The influx of gold, silver, and precious stones was so great that Spain neither had to be concerned with fiscal responsibility, nor did it ever develop civil servants who understood the concept. When the majority of the Spanish colonies in the Americas became independent, 1808–1842, Spain quickly fell on hard times.

It is difficult to quantify the damage done to the Spanish economy by a half century of wars. England and France were able to maintain and improve their industrial bases while Spanish factories, including a promising textile industry, were destroyed by the French and English armies which were conveniently fighting their war in Spain. In addition to the devastation created by the wars, Spain lost most of its colonies in the Americas, and suffered the effects of the incompetency of the various groups that ruled the country during the long convalescing period which followed.

Spanish historian José María Jover points out that during the early part of the nineteenth century the word "Constitution" made no sense to the vast majority of Spaniards since "in 1803 the percentage of illiterate citizens was 94%."[3] Jover also postulates that the Spanish people were accustomed to having a king, for the king to rule, and for the people to obey. One must be careful of what one wishes for, since after the War of Independence Napoleon agreed to recognize Ferdinand VII as the king of Spain. On December 11, 1813, the Spanish people got King Ferdinand VII back, and rule he did.

Don Carlos (1788–1855), Ferdinand's younger brother, wanted to be named as successor to the Spanish throne after the death or incapacity of the King, following Salic law, which stated that women could not inherit the throne. María Cristina of Bourbon, the fourth wife of Ferdinand VII, also wanted to inherit the Spanish crown. Ferdinand resisted the wishes of both his brother and his wife, convinced Parliament to set aside Salic law, and named his daughter (by María Cristina) Isabella, only three years old at the time, as crown princess. Carlos, angered and disappointed, fled to Portugal. Carlos' followers were called Carlists, which later became a political party which endured through Spain's Civil War. In fact, Franco had difficulty with the Carlist Party when he named Juan Carlos of Bourbon as his successor.

Starting in 1833 after Ferdinand's death, three different wars took place between the Absolutists who wanted a monarch with absolute power, and the Constitutionalists who preferred a king who would rule in accordance with a written constitution. The consequence of these wars was that from 1840 through 1875, military officers-turned politicians ruled Spain.

Carlos' invasion of Spain marks the start of the First Carlist War (1833–1839). María Cristina was named regent until her daughter Isabella would come of age, and appointed the experienced and liberal General Baldomero Espartero to fight Carlos' army. The First Carlist War ended with the signing of the Convention of Vergara.

Espartero, viewed as the savior of Spain, demanded liberal reforms from María Cristina, but the regent preferred to resign, and thus Espartero became regent in 1840. Espartero is the only Spanish military man to have been addressed as Your Royal Highness. General Espartero was perceived as too liberal for Spanish politics, and was overthrown in 1843 by Generals Ramón Narváez and Leopoldo O'Donnell, who convinced the Parliament to declare Isabella capable of ruling at age thirteen.

Isabella II was crowned in 1844, but she never was a popular regent. She is the only woman who has been Queen Regent of Spain. She showed favoritism to extremist generals and high-ranking clergy. She was also obsessed with supporting Maximilian and Charlotte in a European monarchical revenge against Mexico.

Carlos' son, the count of Montemolín (1818–1861), refused to accept a woman as Queen Regent. He attempted to take power in 1846, through the Matiners (Second Carlist) War, which started in Catalonia. This conflict was suppressed in 1849.

Wanting to be liked by the Spanish people, Isabella II launched the Liberal Union in 1856 under the leadership of General Leopoldo O'Donnell (who had been Captain-General of Cuba). The Liberal Union was a failure, and Isabella II became even more unpopular.

O'Donnell conducted several military campaigns abroad. A successful war against Morocco (1859–1860) provided territorial gains for Spain. Spanish and Filipino troops fought in Viet Nam (1859–1863), and in 1862, Spanish troops joined the French in Mexico to force the repayment of debts. Isabella's popularity did not improve.[4]

In 1868, generals Francisco Serrano, also a former Captain-General of Cuba, and Juan Prim staged a revolt against Isabella II. Knowing she could not govern, Isabella II, her children, her husband, and her lover du jour went into exile in France. Also in this year, the first Cuban War of Independence (Ten Year War, see Chapter 11) started, as well as an independence movement in Puerto Rico.

Serrano and Prim ruled the destiny of Spain until Prim was assassinated in 1871. Because of the many problems at home, "Prim considered selling Cuba to the United States."[5] Maintaining the war effort in Cuba was expensive and conscription was unpopular. The Spanish Parliament, choosing the lesser of available evils, declared that Spain would again have a king, and the German Prince Amadeo of Savoy was elected and crowned Amadeo I.

Amadeo I did not arrive in Spain at a good moment. He found unstable politics, assassination attempts, and to top it all, Carlos, duke of Madrid (1848–1909), the nephew of the count of Montemolín, tried to take the crown, and the Third Carlist War broke out in 1872. Amadeo was instructed by Parliament to discipline the striking artillery corps, which he did, and then he appeared before Parliament and stated that he found the Spanish to be ungovernable, resigned, and wisely fled the country.

In 1870, while in exile in France, Isabella II had abdicated in favor of her son Alfonso. The 1873–1874 period is known as the First Spanish Republic, and fighting was generalized throughout Spain. During the first year, the Republic was dominated by General Francisco Serrano. "An election in August 1873 brought a Radical majority to the Cortes, which once more went after the Church, reduced the wages of the clergy, and abolished slavery in Puerto Rico."[6] This move further angered Cuban patriots who had been fighting for independence and for an end to slavery.

In early 1874, Antonio Cánovas del Castillo, who would become Prime Minister, appeared on Spain's political scene and supported the return of Alfonso to the Spanish crown. Fighting continued until General Arsenio Martínez Campos, who would later become Captain-General of Cuba, declared his support for Alfonso. The army refused to fight against Martínez Campos and the Bourbon dynasty was returned to Spain. Isabella's son was crowned Alfonso XII in 1874 and his reign would last until 1885.

Cánovas del Castillo, politician, lawyer, and historian, was the prime mover in the development of the Spanish Constitution of 1876, which formalized constitutional monarchy, thus allowing Alfonso XII to assume the throne. Cánovas del Castillo was also instrumental in ending the Third Carlist War in 1876 by merging the key Carlist politicians into his Conservative party.

"Martínez Campos took reinforcements freed by the end of the [Third] Carlist War to Cuba and soon had the rebels confined to the eastern part of the island."[7] Martínez Campos became a public hero after patching up a peace with the Cuban revolutionaries. With peace in Cuba, Alfonso and his government sought a more important role in Europe.

After Alfonso XII's death in November 1885, his widow, Christina of Austria, became the figure-head ruler Spain from 1885 to 1902. Práxedes Sagasta Escolar, a reformer, Martínez Campos and Cánovas del Castillo agreed to take turns at ruling in case María Cristina had a son. In May 1886 she delivered a son, Alfonso XIII, who became king in 1902. Pope Leo XIII agreed to be the baby's godfather.

Christina of Austria relied heavily on her prime ministers for domestic as well as foreign policy. Práxedes Sagasta Escolar became Prime Minister in 1893. The Spanish people were not ready for reformation, and he was replaced in March 1895 as news of the new Cuban Independence War, led by José Martí, reached Madrid.

The people and the military demanded a hard-line government and thus the sixty-seven-year-old Antonio Cánovas del Castillo was taken out of mothballs. He had saved the monarchy twenty years earlier and it was expected that he could save what remained of the empire. Upon assuming power in 1895, Cánovas del Castillo found the damages to Spain's political situation difficult to repair.

Wanting to bring order into a chaotic situation, Cánovas del Castillo utilized repression as a weapon. Valeriano Weyler was dispatched to Cuba with orders to suffocate the Cuban rebellion at any cost. On the domestic side, the Spanish working class was equally repressed, particularly through electoral manipulation, mass arrests, and torture.

The most heinous crime committed during Cánovas del Castillo watch happened after a bomb was thrown, allegedly by Anarchists, in Barcelona during a religious procession. More than three hundred men and women were imprisoned, and while some were Anarchists, most of them were Socialists and trade union leaders. They were subject to abominable tortures, only rivaled by the Inquisition. After the liberal European press took the case, the few remaining survivors were released.

Many Spaniards believe that the nationalist movements in Spain, primarily in the Basque Country and Catalonia were fueled by the repression techniques of Antonio Cánovas del Castillo. It also cost him his life, since he was murdered in 1897 by an Italian Anarchist while he vacationed with his family. Some historians believe that the assassination of Cánovas del Castillo was "funded and egged on by Cuban exiles."[8]

During the rule, in name only, of Cristina of Austria, Spain was plagued with economic woes, internal strife, and the fear of losing their remaining colonies in Asia (Marianas and The Philippines) and the Americas (Cuba and Puerto Rico).

Notes

1. Raymond Carr, ed., *Spain: A History* (Oxford: Oxford University Press, 2000), 194–95.
2. Ibid., 196.
3. Antonio Ubieto and others, *Introducción a la Historia de España* (Barcelona: Editorial Teide, 1974), 535.
4. Peter Pierson, *The History of Spain* (Westport, CT: Greenwood Press, 1999), 101–2.
5. Ibid., 102.
6. Ibid., 106.
7. Ibid., 109.
8. Charles J. Esdaile, *Spain in the Liberal Age: From Constitution to Civil War, 1808-1939* (Oxford: Blackwell Publishers, 2000), 192.

8

Loss of South and Central American Colonies

Spain's loss of South and Central American colonies had an extraordinary impact on the histories of Spain, Cuba, and the United States. It thus seems fitting to devote a chapter to review the struggle for independence of the countries we now call Argentina, Chile, Uruguay, Paraguay, Bolivia, Peru, Ecuador, Colombia, Venezuela, Mexico, Panama, Costa Rica, Nicaragua, El Salvador, Guatemala, Honduras, Dominican Republic, and Puerto Rico.

To put in perspective the size of the territory Spain lost, it was more than twenty-seven times the size of Spain. Considering the size of Mexico before the Mexican-American War, Spain lost a territory equivalent to 1.5 times the size of the 50 States of the United States.

From a military viewpoint, when studying the independence of Spain's colonies in the Americas, the immensity of the geographic theater and the political situation in Spain must be taken into account. Another important factor to consider is that it was impossible for the Spanish crown to send troops to the Americas when Spain was first under France's domination as well as later, when it was involved in bloody civil wars.

It must also be pointed out that these Latin American wars of liberation from Spanish domination were not limited to Spaniards fighting against people born in the Western Hemisphere. A large component of the Spanish armies in the Americas consisted of criollos, Native Americans, and people of mixed races. Conversely, many Spanish-born soldiers fought on the side of independence.

In the late 1700s, after Spain suffered significant military defeats in Europe, Charles III became concerned with the defense of the colonies and instituted important changes in the political, economic, and religious structure of the colonies. It is possible that the changes instituted by Charles III made the colonies easier to defend; however, these changes certainly created a situation propitious for these colonies to seek independence. University of London Professor John Lynch accurately stated that "imperial reform [by Charles III] planted the seeds of its own destruction."[1]

On the political side, Charles III modified the configuration of the viceroyalties by adding the Viceroyalty of the Río de la Plata, with its capital in Buenos Aires, which included the countries we now know as Argentina, Paraguay, and Uruguay. Having lost some territory, the Viceroyalty of Peru, though downgraded in importance, was still large since it included Chile, Bolivia, and Peru. The Viceroyalty of New Granada remained unchanged and included Colombia (Panama was a department of Colombia), Ecuador, and Venezuela. The territory of the Viceroyalty of New Spain also stayed the same and included Mexico, a large territory since it included a significant portion of today's western United States, most of Central America, and the Spanish possessions in the Caribbean.

On the economic side, Charles III lifted some trade restrictions between Spanish ports and the colonies, but still did not allow trade with other countries. Merchants prospered and wondered about the incredible profits they could reap if they would also be allowed to trade with wealthy nations, primarily France, England, and the United States.

On the defense side, Spain created colonial armies and militia units in Latin America. These same armies and militia would later become the armies of independence. To centralize power, Charles III decreed that all important administrative positions had to be filled with *Penisulares*, or Spanish-born officials. The criollos resented this measure, as they felt that the Bourbons were treating them as a recently conquered nation, and this made them more open to independence ideas.

Charles III also believed that the Catholic Church was too powerful and was using its political influence to increase its wealth. The Jesuit order, in particular, controlled vast amounts of land as well as most secondary and university teaching institutions in the colonies. In 1767, Charles III expelled the Jesuits from Spain and from its colonies, and confiscated all their holdings. In 1804, the crown confiscated all the land belonging to the Catholic Church and its charities. Criollos viewed the expulsion of the Jesuits as an act of despotism against their compatriots, for "of the 680 Jesuits expelled from Mexico about 450 were Mexicans."[2] The criollos as well as the clergy clearly became receptive to independence.

Charles III died on December 14, 1788, and his son, the supposedly half-witted, Charles IV became the king. In 1807, Charles IV granted passage through Spanish territory to French troops on the way to invade Portugal. Napoleon soon turned against his Spanish allies, and on March 19, 1808, Charles IV abdicated in favor of his son Ferdinand VII. As described in Chapter 7, Napoleon's answer was to have both Charles IV and Ferdinand VII imprisoned and to appoint his brother Joseph to the Spanish throne.[3]

In 1810, the Spanish Parliament convened in Cádiz and by 1812 had produced a liberal constitution that proclaimed Spain's possessions in the Americas to be full members of the kingdom. The 1812 Constitution granted all persons in the colonies full Spanish citizenship, even if they were not born in Spain.

Ferdinand VII was restored to the Spanish throne in 1814 and he immediately undertook strong actions to reestablish Spanish power in the Americas. Spanish Americans had been given a taste of freedom and they were not prepared to accept a reduction in political autonomy and economic isolation. The stage was thus set for the independence of Spanish possessions in the Americas.

Most independence movements in Spanish America can be traced to economic discrimination on the basis of ethnic and racial ancestry. Following the mandates of Charles III, colonial power was solely in the hands of Peninsulares, but there were not enough of them to appropriately rule. For instance, in Venezuela "whites were 20.3% of the total [population], of which only 1.3% were Peninsulares."[4] In Argentina, "in a total population of 16.9 million, there were 3.2 million whites, and of these only 150,000 were Peninsulares."[5] This racial mix of Venezuela and Argentina speaks for itself as to why these countries led the way to independence. On the other side of the coin, Peru was the last country to be freed of Spanish rule, since "whites totaled 13% of the whole,"[6] thus making it easier to maintain control of the territory.

Since many of the independence wars in the Americas went on for extended periods and in some cases several wars took place simultaneously, it is difficult to present this chapter in a strict chronological order. Therefore, the independence of each country or group of countries (Viceroyalties) will be separately titled.

Viceroyalty of New Granada

Independence movements in Spanish America started in 1806 in the area which is today's Venezuela. Francisco de Miranda launched an invasion from the United States with a single ship, but the would-be revolutionaries were quickly defeated by Spanish troops. In 1810, the Caracas town council proclaimed independence from Spain and sent Simón Bolívar to London to seek support for their cause. Bolívar contacted Miranda and both men returned to Caracas. The conspiracy was defeated by royalist forces and Miranda was captured and sent to prison where he died in 1816. Bolívar escaped to Cartagena, a Caribbean seaport in present-day Colombia, where an independence movement was already underway.

Bolívar took a small army to Venezuela and on August 6, 1813, he entered Caracas after defeating forces loyal to the Spanish crown. This time *Llaneros*, cowboys from the southern plains, defeated the republican forces. Bolívar escaped to Bogotá, the capital of the Viceroyalty of New Granada.

After Ferdinand VII was restored to the Spanish throne, he sent 10,000 experienced Spanish troops and 17 warships under the leadership of General Pablo Morillo to enforce Spanish rule in the colonies. Morillo retook Caracas in May 1815, and then headed to Bogotá. Bolívar escaped to Jamaica and then to Haiti, where he asked Haiti's President Alexander Pétion for help. Pétion agreed to help with the condition that Bolívar must free all slaves as colonies were liberated. Bolívar agreed. Haiti had been the second colony in the Americas to become independent of a European power, while the United States had been the first.[7]

Bolívar's first expedition did not fare well and he returned to Haiti. In his second attempt in 1817, he captured the fortified town we now know as Ciudad Bolívar. His army was reinforced by some 4,000 soldiers from England and other European nations who had become unemployed after Napoleon's defeat at Waterloo. In order to cement his power, Bolívar led his army across the Andes and attacked and defeated Spanish forces in the Battle of Boyacá on August 7, 1819. The Republic of Gran Colombia was proclaimed on December 17, 1819, which included the countries we now know as Venezuela, Colombia, and Panama.

The final defeat of Spanish colonial power in continental America was possibly created by Ferdinand VII himself. Influenced by ultraconservatives and the clergy, he refused to swear to govern in accordance to the liberal Constitution of 1812.

A large contingent of Spanish troops had been assembled at Cádiz by Ferdinand to fight against the independence forces in South America.

When these troops, commanded by Colonel Rafael Riego, learned that Ferdinand had declined to accept the 1812 Constitution, they rebelled on January 1, 1820, took the king prisoner, and were soon joined by military units throughout Spain. Ferdinand finally agreed to rule in accordance to the principles of the 1812 Constitution, but the mutinous troops at Cádiz never left for South America.

Bolívar won the decisive Battle of Carabobo on June 24, 1821. From the former Viceroyalty of New Granada, only present-day Ecuador remained under Spanish control. General Antonio José de Sucre was chosen by Bolívar to liberate Ecuador. Sucre defeated the royalists in the Battle of Pichincha on May 24, 1822. The Republic of Gran Colombia was proclaimed on this date, with Simón Bolívar as its first president.[8]

The three-country union did not work well. Venezuela seceded from Gran Colombia in 1829 and Ecuador did likewise in 1830. Colombia and Panama then became the Republic of New Granada. The Republic of Colombia was proclaimed in 1886. Panama seceded in 1903 due to a conspiracy orchestrated by President Theodore Roosevelt so that the construction of the Panama Canal could proceed.

Viceroyalty of Río de la Plata

In most Spanish colonies, the sense of national identity was created by economic reasons, usually derived from trade restrictions, as colonies could only trade with Spain. The citizens of Buenos Aires, the capital of the Viceroyalty of Rio de la Plata, were very good contrabandists and had found ways to trade with many foreign merchants. The national identity of the region had its origins in military self-sufficiency.

A British expedition invaded the Viceroyalty and captured Buenos Aires in 1806. Instead of defending the city, the Viceroy took the state treasure and hid in Córdoba, a city west-northwest of Buenos Aires. *Criollos* and *Peninsulares* hastily organized a militia, where contrary to Spanish tradition senior officers were chosen by election, and were able to repel the British invaders. A second attempt by the British in 1807 was also pushed out by the locals. The colony had been defended by local inhabitants and not by Spain.[9]

In May 1810, when the news that the French had defeated the forces of Ferdinand VII reached the new world, the residents of Buenos Aires set up a council to govern in the name of the king. Likewise in Santiago de Chile, in September 1810, a junta was installed to govern the territory in Ferdinand's name. Chile was a part of the Viceroyalty of Peru, but its independence is closely tied to that of Argentina.

On July 9, 1816, the former Viceroyalty of the Rio de la Plata declared its independence. Two years earlier, Chile had also declared its independence. The Chilean patriots, commanded by Bernardo O'Higgins, had been defeated by royalist forces coming from Peru on October 12, 1814, at the Battle of Roncagua. O'Higgins and the surviving Chilean patriots had escaped to Argentina, where José de San Martín was leading a similar campaign in the Viceroyalty of the Río de la Plata.

Ferdinand VII had been restored to the Spanish throne in 1815 and thus the independence of the Viceroyalty of Rio de la Plata was in danger. An assembly of representatives from most Argentine Provinces declared Argentina's independence from Spain on July 9, 1816.

Paraguay had declared its independence on May 14, 1811.

Since Uruguay was a part of Argentina, the Argentines drove the Spanish army out of Montevideo in 1814. In 1816, Uruguay was taken over by Brazil. In 1828, Argentinean and Uruguayan patriots fought and defeated the Brazilians. Uruguay became an independent country in 1828.

Viceroyalty of Peru

San Martín was convinced that a lasting independence depended on a totally independent South-American continent. Further, San Martín believed that Peru was the key to South-American victory over Spain and that Peru had to be taken from the south, which meant coming from Chile. Therefore, San Martín organized an army composed of Argentines and Chileans, and marched in the direction of Santiago de Chile over the Andes. The Spanish were expecting an attack from sea and were surprised and defeated at the Battle of Chabuco. Chile declared its independence from Spain on February 12, 1818.

San Martín's army sailed for Lima and after taking the city on July 21, 1821, Peru proclaimed its independence on July 28, 1821.

On July 26, 1822, Bolívar and San Martín had a secret meeting in Guayaquil, Ecuador, to determine the strategy for the total liberation of Peru. San Martín returned to Argentina, while Bolívar concentrated on strategy planning. Many historians have offered versions of this enigmatical meeting. It is generally believed that Bolívar wanted to create democratic countries, while San Martín advocated a monarchical form of government.[10]

In September 1823, Bolívar arrived in Lima with Sucre. The royalists regained control of Lima in February 1824. Bolívar defeated the Spanish on August 6, 1824, at the Battle of Junín. This was an interesting battle, in that it involved only cavalry charges and no firearms were used. The weapons utilized were lances and sabers.

By decree of the Congress of Gran Colombia, Bolívar turned command of the insurrect troops to Sucre. The royalist concentrated all their remaining troops at the city of Ayacucho, southeast of Lima.

The decisive Battle of Ayacucho took place on December 9, 1824. The 5,700 men combined forces of Peruvians and Gran Colombians under the command of General Antonio José de Sucre defeated the 6,900-strong royalist troops commanded by the Viceroy of Peru, General José de la Serna.

The independence of Bolivia (then called Upper Peru), which had remained dormant for some years, gained new life after the royalists defeat at Ayacucho. Bolivians wanted to be independent, and not a part of a multicountry union, such as Gran Colombia. Bolívar left the decision to Sucre, who proclaimed Bolivia's independence on August 6, 1825. And on this date, the South-American continent became free of Spanish rule. In honor of Simón Bolívar, Upper Peru was renamed Bolivia on August 11, 1825.[11]

The map of South America shown in Figure 8.1 provides the year that each territory held by Spain became an independent nation.

Viceroyalty of New Spain

At the time of its independence, the Spanish Viceroyalty of New Spain included today's Mexico (minus the Mexican state of Chiapas), most or all of current U.S. states of California, Texas, New Mexico, Arizona, Nevada, Utah, Colorado, and Wyoming, a portion of the Canadian Province of British Columbia, as well as all Spanish possession in the Caribbean.

Upon Napoleon's invasion of Spain in 1807, and the installation of his brother Joseph to Spain's throne, a group of Peninsulares living in Mexico staged a coup d'état demanding a more stable government. In 1808, the Peninsulares deposed the viceroy and persecuted criollos as well as people of mixed races.

There were a number of features of New Spain which rendered it quite different to other Spanish American colonies. It had the largest population, including more than one million whites; its territorial extension made it the largest Spanish colony; and Mexico City was

Figure 8.1 Independence of Spanish South American Colonies

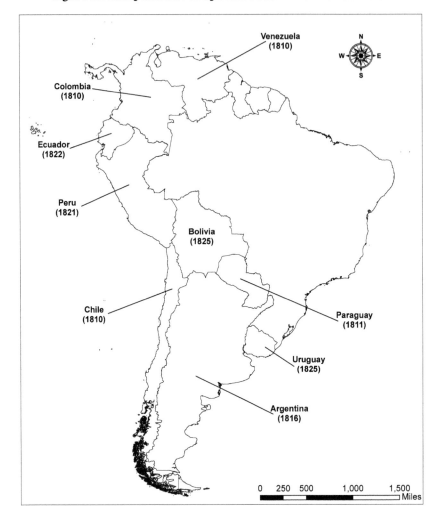

and still is the largest city in the Western Hemisphere. But the key peculiarity of New Spain was the power of the Church, which, in fact, sometimes exceeded that of the state.[12]

In 1810, a criollo priest named Miguel Hidalgo started a revolt against the Peninsulares and criollos in the name of Ferdinand VII. Hidalgo declared Mexican independence on September 16, 1810, in the village of Dolores, with a proclamation entitled The Cry of Dolores. This conspiracy was supported by Native Americans, mestizos, and mulattoes. The criollos joined the Peninsulares as the crown-sponsored government, though corrupt, offered more stability. Hidalgo's army was defeated by the royalists in January 1811, captured and executed on July 30, 1811.[13]

A mestizo priest, José María Morelos replaced Hidalgo under an agenda of independence from Spain and social equality. Morelos had a measure of success and captured some territory, but he was apprehended in 1815 and executed.

Native Mexicans, criollos, and even some Spaniards declared Mexico's right to independence from Spain. The guerrilla warfare was led by Vicente Guerrero, who was a follower of Morelos.

Agustín de Iturbide, a colonel in the royal army, was charged with the responsibility of destroying the guerrillas led by Vicente Guerrero. Instead, Iturbide and Guerrero decided to negotiate a settlement which would guarantee the independence of the Mexican Empire, naming the Catholicism as the official religion of the state, and insuring equality under the law for all Mexicans. On February 24, 1821, General Agustín de Iturbide signed the Pact of Iguala to establish the new nation. In July 1821, the last Spanish Viceroy Juan O'Donojú recognized Mexican independence in the Treaty of Córdoba. The Spanish Parliament as well as Ferdinand VII rejected the Treaty of Córdoba. The final break with Spain came on May 19, 1822, when the Mexican Congress proclaimed Iturbide to be Agustín I, Emperor of Mexico.[14]

Iturbide's government only lasted eighteen months. A revolt led by Guadalupe Victoria, a former follower of Guerrero and Antonio López de Santa Anna, established the United Mexican States. In 1824, Guadalupe Victoria became the first Mexican President. Vicente Guerrero was the next president, but was deposed by a coup, which became the norm in Mexican politics. Three strong men emerged in Mexican politics during the nineteenth century. Santa Anna was president eleven times from independence until 1855; Benito Juárez led the nation during the 1850s and 1860s; and Porfirio Díaz was the strong man during the last quarter-century.

Central America

The Captaincy-General of Guatemala, also known as the Kingdom of Guatemala, at the time of its independence included the current nations of Costa Rica, El Salvador, Guatemala, Honduras, Nicaragua, and the Mexican State of Chiapas.

On September 15, 1821, Gabino Gainza, the Captain-General, declared independence from Spain and later joined Iturbide's Mexican Empire in 1822. When the Mexican Empire failed, Central America declared its independence once again and created a federation which did not include the State of Chiapas which had been annexed by Mexico. By the late 1830s, the federation had been disbanded and was replaced by five independent republics: Costa Rica, El Salvador, Guatemala, Honduras, and Nicaragua.

The map of Mexico and Central America, minus Panama, depicted in Figure 8.2, contains the date that each Spanish-held territory became an independent country.

Figure 8.2 Independence of Mexico and Central America

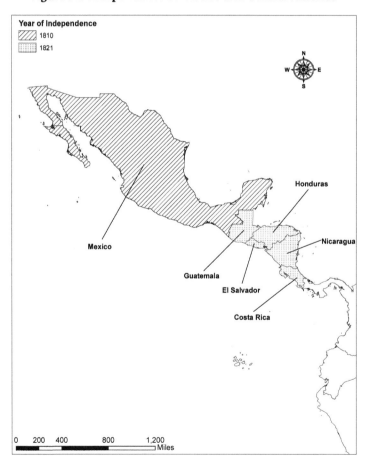

Dominican Republic

After Haiti's independence from France in 1804, the Haitians had invaded the Spanish territory of the Dominican Republic (then known as Santo Domingo). Spain fought back, and Santo Domingo reverted to Spanish domination from 1809 to 1821. The Dominicans declared their independence from Spain, but the Haitians again invaded in 1822 and annexed the colony. In 1844, Santo Domingo declared its independence and became the Dominican Republic.

Pedro Santana, a Dominican dictator, unable to defend his country against attacks by Haiti, invited Spain in 1861 to rule the Dominican Republic. The United States, at the time involved in its Civil War, was unable to enforce the Monroe Doctrine. Following a protracted Dominican revolt, and since the U.S. Civil War was over, Spain withdrew and Dominican patriots proclaimed for the second time the independence of the Dominican Republic on March 3, 1865.

After 1865, Spain only had two remaining colonies in the Americas: Cuba and Puerto Rico.

Puerto Rico

The Captaincy-General Puerto Rico was under the administrative control of the Viceroyalty of New Spain, with its capital in Mexico City. After Mexico's independence in 1821, Puerto Rico was administered as an Autonomous Captaincy-General. Puerto Rico's Captain-General was appointed by the Spanish Crown and reported directly to Madrid.

Puerto Ricans had, in general terms, better treatment from Spain than did citizens from Cuba, Philippines, or Mariana Islands. For instance, the Spanish Constitution of 1812 granted all Puerto Ricans conditional Spanish citizenship.

During the second half of the nineteenth century, Puerto Ricans started to demand additional autonomy and reductions of the taxes and tariffs imposed by the Spanish crown. Spain's answer to those demanding reform was either prison or forced exile.

Dr. Ramón Emeterio Betances had founded the Revolutionary Committee of Puerto Rico in early 1868. He was forcibly exiled to the Dominican Republic. On September 23, 1868, hundreds of citizens of the impoverished town of Lares took to the streets in what would later be called the *Lares Cry*. This significant uprising was led by Dr. Betances, Lola Rodríguez de Tió, Mariana Bracetti, Mathias Brugman, Manuel Rojas, and Francisco Ramírez.

Wisely, Spanish authorities answered some of the demands made by the participants in the Lares Cry. On March 22, 1873, with only minor exceptions, slavery was abolished in Puerto Rico.

The last major uprising in Puerto Rico during Spanish rule was in 1897 at the town of Yauco, and it included displaying, for the first time, the current Puerto-Rican flag in Puerto-Rican soil. Spanish authorities swiftly squashed the insurrection.

On July 17, 1898, Puerto Rico was authorized by Spain to have an autonomous government. It would not last long.

Shortly after the surrender of Spanish forces at Santiago de Cuba, during the Cuban-Spanish-American War, U.S. General Nelson A. Miles landed at Guánica, Puerto Rico, on July 25, 1898. Opposition was minimal and by the end of August 1898, Puerto Rico was under U.S. control.

U.S. negotiators had to walk a tightrope during the drafting of the Treaty of Paris. The Teller Amendment to the U.S. Declaration of War with Spain made it difficult to annex Cuba. This was not the case with Puerto Rico; therefore, Spain ceded Puerto Rico to the United States in the Treaty of Paris. John R. Brooke became the first U.S. military governor of Puerto Rico.

The United States has instituted several improvements to the status of Puerto Ricans, such as the Foraker Act of 1900 and the Jones Act of 1917. All Puerto Ricans have a restricted U.S. citizenship. The Commonwealth of Puerto Rico, which allowed Puerto Ricans to draft their own constitution, was established on July 4, 1950, by Public Act 600, signed by President Harry S. Truman (1945–1953).

Several plebiscites, such as the ones in 1967, 1993, and 1998 have been conducted in Puerto Rico to determine how the voters feel about Commonwealth versus Statehood versus Independence. In every case the voters overwhelmingly desired the continuation of the Commonwealth status. Voting for statehood is an academic exercise since there is no provision in the U.S. constitution to obtain statehood by popular demand.

Notes

1.   John Lynch, *The Spanish American Revolutions, 1808-1826* (New York: W. W. Norton and Company, 1973), 2.
2.   Ibid., 10.
3.   Esdaile, *Spain in the Liberal Age*, 21–31.
4.   Lynch, *Spanish American Revolutions*, 190.
5.   Ibid., 19.

6. Ibid., 158.
7. Robert Harvey, *Liberators: Latin America's Struggle for Independence, 1810-1830* (New York: The Overlook Press, 2000), 141–43.
8. Ibid., 193–98.
9. Lynch, *Spanish American Revolutions*, 37–45.
10. Harvey, *Liberators*, 199–207.
11. Robert L. Scheina, *Latin America's Wars, Volume 1: The Age of the Caudillo, 1791-1899* (Washington, DC: Brassey's, 2003), 65–70.
12. Harvey, *Liberators*, 434–35.
13. Scheina, *Latin America's Wars*, 71–75.
14. Harvey, *Liberators*, 445–52.

9

Spain's Flawed Cuba Policies

There is no doubt that Spanish people had, and still have, a deep love for the island of Cuba and to a large extent for the people of Cuba. Spain did not appear to be devastated when the country lost the Viceroyalty of New Spain, which included Mexico, a good portion of today's western United States, Guatemala, Nicaragua, El Salvador, Honduras, and Costa Rica, even though this loss represented a terri tory of approximately nine times the size of Spain itself.

To put Spain's total territorial loss in perspective, the country lost a significant portion of North America and all of Central America and South America, with the exception of Brazil and the three Guiana's, which were colonies of other European countries. Perhaps, Spain's indifferent attitude can be attributed to the fact that Spain suffered many military defeats during the first half of the nineteenth century, as well as an invasion by France and devastating civil wars.

Cuba is approximately 22 percent the size of Spain; nevertheless, in the late 1890s when it became evident that Cuba would be lost, there was an outcry even in the most remote regions of Spain encouraging the government to find a way to keep the beloved Cuba. Spain sent its toughest and most merciless general, Valeriano Weyler, as the Captain-General of Cuba in February 1896. And when Prime Minister Antonio Cánovas del Castillo was asked if the ownership of Cuba would be defended, he answered with the famous phrase: "*Hasta el último hombre y la última peseta.*"[1] In translation: until the last man and the last peseta.

Spain selected the best of its military establishment to be Captains-General of Cuba. Some examples are: Dionisio Vives, Leopoldo O'Donnell, Francisco Serrano, Arsenio Martínez Campos, and Valeriano Weyler, among others. Perhaps, if Spanish rulers had trained professional administrators for their colonies, like Britain had done, the colonies would have remained faithful to Spain and the good relationship would have lasted even after independence. In general terms, this is true of most former British colonies, the United States included.

Did Spain consider Cuba to be a colony or a possession? For many years Britain was considered to be the optimum colonizer, for going through great lengths to teach the natives how to rule themselves. To some extent, France came second to Britain as a quality colonizer, although an old joke tells that Frenchmen held on to their colonies by teaching native men how to steal and native women how to make love. Were Spaniards good colonizers? History books are replete with stories about the "Black Legend" which places Spanish colonial rulers at the level of the most brutal Roman conquerors.

The first author to coin the phrase Black Legend was Julián Juderías in his 1914 book *La Leyenda Negra y la Verdad Histórica.*[2] Juderías' work covers an extensive timeframe, commencing with the Inquisition and ending at the time of publication of his revealing book which describes Spaniards as cruel, intolerant, and fanatical.

A frightening example of the Black Legend is seen when reading descriptions of how Spanish colonizers treated Native Americans (Indian tribes) and African slaves. One of Spain's endeavors of colonial expansion was to convert the native people to Christianity. The men sent to the New World by the Spanish crown often used violence and brutality to instill the Catholic faith in the natives while working these poor souls into a very early grave.

Setting aside the Inquisition and the early colonial times, and moving on to the second half of the nineteenth century, how did Spain view colonization? According to Juan Gualberto Gómez, one of the most intelligent and least studied Cuban patriots of the late nineteenth century, Spain's definition of colonization was: "to submit, by force if necessary, a given people to the rule of another."[3] Clearly, Spanish administrations confused colonization with conquest.

J. G. Gómez went on to add that under Spain's definition, the colonizing (or conquering) country must resort to force to maintain its sovereignty, and must utilize a system of government which centralizes the entire life of the colony under the power of the ruling country. Under J. G. Gómez's description, the ruling country would consider any attempt of self-rule as dangerous, which inexorably translates into the systematic exploitation of the colony.[4]

It became clear to many enlightened Cubans that in Spain's opinion, Cubans had no rights. Even when Cuban deputies were elected to represent Cuba in the Spanish Parliament of Cádiz, Spanish ministers did not allow the Cubans to take their seats.

At the end of the Ten Year War (1868–1878), which will be covered in detail in Chapter 11, Spain did not fully comply with any of the terms of the negotiated peace treaty. On February 9, 1878, Cuba's Governor-General Arsenio Martínez Campos proposed peace terms in what would later be known as the Pact of Zanjón. The proposal included a *general pardon* for all rebel fighters, political equality of Cuba with Puerto Rico, freedom for the slaves and Chinese workers who fought with the rebel forces, and amnesty for all rebels. After the Pact of Zanjón was signed, amnesty was granted only to rebels who agreed to leave Cuba, freedom was granted only to slaves born in Cuba, and Cuba did not achieve the same political status as Puerto Rico. Cuban rebels had been fighting for total independence and abolition of slavery, terms which were never discussed by Spanish authorities during peace negotiations.[5]

It was patently clear to Cubans that Spain considered Cuba solely to be a possession and that war was the only alternative. J. G. Gómez referred to war against Spain as: "the necessary solution [brought about] by desperation."[6]

On the political side, costly mistakes made by Spanish ruling authorities were: civil service jobs were reserved for people born in Spain; Cuba had no representation in the Spanish Parliament; Cuban businesses were encouraged to trade only with Spain by an abusive system of duties and taxes on goods from third countries; the Cuban educational system had low standards and was reserved for the wealthy; and finally, Spain maintained slavery for many years after other European powers abolished this abominable trade.

The military blunders made by Spain during Cuba's various attempts at independence could fill many volumes. Even though Spain kept many high-ranking officers in Cuba, at times as many as forty generals, the quality of the troops was miserable. Spain conscripted young farmers sometimes adolescents only aged sixteen, and shipped them to Cuba with little or no training. Medical services for the Spanish troops were Spartan, and as a consequence of this, as many as one-quarter of the troops at a given time would be in hospitals and infirmaries. The creation of the Spanish Volunteer Corps during the Ten Year War, and the failure to check the excesses of these blood-thirsty groups were significant mistakes. The establishment of concentration camps (*reconcentración*) by Valeriano Weyler during the War of Independence opened the eyes of the world to the barbaric behavior of Spain against Cuban patriots and innocent civilians alike. Finally, during the final days of the War of Independence (1895–1898), to be covered in Chapter 12, Spanish troops were moved to large cities, allowing the Cuban patriots to own the countryside. Even without the American invasion, it is likely that Spanish troops would have starved and surrendered in a few months.

During the Cuban-Spanish-American War, Admiral Cervera, the head of the Spanish Fleet, was ordered by Captain-General Blanco to exit Santiago Bay and to try to outrun the American fleet. It was well known that Spain's wooden-decked, obsolete and poorly maintained ships were incapable of outrunning America's modern steel-hulled vessels. Moreover, had the Spanish fleet stayed in port and moved some of the ship's artillery to Santiago, 10,000 Spanish sailors could have shifted the balance of power in the defense of Santiago.

Incredible information was revealed during the court martial of Admiral Cervera for having lost his fleet during the battle of Santiago de Cuba. Even though Cervera had begged for time to refit his ships, the political powers of the day ordered him to set sail immediately, as something had to be done. Some of Cervera's vessels were being used for training and many of the cannon shells were filled with sand or sawdust. The ship decks were wooden and readily caught fire. One of the vessels even had some wooden cannons since the artillery pieces were in shops in Spain for repairs.

Perhaps, the most influential Spanish politician of the time, Antonio Cánovas del Castillo, around the year 1890 stated that in his opinion, since Cubans and Spaniards did not agree with one another during peacetime, war in Cuba was indeed inevitable.[7]

To the average Spaniard, the loss of Cuban was a devastating event. Even to this day, more than one hundred years later, when a large magnitude catastrophe occurs, Spaniards console themselves with the expression: *"Más se perdió en Cuba,"* which in translation is: "More was lost in Cuba."

Notes

1. Ubieto et al., *Introducción a la Historia de España*, 772.
2. Julián Juderías, *La Leyenda Negra y la Verdad Histórica*, 1st ed. (1914; repr., Castilla y León: Conserjería de Educación y Cultura, 2004).
3. Juan Gualberto Gómez, *Por Cuba Libre* [For a Free Cuba] (Municipio de La Habana: Oficina del Historiador de la Ciudad, 1954), 15.
4. Ibid., 15–17.
5. Thomas, *Cuba or the Pursuit of Freedom*, 265–67.
6. Gómez, *Por Cuba Libre*, 17.
7. Ibid., 18.

Part 3

Cubans Fight for Independence

10

Initial Attempts

Many people in the United States believe that Cubans never made serious attempts to become independent from Spain. The next three chapters will enumerate and describe in detail the many Cuban struggles for freedom. And yet, still freedom has eluded the Cuban people for more than 500 years.

Cubans began considering rebelling as a way to obtain independence from Spain early in the nineteenth century. Initially, some of these rebellions were led by slaves demanding more humane conditions. They were later joined by enlightened Cubans who understood that the Cuban people were economic slaves of Spain.

There were quite a few, perhaps too many to enumerate, localized rebellions by slaves in Cuba during the late 1700s and early 1800s. These revolts were primarily to protest slavery itself and/or to demand better conditions. There is no evidence that any of these rebellions was for the purpose of obtaining Cuba's independence from Spain, and they were suffocated quickly and violently by Spanish authorities.

The only such rebellion to cover a large geographic area was one organized by Nicolás Morales in 1795. Morales was a free Afro-Cuban and his conspiracy started in Bayamo and rapidly spread to the entire eastern section of Cuba. This conspiracy was supported by a handful of whites and demanded equality between blacks and whites, abolition of taxes, and distribution of land to the poor. The Captain-General of Cuba Luis de las Casas imprisoned Morales and other leaders and east Cuba promptly returned to normality.[1]

The first true Cuban attempt at gaining independence from Spain was in 1809 and its leaders were Román de la Luz, a wealthy Freemason from Havana, and Joaquín Infante, a lawyer from Bayamo. The conspirators needed the support of criollo planters, and in order to gain this support, attempted to convince the planters that the preservation of slavery was guaranteed. Infante and de la Luz even drew up a constitution for the independent Republic of Cuba which stated that it would be dominated by the wealthy landowners, Catholicism would be the official religion, and only wealthy people (*personas pudientes*) could be officers in the army. Slaves and free Afro-Cubans supported the conspiracy but the key criollo planters refused to participate. Spanish military rulers had done an excellent marketing job of convincing criollo planters that once free from Spain, Cuba could become another Haiti.

Cuba's Captain-General Salvador de Muro Salazar, Marqués de Someruelos, discovered and suppressed the conspiracy. Román de la Luz and other conspirators were condemned to ten years of hard labor followed by permanent exile. Joaquín Infante escaped to the United States; from there he went to Venezuela and then to Mexico.[2] While in Venezuela, Infante wrote a draft Cuban Constitution in which he proposed four branches of government: executive, legislative, judicial, and military. Infante fought alongside Bolívar, was captured by Spanish forces and sent to Cuba to be tried. In 1813, he was released from prison, traveled to Venezuela and rejoined Bolívar. It is not known when or where he died and he does not appear in the list of patriots in Cuban history books.

In the rebellion of 1810, free Afro-Cubans joined with a white militia, all of them Freemasons, to rebel against Spanish domination of the colony. This unnamed conspiracy had no plans to change the island's social structure. White people would continue to rule, and slaves would remain slaves. The rebellion was crushed by a white militia with heavy involvement of the French refugees from *Saint Domingue* and the strong leadership of Someruelos who came into the streets of Havana to fight against and defeat the rebels.

In 1812, the first country-wide efforts aimed at independence took place. The mastermind behind the movement was José Antonio Aponte, a free Afro-Cuban from Havana who was a skilled carpenter and wood carver. This uprising is known as the Aponte Conspiracy. Rumors had started to circulate in the island that the Spanish Parliament at Cádiz had abolished slavery. The conspiracy originated when the rumors about abolition of slavery turned out to be unfounded.

The plan was to start a large-scale revolt in sugar mills and coffee plantations in eastern Cuba. The conspirators expected that Spanish authorities would move a large number of troops to that area, at which time the rebels would take Havana.[3] The Aponte Conspiracy had an international component since abolitionists from the United States, Haiti, and Brazil were kept informed.

In mid-February 1812, Aponte and eight of his main coconspirators, five free Afro-Cubans and three slaves, were apprehended and hanged by Someruelos' forces. As a warning to those considering independence, Someruelos had the heads of the nine men severed and prominently exhibited in public places.[4] For many years after 1812, when Cuban white children misbehaved, in order to shame them, they were told: "You're worse than Aponte."[5]

During the quarter century from 1817 through 1842, Cuba's independence movements were masked by antislavery movements. Cuban slave owners were convinced that Cuba's economy, and their standard of living, depended on a continued supply of slave labor. Britain had stopped the trade in 1807 and the United States in 1808, with Cuba becoming the distribution center for this "odious commerce" in the Caribbean.[6] Argentina abolished slavery in 1816; Colombia and Chile in 1821; and Guatemala, Peru, and Uruguay in 1828.

Spain was tightening its grip on its profitable colony of Cuba and in 1825, by royal decree, gave absolute authority to the Spanish Captain-Generals. The first Captain-General to be so elevated was Dionisio Vives, followed by Mariano Rocafort in 1832 and Miguel Tacón in 1834. Their absolute power kept the slaves coming and independence movements in check.

Cubans were aware of the political problems which plagued Spain and this may have caused independence inclinations to diminished. The desire to be allied to a stronger and geographically closer nation, to some extent replaced the hunger for freedom with a desire to be annexed to the United States. "Annexation sentiment increased both in Cuba as well as in the U.S. during the 1820s and 1830s."[7]

Britain ended slavery in its territories in the Caribbean in the 1830s and pressured Spain to do likewise in Cuba. Cuba's Captain-Generals ignored the British. The reply of the British in 1836 was to appoint Dr. Richard Madden, an activist abolitionist, to the post of Superintendent of Liberated Africans in Havana. Madden had been in Cuba in 1833 representing the British and Foreign Anti-Slavery Society. During this visit to Cuba, Madden had been presented a collection of poems written by slaves in Cuba. He later translated these poems and they were published in London and clandestinely circulated in Cuba. Captain-General Tacón was alarmed with Madden's appointment, but he did not question decisions being taken in London and Madrid.

Madden was replaced in 1840 by David Turnbull, an even more ardent human rights campaigner. In turn, Tacón was replaced in 1838 by

Joaquín Ezpeleta, who in 1840 was replaced by Pedro Telles. In 1841, Gerónimo Valdés was appointed Captain-General. The absolute power royal decree was no longer applicable, and Valdés closed the Havana slave market to new arrivals and freed a number of slaves.[8]

Under pressure by white Cuban planters, Telles had declared Turnbull *persona non grata* in 1841; however, when Valdés took over, he revoked Turnbull's expulsion and recognized Turnbull as British Consul. Turnbull began organizing a revolt against Spain with the objective of obtaining the total abolition of slavery. He found some white Cubans who supported his conspiracy as well as a free Afro-Cuban, José Miguel Mitchell. The conspiracy never got off the ground. Mitchell, a *protégé* of Turnbull, was arrested and condemned to death, although his sentence was later commuted to ten years' imprisonment in Africa.

Turnbull had left for Jamaica but attempted to return to Cuba in late 1842. Upon Turnbull's arrival in Cárdenas his black associates were shot, and he was arrested, put on board a British steamer, and notified that he was being expelled and was not to visit the Island of Cuba under any pretext whatever. Turnbull had many Cubans convinced that the British might invade the island if the slave trade continued.[9]

The most far-reaching and violently suppressed conspiracy was *La Escalera* or *The Ladder*. It was so named because detainees were tied to a simple wooden ladder and then lashed and/or tortured.

In October 1843, Leopoldo O'Donnell, Duke of Tetuán, became Captain-General of Cuba and would remain in this post for five years. O'Donnell, who was considered a war hero in Spain, governed Cuba with an iron fist and a greedy hand.

There are several hypotheses regarding the origin of *La Escalera*, although many believe that the frequent journeys into the Cuban countryside by Turnbull and his assistant Francis Cocking led many slaves and free Afro-Cubans to the belief that Britain would indeed come to their rescue if they rebelled.[10]

The general slave insurrection of *La Escalera* started at the sugar mill *La Alcancía* in Cárdenas on March 27, 1843, and it involved the full crew of 250 slaves.[11] The rioters, after destroying practically the whole mill, moved on to nearby plantations *La Luisa*, *La Aurora*, and *La Trinidad*, where the entire crews of those plantations joined them. The rebels continued on to the *Moscú* coffee plantation and the *Ranchuelo* horse-breeding farm where the slaves also joined the revolt. The slaves who were building the rail track between Cárdenas and Júcaro (a small town north of Sagua la Grande, Las Villas) also rebelled that evening, but were unable to join with the other group.

Spanish authorities reacted quickly and mercilessly. Well-armed troops on horseback and men with bloodhounds specially trained to track *cimarrones* (runaway slaves) pursued and attacked them. The slaves, armed only with machetes and sticks, were overpowered. Scores were killed on the spot. Hundreds were flogged. The first act of the Conspiracy of *La Escalera* ended there, but the play would run for at least another year.

In November 1843, another general slave uprising broke out at the *Triumvirato* sugar mill in Matanzas. "The legend has it that it was spearheaded by a black slave woman 'La Negra Carlota' who died fighting with machete in hand. Her name was later given to 'Operation Carlota', the Cuban military intervention in Angola."[12] The rebels were attacked by regular Spanish troops and the uprising was brutally crushed.

Again near Matanzas in December 1843, a slave betrayed a conspiracy at the *Trinidad* sugar mill. O'Donnell conducted a cursory investigation which concluded with the execution of sixteen slaves at the mill. "The crews of the neighboring mills were forced to witness the executions."[13]

In January 1844, a new and wider-scoped conspiracy was uncovered in Matanzas. The conspirators were primarily free Afro-Cubans, slaves, and a handful of whites. They had been meeting for three years and the plan was to start in Matanzas, where they would soon be joined by conspirators in Havana. Their goal was to establish a republic in which slavery would be abolished and Afro-Cubans would enjoy full equality with whites.[14]

The conspiracy was exposed by informants and Captain-General O'Donnell took the opportunity to terrorize the population to make sure that, at least during his watch, a similar event would not take place again. Thousands, including foreigners, were arrested and tortured even before being tried. "All told, 4,039 individuals were arrested; 2,166 were listed as free Negroes, 972 as slaves, 74 as white, and 827 were not classified."[15]

Considering that whatever evidence was available had been obtained by torture, the sentences were incredibly harsh. There were 78 death sentences, 1,292 were sent to prison, and over 400 forcibly sent into exile. A conservative estimate of how many died under the lash is 300.[16]

Within the context of the time, the penalty of forced exile was a euphemism for prison outside Cuba, usually in Spanish enclaves on the coast of Africa. The over 400 condemned to "exile" were sent to secure Spanish prisons in Ceuta (in current Morocco), Oran (in current Algeria), and the island of Fernando Po (now called Bioko in Equatorial Guinea).

Among the free Afro-Cubans executed were the well-known musician José Miguel Román, the dentist Andrés Dodge, and the famed poet Gabriel de la Concepción Valdés, better known by his *nom de plume Plácido*. To a large extent, the more brilliant and attractive free Afro-Cubans were targeted by O'Donnell. Other than names or descriptions given under torture, the culpability of these men was never established. In fact, it is possible that there was no conspiracy of *La Escalera*. It may have been an excuse by O'Donnell to free the country of people he considered undesirable or troublemakers.

Some Cuban historians, including Francisco González del Valle and Vidal Morales, label the conspiracy a mirage, precipitated by distrustful Spanish authorities. Others, like José Manuel Pérez Cabrera suggest that there is not enough information to draw a conclusion. A third group, which includes José Manuel Ximeno, considers La Escalera to be the first major Cuban conspiracy of a secessionist nature, with representation throughout the island.[17]

O'Donnell also targeted liberal antislavery white Cubans. José de la Luz y Caballero, Professor of Philosophy at the College of San Francisco was among those accused, but he was acquitted.

The execution of Plácido was a severe blow to Cuban literature of the time. Plácido was the illegitimate son of a mulatto barber from Havana and a Spanish dancer from Burgos. A printer by training, he won the 1834 Havana poetry prize. He was the best-known romantic poet of the 1830s and 1840s, until his death in 1844.[18]

Plácido was accused of being Turnbull's agent and of having been selected as President of the Republic being set up by the conspirators. Perhaps, Plácido's only crime was to have written a poem in honor of Queen Isabella II with some hidden sarcasm:

> As before the altar of Supreme
>> Jove
> Hasdrubal swore hatred against
>> The Romans
> And showed them the fierceness of
>> Mars.

> I, before God, swear eternal
> Hatred against all tyrants.[19]

O'Donnell's ferocity was applauded by Cuba's white elite. The fear of another Haiti coupled with the knowledge that whites were a minority certainly made whites apprehensive about a black-led conspiracy.

La Escalera had the immediate effect that harsher slave regulations were adopted. The movement of slaves was further restricted and O'Donnell exiled free blacks that had not been born in Cuba.

As wealthy white Cubans became alarmed at the black to white ratio, the slave trade decreased significantly. At the same time, in February 1845 a royal decree directed Spanish consular agents to arrange free passage for white migrants to Cuba. It is possible that some of these measures worked, for the U.S.-organized 1899 census showed that the black population had diminished to as little as 32 percent.[20] It had been as high as 73 percent in 1846.[21]

Another effect of *La Escalera* is that it made many Cubans, black as well as white realize that annexation to the United States might not be such a bad idea after all, especially given O'Donnell's brutality and corruption. How many more O'Donnells was Spain prepared to send to Cuba? O'Donnell took bribes not only from the slave traders but from the large slave owners as well. When he retired as Cuba's Captain-General in 1848, he had accumulated a fortune of one-half million dollars.[22]

La Escalera also demonstrated that the whites could be rallied for independence as long as they were given assurances that Cuba would not become a black-led republic. The blacks would certainly rally for an end to slavery, but they wanted assurances that they would have equal rights in an independent Cuba. At the time it was difficult, if not impossible, to get the blacks and the whites to work together. That is perhaps why the South so artfully disguised Narciso López's annexationist expedition as an independence conspiracy. This stratagem worked so well that even many Cuban historians were fooled. To this day, Narciso López is revered by many Cubans as one of the fathers of Cuban independence from Spain.

The country was now ready to formally organize to fight Spain for independence, commencing with the War of 1868.

Notes

1. Richard Gott, *Cuba: A New History* (New Haven, CT: Yale University Press, 2004), 48.
2. Phillip S. Foner, *A History of Cuba and its Relation with the United States*, vol. I (New York: International Publishers, 1962), 88–90.
3. Ibid., 90–94.
4. Gott, *Cuba*, 50–51.
5. Sergio Aguirre, *Lecciones de Historia de Cuba, Primer Cuaderno* (La Habana: MINED, 1960), 41.
6. Laird Bergad, *The Cuban Slave Market, 1790-1880* (Cambridge: Cambridge University press, 1995), 38.
7. Louis A. Pérez Jr., *Cuba and the United States: Ties of Singular Intimacy* (Athens: The University of Georgia Press, 1990), 38.
8. Ibid., 65.
9. Foner, *History of Cuba*, 201–11.
10. Gott, *Cuba*, 64.
11. Foner, *History of Cuba*, 212/213.
12. Gott, *Cuba*, 65.
13. Foner, *History of Cuba*, 213.
14. Mario Hernández y Sánchez Barba, *David Turnbull y el Problema de la Esclavitud en Cuba, Anuario de Estudios Americanos* (Sevilla, 1957), vol. XIV, 52–53.
15. Hubert H. S. Aimes, *History of Slavery in Cuba, 1511 to 1868* (New York: G.P. Putnam's, 1907), 146.
16. Foner, *History of Cuba*, 215.
17. Ibid., 217.
18. Thomas, *Cuba or the Pursuit of Freedom*, 204–6.
19. Fernando Portuondo, *Curso de Historia de Cuba* (La Habana, 1941), 105.
20. Gott, *Cuba*, 105.
21. Foner, *History of Cuba*, 187.
22. William L. Mathieson, *Great Britain and the Slave Trade, 1839-1865* (London: Longmans, Green, 1929), 141.

11

Ten Year War (1868–1878)

The first organized movement to claim Cuba's independence from Spain started on October 10, 1868. The uprising was scheduled for a later date, but the Spanish had discovered the plans of the Cuban patriots.

The Spanish had been defeated in the Dominican Republic in 1865, and the French Army was crushed in Mexico in 1867, with the subsequent execution of the Emperor Maximilian I. Armed with these data, Cubans had concluded that European powers were weak and unable to control independence movements in the Americas.

Carlos Manuel de Céspedes was a lawyer and land owner born in 1819 in Bayamo, Oriente Province. On October 10, 1868, he assembled his friends at his small sugar mill called La Demajagua, near Manzanillo, freed his thirty slaves, and declared that Cuba had the right to be independent from Spain and to rule its own destiny. The Ten Year War started on this date, and Céspedes' action won him the title of Father of the Nation.

The initial army, composed of Céspedes, his friends, and slaves for a total of 147 men, moved on to try to seize the nearby town of Yara. They were soundly defeated by the Spanish Army, and significant casualties were inflicted on the Cuban patriots. Only Céspedes and twelve men escaped. After obtaining firearms and recruiting many new volunteers, they did eventually take Yara and also Bayamo. Céspedes declared Bayamo the provisional capital of Cuba and appointed himself as Captain-General, with the same legal authority as that of a Spanish colonial governor.

Many inhabitants joined the cause of freedom in Camagüey and Oriente provinces, and by the end of October, Céspedes' army had 12,000 men, and had also taken over the city of Holguín. On August 14, 1867, Céspedes' friend and follower Pedro "Perucho" Figueredo composed a martial song at Bayamo which would later become the Cuban national anthem.

Soon the Province of Camagüey would join in the fighting, with Ignacio Agramonte and Salvador Cisneros Betancourt as political leaders. Manuel de Quesada, a Cuban who had attained the rank of General in the Mexican Army, would later be in charge of the military. Quesada had fought in the first battle against French forces near Veracruz.

The Cuban rebels, though brave and patriotic, possessed very little military knowledge. A small group of former Dominican military forces who were living in the Bayamo area had joined the Cuban rebels and provided their invaluable war expertise. Luis Marcano organized the Bayamo battle. Máximo Gómez, a gifted general, taught the Cubans the use of the machete as a weapon of war. A third Dominican, Modesto Díaz, conducted several victorious battles during the ten-year conflict.[1]

Ignacio Agramonte was born in Camagüey in 1841, and earned his law degree at Havana University in 1866. Agramonte had more liberal ideas than Céspedes, for he believed in the total abolition of slavery, as did most of the rebels in Camagüey Province. Céspedes was opposed to the radical abolition of slavery, and his ideas of governing the future Republic of Cuba were similar to the rule by Spain, but with Cubans instead of Spaniards in power.

Salvador Cisneros Betancourt was born in Camagüey in 1828, and was one of the richest men in Cuba. His family had the nobility title of Marqués de Santa Lucía, granted by Ferdinand VII King of Spain. Cisneros Betancourt studied in Philadelphia, where he obtained a degree in civil engineering. After graduation, he returned to Cuba to run the many businesses of the family.

Máximo Gómez was born in 1836 in Baní, a small town in the Dominican Republic. He fought against the Haitians when they invaded the Dominican Republic in the mid-1850s, and afterwards became a captain in the Dominican army reserve, during the second Spanish domination. When the Dominican Republic obtained its second independence from Spain in 1865, Gómez moved to eastern Cuba.

Cuba's Captain-General Francisco Lersundi only had about 22,000 regular Spanish soldiers stationed in Cuba, but many were permanently off-duty on civilian jobs as they could not survive on their military pay.[2] It is estimated that Lersundi's fighting troops amounted to only about 7,000 men.[3]

The political situation in Spain was abysmal. A new revolution had started on September 18, 1868, and by October 3, 1868, General

Francisco Serrano, a former Captain-General of Cuba, had taken over Madrid. Queen Isabella II had been sent into exile, while Generals Serrano and Juan Prim ran the government. Internal wars were raging in Spain, thus Spain could not afford to send any troops to Cuba, and it was therefore unlikely that Lersundi would obtain reinforcements.

Lersundi's solution was to recruit young, white, Spanish-born immigrants, and band them together in killer battalions of *voluntarios*, or volunteers. These volunteers had no mercy toward any Cuban rebel, or anyone suspected of being one or aiding the cause of Cuban independence. The feeling was mutual, for any volunteer caught by Cuban rebels would be hanged. Clearly, these volunteers drove the wedge of separation between Spaniards and Cubans even deeper.

Lersundi had no idea if anyone was running the government of Spain. But his only concern was that Cuba should remain Spanish. British historian Richard Gott quotes a telegram that Lersundi sent to Madrid shortly after the Céspedes revolt, "*La isla de Cuba es de España, mande quién mande en la Península, y para España es preciso defenderla cueste lo que cueste.*"[4] In translation: Cuba belongs to Spain, no matter who rules Spain, and we must defend it for Spain whatever the cost.

There had been volunteers in Cuba at previous times, but always under the command of the Spanish military. The Lersundi volunteers became a law unto themselves. They started in Havana and then spread to all important towns throughout the country. Italian historian Antonio Gallenga, who spent some time in Cuba during those days, estimated that there were about 11,000 volunteers in Havana, and as many as 60,000 in the rest of the island. They were as much concerned with internal repression as with fighting the war. Known anti-Spanish dissidents in Havana and Santiago were rounded up and executed without a trial.[5]

After learning of the volunteers' excesses, Spain's Prime Minister General Serrano dismissed Lersundi and appointed the mild-mannered General Domingo Dulce as Cuba's Captain-General. The powerful volunteers forced Dulce to resign, and he was replaced by General Antonio Fernández y Caballero de Rodas, who gladly accepted the demands of the volunteers.

During the first half of 1869, two new military leaders arrived at the rebel ranks, Antonio Maceo and Thomas Jordan.

Antonio Maceo was a twenty-year-old mulatto from Oriente Province. A daring captain who was always in the first line of battle, he soon emerged as the leader of the black and mulatto rebels supporting Céspedes. Antonio Maceo was born near Santiago de Cuba in 1845, at a small farm run by his family. Maceo was educated at home by private tutors, and his only contact with the outside world was during trips to Santiago to sell products from his family's farm. Under the command of Máximo Gómez, soon Maceo showed uncanny command abilities, and became one of the most daring and successful fighters in the Cuban rebel army. By 1872, Maceo had achieved the rank of general, but many white Cubans resented serving under the command of an Afro-Cuban.

The entire Maceo family became icons of Cuban independence in the struggle against Spain. Maceo's father, Marcos was killed in action in May 1869. Maceo's mother, Mariana Grajales had three sons by a prior marriage whom Marcos welcomed in the family. Mariana's two eldest sons, Justo and Fermín Regüefeiros were killed in action, and the youngest son, Felipe was captured and deported to Spain. Maceo had six brothers: José, killed in July 1896; Rafael, was captured and died in prison; Miguel, killed in April 1874; Julio, killed in December 1870 at the age of sixteen; Tomás, wounded and became an invalid; and Marcos Jr., killed in action at an unknown time and place.

In May 1969, Confederate General Thomas Jordan joined the rebels. Jordan was born in Virginia in 1819, and graduated from the U.S. Military Academy at West Point in 1840. Jordan had fought in the Second Seminole War, having been involved in the capture of Chief Tiger Tail near Cedar Keys, Florida. During the U.S. Civil War, Jordan resigned from the U.S. Army and joined the Confederate Army. He fought in the First Battle of Manassas, and distinguished himself in the Battle of Shiloh. He attained the rank of brigadier general, before retiring from military service.

Jordan landed in Mayarí, eastern Cuba in May 1869 with 300 men and enough arms, ammunition, and supplies for an additional 6,000 men. By December 1869, Jordan had been promoted to Chief of the Cuban Army of Independence. Against a much larger Spanish force, Jordan scored a major victory at the Battle of Guáimaro in January 1870. With a force of only 580 poorly armed men, Jordan ambushed two Spanish columns several thousand men strong. The Spanish suffered approximately 700 casualties, and shortly thereafter Spain posted a reward of $100,000 for Jordan's head. In February 1870, running low of supplies, and closely followed by Spanish bounty hunters, Jordan resigned and escaped out of Cuba in an open boat.

After Jordan's resignation, Quesada reassumed military command, while Céspedes remained nominally in charge of political matters. The Revolutionary Junta had a dim view of both Céspedes and Quesada. Céspedes, deemed too conservative to lead a revolution politically, did not have a strong stance on abolition, while Quesada was feared as someone who was likely to become a military dictator.

On the other side of the coin, Maceo and Gómez were in complete agreement on the strategy for success. They believed that slaves would be a necessary part of the rebel army; therefore, the slaves had to be freed. They further believed in destroying the economy of the island by wrecking mills and torching crops, for Spain would lose interest in Cuba without its tax revenues.

Camagüey Province planters resented the torching concept advocated by Maceo and Gómez. They also resented the facts that Maceo was an Afro-Cuban and that Gómez was not a Cuban. Ignacio Agramonte found himself with little support while conducting military activities in Camagüey. Many rebels abandoned the fight and fled to Jamaica. In the large-scale battle of Jimaguayú on May 11, 1873, Ignacio Agramonte was killed.

Carlos Manuel de Céspedes was made the scapegoat for all the defeats of the revolution, and was deposed *in absentia* on October 1873 by the revolutionary House of Representatives. The Cuban government at-arms, now presided over by Salvador Cisneros Betancourt, instructed Céspedes not to go into exile, and denied him an escort. Céspedes hid in a mountain refuge near San Lorenzo, Oriente Province. Spanish troops found Céspedes and killed him in March 1874.

The Spanish military strategists knew that it was important to keep the rebels in the eastern part of the island, while Maceo and Gómez were equally aware that they had to move on to the central and western parts of Cuba. The Spanish Army constructed a *trocha* or barricade on the narrow portion of Camagüey Province.

Colonel Ramón Barquín, an expert in military strategy, described the trocha. "It extended from Júcaro to Morón (approximately 70 kilometers) and it was the first strategic barrier of its type in the Americas. It contained 68 towers, 400 sentry boxes with shooting loopholes, and 68 block-houses laid out in such a way they could support one another visually as well as with firepower. There was a deep trench on either side (of the trocha) with triple rows of barbed wire."[6]

In spite of ideological and racial differences, the rebels were gaining on the Spanish Army. The Spanish tried negotiations, but after failing to reach an agreement, they started a war of extermination. The Captain-General enacted a number of laws, including those stating that all arrested leaders and collaborators would be executed on the spot; ships carrying weapons would be seized and all on board immediately executed; males above the age of fifteen caught outside their plantation or place of residence without justification would be summarily executed; and any woman caught away from her place of residence would be sent to a concentration camp in a city. To make matters worse, these laws were to be upheld by the blood-thirsty volunteers.

Many excesses were committed by the volunteers, but two are particularly heinous. The volunteers had a newspaper, *La Voz de Cuba*. Its founder and director, Gonzalo Castañón, who also held the rank of colonel of the volunteers, went to Key West in late January 1870 looking for José María Reyes, a Cuban exile journalist who had written an article Castañón considered insulting. He was accompanied by his physician and his second, Felipe Alonso who was a captain of the volunteers. Castañón stated that all Cuban women were prostitutes and challenged Reyes to a duel, but instead a Key West baker, Mateo Orozco, accepted the challenge. Castañón decided to leave town instead of dueling Orozco, but Orozco went to Castañón's hotel on January 29, 1870, a shooting battle ensued, Castañón and Alonso having fired first, and Castañón was killed.

Castañón's body was sent to Havana in early February 1870 and he was given an impressive State Funeral. Spanish newspapers claimed that Castañón had been murdered by Cuban exiles. U.S. authorities dropped charges against the Cuban exiles involved in the shootout. Mateo Orozco, fearing that a volunteer death squad would be sent to Key West to kill him, escaped to Jamaica where he settled and lived. The volunteers swore they would avenge Castañón's "murder."

On the afternoon of November 24, 1871, several medical students from Havana University, after learning that their professor was running late, went for a walk on the graveyard. One of the students took a flower which had been recently planted. The caretaker was furious that his garden had been disturbed and informed the volunteers that the students had scratched the glass covering the crypt of Castañón's tomb. The entire class of forty-five students was arrested by volunteer Captain Felipe Alonso, who had been Castañón's second in the Key West duel. The students were tried and convicted of desecration, with the mild penalty provided in the Spanish Civil Code. The volunteers were not satisfied and demanded a Court Martial. In the second trial, thirty-seven students were given prison terms and eight students were given the death sentence, including one who was not in Havana at the time. The eight students were executed for desecration on November 27, 1871. Since all the executed students had been born in Cuba, the volunteers felt that Castañón's death had been properly avenged.

The second incident involved the USS *Virginius*, a Civil War paddle wheeler flying the American flag and carrying weapons to the rebels. The *Virginius* was captured on October 31, 1873, by the Spanish vessel *Tornado* in international waters off Jamaica, and taken to Santiago. The master was Joseph Fry, an American, a graduate of the U.S. Naval Academy and former officer of both the Union and Confederate navies, with a crew of 52, mainly Americans and Britons, and 103 passengers, mostly Cubans. After a summary court martial, 53 of the crew and passengers were executed, including Fry and some Americans and Englishmen. The intervention of the British Navy vessel HMS *Niobe* prevented further deaths.[7]

The *Virginius* incident almost caused an early Spanish American War. U.S. Secretary of State Hamilton Fish kept a cool head throughout the affair, thus avoiding an armed conflict. The Spanish were able to prove that the vessel was under charter to Cubans and thus had no right to fly the U.S. flag. Spanish authorities released the surviving crew and passengers to an American ship, and Spain paid indemnities to both the American and British governments.

The Cuban rebels were supported by Cuban exiles in New York, Washington, Tampa, and Key West. By the fall of 1873, Cuban exiles in the United States became less willing to offer their support, as the rebels were making little progress and internal divisions within rebel ranks were affecting the outcome of battles. Salvador Cisneros Betancourt was replaced by Tomás Estrada Palma.

Tomás Estrada Palma was born near Bayamo in 1835. He studied in Havana and at Seville University in Spain. He did not obtain a degree because he returned to Cuba after learning of his father's death. As soon as hostilities broke out in 1868, Estrada Palma joined the rebels. He was elected president of the provisional government in 1877, but shortly thereafter he was captured by Spanish forces and exiled to Spain, where he remained until the end of the war.

Sadly, the rebels were divided along national, regional, and racial lines. As an example, when the war was finally extended to Las Villas Province in Central Cuba, "the locals refused to accept Máximo Gómez as their leader because he was not Cuban; they also rejected Julio

Sanguily because he was from Camagüey Province; and they would not accept Antonio Maceo because he was a mulatto and from Oriente Province."[8] This situation made it difficult to create a centralized and unified military chain of command, without which appropriate planning is impossible.

Cuban rebels fought the typical guerrilla warfare. They traveled at night and attacked at dawn, taking advantage of the Spanish infantry formation. Under the leadership of Máximo Gómez, Cuban rebels mastered the cavalry charge, with a revolver in one hand and the machete in the other. They did not attack the enemy frontally, their preference being the rearguard or the flanks. They shot with great accuracy while simultaneously screaming *al degüello*, or "off with their heads," with their horses galloping at full speed. There were not many rebels in the Cuban infantry; they were poorly armed, normally barefooted, and always on the hunt for a horse so they could join the cavalry. "Only Ignacio Agramonte, Máximo Gómez, Calixto García, and Antonio Maceo achieved a sufficient tactical military level to allow them to engage Spanish forces in conventional battles."[9]

The Spanish army was organized, trained, and supplied in the European style. They depended on military bases located in cities, and their fighting strategy consisted of strong infantry columns, occasionally reinforced with field artillery. Their ammunition and supplies were moved by oxen-driven carts. The fighting style of the Spanish army was the classic infantry stance. They would form three rows of riflemen with the front row lying down, the middle row kneeling, and the back row standing up. Since single shot rifles were the norm, once the infantry was overrun by the rebel cavalry, the machetes would always win. This Spanish occupation army was infinitely superior in numbers, training, and weaponry to the revolutionary army, but no better than its criollo adversary in morale and combativeness.[10]

The political situation in Spain had a significant effect on the conduct of the war in Cuba. General Prim was assassinated in 1870 and the brief Spanish Republic was overthrown by a military coup in 1874, thus allowing Alfonso XII to return to the Spanish throne in late December 1874.

General Arsenio Martínez Campos, who had been instrumental in restoring the monarchy in Spain, was appointed Captain-General of Cuba and arrived in Havana in October 1876, with 25,000 fresh troops. Including the new arrivals, Martínez Campos had a total of 70,000 men and immediately offered promises of reform.

After Estrada Palma's capture, Máximo Gómez called for a cease-fire in December 1877. Peace negotiations took place in February 1878 at the villa of Zanjón, east of the city of Camagüey. Martínez Campos offered freedom for all slaves and Chinese immigrants who had fought on the side of the rebels, freedom for all leaders who agreed to leave Cuba, and vague promises of political reforms, including granting Cuba political and social rights similar to the ones given to Puerto Rico in 1873. The Pact of Zanjón ended the Ten Year War, but Spain did not fully comply with any of the terms of the peace agreement.

A particularly sad story after the Pact of Zanjón is that of Salvador Cisneros Betancourt. As a political leader of the Ten Year War, he had to leave Cuba. Spanish authorities offered to return all his property as well as his title of Marqués de Santa Lucía if he agreed not to ever engage in anti-Spanish activities. He refused. Alone and penniless, he took a ship to New York. He scratched a meager living selling cigars and candy from a kiosk he built himself, since he was too proud to accept charity from wealthy Cuban exiles. At age sixty-seven, he had turned down his second chance to be a wealthy Spanish Marqués so he could be a Cuban.

Maceo was not happy with the Pact of Zanjón and asked to meet with Martínez Campos. They met in March 1878 in a mango grove in Baraguá, north of the city of Santiago. Maceo told Martínez Campos that his objectives were Cuba's independence from Spain and an immediate end to slavery. This so-called *Protest of Baraguá* did not result in war, as the Cuban provisional government convinced Maceo to go into exile, and prepare for future resistance. The war stopped at all fronts in May 1878. Slavery was finally abolished in October 1886.[11]

The Ten Year War took place during the presidencies of Andrew Johnson, Ulysses S. Grant, and Rutherford B. Hayes (1877–1881). Throughout the entire conflict, "the United States continued to proclaim its commitment to Spanish Rule."[12] Developments during the Ten Year War were closely watched by President Grant's Secretary of State Hamilton Fish, who showed optimism that a lengthy and costly Cuban Independence War would encourage Spain to sell the island to the United States.

In August 1879, the *Guerra Chiquita*, or Small War broke out in eastern and central Cuba. Spanish authorities, having learned of the conspiracy, were able to stop significant arms shipments to the rebels. On the marketing side, they warned the population that this was a black conspiracy and reinstilled the fear of another Haiti. General Calixto

García went as far as to convince Antonio Maceo not to participate in this insurrection in order to dispel the rumor of a black uprising.

Calixto García was born in Holguín, Oriente Province, in 1839. His mother's last name was Íñiguez, which suggests he may have been a descendant from Íñigo Arista, a Navarre king, whose forces are described as demons in the *Chanson de Roland*. García joined the Ten Year War at its inception, and soon distinguished himself for his bravery, as well as his leadership ability. Together with Máximo Gómez, they captured Holguín in 1872. In September 1873, surrounded by a superior Spanish force, and with most of his soldiers dead, García put his .45 caliber pistol in his mouth and shot himself. The bullet came out of his forehead, between his eyes, but he survived. Spanish soldiers came to see his mother, Lucía Íñiguez, to tell her that her son had been captured. According to the anecdote, she replied that they were mistaken, that that was not her son. When they further explained that the man in question had tried to commit suicide rather than be taken prisoner, she replied that this man was indeed her son, *mejor muerto que prisionero*, or "better dead than captured."

García was imprisoned in Spain, and released after the Pact of Zanjón. He traveled to Paris, where he befriended Dr. Ramón Emeterio Betances, an exiled Puerto-Rican proindependence leader. On September 1868, Dr. Betances had led the Lares Uprising, a significant movement seeking Puerto Rico's freedom from Spanish rule. From Paris, García traveled to New York to help organize the Guerra Chiquita.

Other than the error of not allowing Antonio Maceo to participate, the failure of the Guerra Chiquita is obvious. The war started in August 1879, and Calixto García, the chief of military operations, did not arrive on Cuban soil until May 7, 1880. The majority of his troops had already given up the fight, and García could not contact any of his men. He was captured in Bayamo, on August 4, 1880, and on August 11, 1880, he was delivered to a ship bound for Spain, where he would again be a war prisoner.

Juan Gualberto Gómez, a patriot, thinker, and journalist, explained the reasons why the Guerra Chiquita failed. "The Guerra Chiquita failed because its commander-in-chief, Calixto García, arrived late. (The War) nevertheless lasted for several months and was significant. For instance, General Guillermo Moncada had a force of 4,000 men, and many Spanish garrisons, such as the one in Mayarí, joined the revolutionary forces. The war failed because it needed a chief and did not have one."[13]

During the wars of independence in Latin America, Spain placed approximately 100,000 soldiers in a war theater of 10 million square kilometers. It was the year 1820, and at the same time, Spain's army in Mexico consisted of 45,000 men to protect a territory of 2 million square kilometers. George Washington fought against 50,000 Englishmen. Simon Bolívar faced 25,000 Spanish soldiers, and José de San Martín battled against a Spanish army of 20,000 men. The Cuban rebels fighting for independence in 1878 faced the largest European force to ever operate in the Western hemisphere, with nearly 250,000 men, including volunteers, commanded by 40 professional generals, with the best weapons available at the time and complete control of all means of transport and communication. Considering that the Ten Year War was limited to the Provinces of Las Villas, Camagüey, and Oriente, the theater of operations was 80,000 square kilometers. In spite of Spanish superiority, the Spanish Army had 80,000 casualties during the war, which was about 30 percent of the effective troops. It is estimated that rebel forces had 12,000 casualties.[14]

Notes

1. Colonel Ramón M. Barquín, *Las Luchas Guerrilleras en Cuba: De la Colonia a la Sierra Maestra*, vol. I (Madrid: Editorial Playor, 1975), 5.
2. Joan Casanovas, *Bread or Bullets: Urban Labor and Spanish Colonialism in Cuba, 1850-1898* (Pittsburgh, PA: University of Pittsburgh Press, 1998), 97–106.
3. Thomas, *Cuba or the Pursuit of Freedom*, 247.
4. Gott, *Cuba*, 74.
5. Antonio Gallenga, *The Pearl of the Antilles* (Oxford: Oxford University Press, 1873), 17.
6. Barquín, *Las Luchas Guerrilleras en Cuba de la Colonia a la Sierra Maestra*, 17.
7. Richard H. Bradford, *The Virginius Affair* (Boulder: Colorado Associate University Press, 1980), 1834.
8. Barquín, *Las Luchas Guerrilleras en Cuba de la Colonia a la Sierra Maestra*, 7.
9. Ibid., 11.
10. Ibid., 12–15.
11. Gott, *Cuba*, 77–83.
12. Louis A. Pérez Jr., *Cuba and the United States: Ties of Singular Intimacy* (Athens: The University of Georgia Press, 1990), 53.
13. Juan Gualberto Gómez, *Por Cuba Libre* (Municipio de La Habana: Oficina del Historiador de la Ciudad, 1954), 28–29.
14. Barquín, *Las Luchas Guerrilleras en Cuba de la Colonia a la Sierra Maestra*, 19–20.

12

War of Independence (1895–1898)

The Ten Year War had been a closely fought contest, but Spain's treachery insured their victory. Spain had agreed to amnesty for all Cuban patriots in the Pact of Zanjón, only to add, after the peace treaty was signed: "...amnesty for all Cuban patriots who go into exile." The Guerra Chiquita was stillborn. Both wars had been lost for lack of political leadership. That political and leadership vacuum would be filled by José Martí and to a different extent by Juan Gualberto Gómez.[1]

The fifteen-year period from 1880 to 1895, though full of anti-Spain conspiracies, was also defined by differences of opinion among Cubans. Spain did not appoint their best and brightest to Cuba's Captaincy-General, corruption being their only common denominator; the Cuban economy was weak, and many Cubans chose exile rather than the fight for independence.

Cubans, both in Cuba and in exile, while united by the idea of Cuban independence, were deeply divided by the different ways they advocated to free Cuba from Spain's domination. There were Annexationists, who were convinced that the way to the future was to become another state of the United States. Then there were those that thought that the United States should fight Spain, force Spain to abandon Cuba, and immediately organize elections, which would allow Cubans to run the destiny of the island-nation.

Another large group, primarily consisting of large landowners, were the Autonomists, who thought Cuba should remain a Spanish possession, but be allowed self-rule. This Cuban elite group believed that Spain was capable of defending criollo interests from internal challenges, but they were not so sure of Spain's ability to defend them from external confrontations.

The die-hard pro-Spanish thought the status quo was fine, but believed that Cuba should just become another province of Spain, and since Cubans were Spanish citizens, Cuba should be represented in the Spanish Parliament.

Around the mid-1890s, it appeared that most Cubans in exile were in agreement with Martí's ideas of fighting Spain to obtain Cuba's independence.

In August 1890, Spain appointed General Camilo Polavieja as Captain-General. Polavieja was good at dividing and conquering. He revived the racist marketing propaganda, convincing most well-to-do Cubans that Antonio Maceo's idea was to create a country similar to Haiti, which would, in turn, bring an American invasion.[2]

Cuban military leaders of the Ten Year War, after the Pact of Zanjón, were in exile, mostly in the United States or nearby Latin American countries. The military commanders who participated in the Guerra Chiquita were incarcerated, either in Spain or in the Spanish prison on the African island of Fernando Po, in the Gulf of Guinea.

José Martí was born in Havana on January 28, 1853. His father was born in Valencia, Spain, and was a policeman in Havana, while his mother was born in Tenerife, Canary Islands. Martí was first arrested at age sixteen for anti-Spanish activities and was deported in 1871 to exile in Spain. Martí obtained a degree in law and philosophy at Zaragoza University in 1875 and afterwards lived in Mexico and Guatemala, where he learned firsthand the negative aspects of military dictatorships and decided that the future government of a free Cuba should be in the hands of civilians.[3]

After meeting Antonio Maceo and Máximo Gómez, Martí became concerned that these two men were likely to establish a military dictatorship in a free Cuba. In 1884, Martí distanced himself from these two leaders, but by 1887 the three men were conspiring together, under Martí's able political leadership.[4]

In 1878, after the Pact of Zanjón, Martí returned to Havana where he met and developed a close friendship with Juan Gualberto Gómez. The two patriots conspired together for the Guerra Chiquita, but Martí was apprehended and sentenced to exile in Spain. He soon made his way to New York, where he joined the Cuban Revolutionary Committee, set up by Calixto García. J. G. Gómez was likewise tried for his participation in the Guerra Chiquita in 1890, and condemned first to prison in Ceuta, a Spanish enclave on the northern African coast, and later in 1892 to Spain, under controlled freedom, where he was required to report to the authorities every week.[5]

J. G. Gómez was born on July 12, 1854, at a sugar mill in Matanzas Province. He was the free child of mulatto slave parents and was educated in France. J. G. Gómez dedicated his life first to the abolition of slavery, and later to racial equality. He wanted Cuba to become an independent nation, but through the rule of law. Eventually he fought in the Independence War, where he rose to the rank of General.

Under Martí's leadership and brilliant oratory, the Cuban Revolutionary Party gained thousands of members within the Cuban exile community, primarily in New York, Philadelphia, Key West, and Tampa. Many workers agreed to contribute one-tenth of their earnings to the cause of Cuban freedom from Spain. War preparations began in earnest both in Cuba and abroad. In August 1892, Martí traveled to Santo Domingo, and offered Máximo Gómez the job of military commander. Martí then traveled to Costa Rica and asked Antonio Maceo to join in the forthcoming Independence War as Gómez's deputy. Both men agreed. Maceo was recovering from a gunshot wound, allegedly inflicted by Spanish would-be assassins. Juan Gualberto Gómez became the political leader inside Cuba.[6]

Martí assembled an expedition at the port of Fernandina, near Jacksonville, Florida. The original date for the start of the revolution is believed to have been December 25, 1894. Martí's invasion force consisted of three vessels, *Almadis*, *Lagonda*, and *Baracoa*, loaded with soldiers and weapons. The commander of this force was Colonel Fernando López Queralta. Apparently concerned with the U.S. Neutrality Law and/or his own safety, López Queralta contacted the American authorities. Two of the ships were seized by U.S. authorities on January 14, 1895, the crews arrested, and weapons and supplies confiscated. One ship got away. Martí, saddened by Lopez Queralta's betrayal, changed the starting date of the rebellion to February 24, 1895.

The Cuban War of Independence did not have an auspicious start. The rebel commanders in the western region, Pedro Betancourt, and the brothers Julio and Manuel Sanguily, along with Juan Gualberto Gómez were promptly arrested in Havana by Spanish authorities.

In Spain, once the news of the Cuban insurrection arrived, Antonio Cánovas del Castillo was reappointed as Prime Minister. Arsenio Martínez Campos was tapped to succeed Calleja as Captain-General of Cuba and departed from the port of Cádiz on April 4, 1895, along with 7,000 well-trained fresh troops.

The brothers Antonio and José Maceo, accompanied by Flor Crombet and some nineteen combatants set sail from Costa Rica to Jamaica and Bahamas, where they boarded the ship *Honor* on their way to Cuba. A few days earlier, Martí, Máximo Gómez, and four companions had departed Santo Domingo for eastern Cuba. With the key players on their way to Cuba, the Independence War had started.

Francisco Adolfo Crombet, better known as Flor Crombet, was an Afro-Cuban born near Santiago de Cuba. He was a descendant of Haitians who had immigrated to eastern Cuba during the fighting in *Saint Domingue* against Napoleon's forces. He joined the Ten Year War in 1868 and was soon promoted for his bravery and organizational skills. He was critical of his boss, Antonio Maceo for having met with Arsenio Martínez Campos during the Protest of Baraguá, as Crombet believed that there should be no contacts with the enemy. He was involved in planning the Guerra Chiquita, captured and sent to prison in Spain. Upon release, he joined Antonio Maceo in Costa Rica and soon they were on the way to the Independence War.

Before sailing from the Dominican Republic to Cuba, Martí and Máximo Gómez signed a document which had been drafted by Martí. This document, known as the Manifesto of Montecristi, was signed on March 25, 1895, and it outlines the reasons why the Cuban people were organizing the War of Independence. With his clear prose, Martí stated that the war was not against the Spanish people, but rather against the colonial regime in effect on the island for more than three centuries. The policy for Cuba's War of Independence is covered in the five points of the Manifesto of Montecristi.

+ The war was to be waged by blacks and whites alike
+ Participation of all blacks was a crucial element to achieve victory
+ Spaniards who did not object to the war effort were to be spared
+ Private rural property was not to be damaged
+ The revolution should inject new economic life to Cuba

Martí, Gómez, and their companions arrived in Playitas, east of Guantánamo Bay, in early April, and immediately took to the hills. The rebellion had already started in Oriente Province. Bartolomé Masó and Guillermón Moncada, a black leader from Santiago, had started battling Spanish forces in February 1895.[7]

Bartolomé Masó was born in Catalonia, Spain. He participated in Céspedes' 1868 rebellion and was second in command to Dominican-born General Luis Marcano. After the Pact of Zanjón, he left Cuba and traveled in Europe. He returned to Cuba in 1879 to help organize the Guerra Chiquita, was taken prisoner and sent to Spain. He again returned to Cuba in 1895 and after fighting in some battles he was asked to join the political organization of the Cuba Republic-at-Arms.

His name was Guillermo Moncada, but because he was very tall and muscular, he was called Guillermón. He was born in Oriente Province and fought in the Ten Year War, the Guerra Chiquita, and the War of Independence. Moncada was one of twenty-nine Cuban generals in the War of Independence. He was always in front of his troops and could not wait for the official start of the war since he was quite ill. He started fighting on February 22, 1895, and died of tuberculosis on April 5, 1895.

The Maceo brothers and Flor Crombet landed at Playa de Derata, near Baracoa. They were spotted by a contingent of Spanish military, divided, and pursued. Flor Crombet was killed. The Maceo brothers were able to get away and lived off the land until they were able to reunite with their followers, thirteen days later.[8]

Martí, Maceo, and Gómez met at *La Mejorana* sugar mill near Bayamo in early May. Maceo advocated that a military junta should rule Cuba until final victory, but Martí strongly disagreed. They parted without reaching an agreement.

Martí and Gómez were on their way to meet Bartolomé Masó, when a Spanish column under the command of Colonel Ximénez de Sandoval surprised them at Dos Ríos. Martí was killed on May 19, 1895, thus depriving the nascent republic of its most clear thinking and eloquent politician.

Martí was replaced by Salvador Cisneros Betancourt, Marqués de Santa Lucía, as President of the Cuban Republic-at-Arms. Bartolomé Masó was appointed as Vice President, and Máximo Gómez remained as Commander-in-Chief, with Antonio Maceo as his second in command.

Without its charismatic political leader, the Cuban independence movement was instantly weakened. Military chiefs Gómez and Maceo had the upper hand, which was precisely what Martí had tried to avoid. On the positive side, Gómez and Maceo, both veterans of the Ten Year War, knew not to make the same mistakes twice. They were painfully aware that they could not defeat the powerful Spanish army by battling only in one province (Oriente), out of six provinces. They had to move the war west, and force the Spanish to split their forces into many fronts.

Gómez and Maceo went through the, by then, poorly maintained Camagüey trocha between Júcaro and Morón, with 1,000 cavalrymen and 500 foot soldiers, by simply moving faster than the Spanish defenders. By mid-October, the rebels had crossed Camagüey Province, and had entered Sancti Spíritus and Santa Clara in central Cuba. They burned every crop in their path, while avoiding frontal encounters with sizeable Spanish troops.[9]

At the end of November, the Cuban Provisional Government was in place. Polish-born Carlos Roloff, who had joined the rebels in Las Villas Province, was appointed Secretary of War. Practically the entire Cuban population was aiding the rebels.

By Christmas 1895, the Gómez and Maceo troops were at Coliseo, not far from Matanzas and only 110 kilometers due east from Havana. Spanish authorities came to two momentous conclusions, that the 1896 sugar harvest would be ruined, and that the city of Havana was being threatened.

In early January 1896, Maceo had bypassed Havana and entered Pinar del Río Province, while Gómez's camp was practically on the outskirts of Havana. At this point in 1896, with Spanish forces on the run, the rebels appeared assured of victory. Cuba's Captain-General Arsenio Martínez Campos was well aware that the only way to prevent Spain's loss of Cuba was radical repression, a measure he was not prepared to execute. He tendered his resignation to Prime Minister Cánovas del Castillo, and returned to Madrid after only nine months on the post.

At this point in the War of Independence, Cubans were winning. Peninsulares and wealthy criollo landowners became Annexationists and openly advocated North American intervention. Clearly, they preferred U.S. domination to government by Cubans. Simultaneously, many U.S. politicians became convinced that the annexation of Cuba was inevitable. Manifest Destiny proponents perceived control over Cuba as a natural extension of expanding boundaries.

It is likely that when Cánovas del Castillo appointed Martínez Campos to the highest office in Cuba, he was expecting another Pact of Zanjón, perhaps with Spain coming closer to complying with the terms of the agreement this time. Now that Martínez Campos had resigned, Cánovas del Castillo had no choice but to follow the advice given by Martínez Campos. Cánovas del Castillo appointed Valeriano Weyler, of Prussian origin, the most brutal general in the Spanish Army, as Cuba's Captain-General. "He was intelligent and serious, had been military attaché in Washington during the American Civil War, and much admired Sherman...he was ruthless to men but loved horses...he had fought in the (Ten Year) Cuban war, and also against the Carlists."[10]

Upon his arrival in Cuba, Weyler hit the ground running. His highest priorities were to push Gómez away from Havana, and to force Maceo out of Pinar del Río. Weyler sent a large contingent of troops to the Gómez camp, to force the rebels to fight an open battle in conventional style. Gómez's forces were defeated, and the rebels retreated in the direction of Santa Clara in central Cuba. Simultaneously, Weyler ordered the refurbishment of the old trocha from Júcaro to Morón in Camagüey, and the construction of a new trocha in the narrowest portion of the island in Pinar del Río Province, from Mariel to Majana. The east and west trochas along which the Spanish forces intended to contain the Cuban insurgents are depicted in Figure 12.1. Also cities that were important to the Cuban wars for independence are indicated in this map.

On July 5, 1896, José Maceo was killed in Oriente Province. The only good news the rebels had in early 1896 was the arrival of Calixto García from the United States in Oriente Province, with men and a

Figure 12.1 Cuba

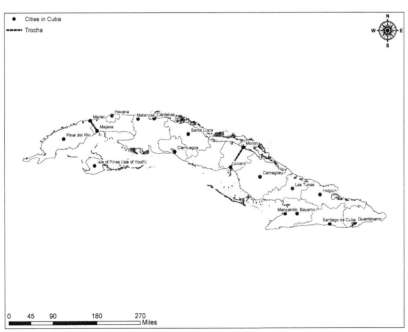

large cargo of weapons. García was appointed military commander of the eastern region, and would remain in that area until the end of the war.[11]

The most cruel and controversial measure taken by Weyler, was the policy of *reconcentración*, which essentially converted the entire island into concentration camps. His idea, which he had suggested and experimented with during the Ten Year War, was now to be implemented in a merciless fashion. Entire populations of towns and villages would be *reconcentrados* in well-defended population centers, thus depriving the rebels of food and support. Food for the reconcentrados would be provided locally, and if there was no food available, Weyler was content to see them starve. There were other even more onerous conditions for the reconcentrados. They had to submit to registration, and those failing to obey military authorities, were deemed guilty of treason and executed.[12]

Weyler also implemented another policy, not well covered in history books, which was the killing of livestock by the Spanish army. He ordered his army to kill all horses and cattle in the country that could not be utilized by the Spanish army. This would prevent the Cuban army's accession to them, but would also deprive the Cuban civilian population of an important source of food. Apparently, the Spanish army took this order seriously, since of the three million head of cattle estimated in the island in 1895, only 10 percent remained in 1898 at the end of hostilities.[13]

Gómez was in trouble in Las Villas, both with the local leadership and planters, as well as with the civilian leadership in New York. The planters were being ruined by the burning of their crops, and Gómez was promoting those who distinguished themselves in the field of battle. These were usually blacks, mulattoes, and lower-class whites. Gómez was encouraged to promote upper-class whites with no military experience, which upset him so much that he was threatening to resign.

Meanwhile, Maceo was leading a successful campaign in Pinar del Río, while Weyler's engineers feverishly built the Mariel to Majana trocha. In October 1896, Maceo received an urgent message from Gómez, asking him to travel to Las Villas and join Gómez's forces. Gómez needed Maceo's political support, but his military help would also be welcome. Maceo had received a reinforcement of men, which included Panchito, Gómez's son, weapons, and ammunition sent by Estrada Palma from the United States.

On October 8, 1896, Weyler first ordered *reconcentración* in Pinar del Río Province, where Maceo was quite active. The entire population had eight days to move into fortified towns. Anyone outside the fortifications would be considered a rebel and treated accordingly. Two weeks later, Weyler traveled to Mariel to personally hunt down Maceo.[14]

Maceo felt that his duty was to join forces with Gómez, but he was concerned about the risk of crossing the new trocha from Mariel to Majana. Instead, he selected a small group of men which included Panchito Gómez, and decided to go by boat from the port of Mariel, to a point near Havana where they set their camp.

On the early morning of December 7, 1896, Maceo's small group was surprised by a much larger Spanish column commanded by Major Cirujeda. Maceo was killed as well as Panchito Gómez. "Panchito Gómez was hit by two bullets, but his wounds were not necessarily life-threatening. He did not want to abandon the corpse of General Maceo, and when it was obvious that he would be captured alive, he committed suicide."[15]

Maceo's death was a watershed event in the Cuban War of Independence. Máximo Gómez was in Oriente Province when he learned of Maceo's death, and that of his son. He would no longer talk about resigning. The liberation of Cuba was now his sacred duty.

Weyler, on the other hand, believed that he had gained the upper hand, and he could sense that he was defeating the rebels. Weyler was probably correct in his assessment, since by the middle of 1897, Gómez's guerrillas were on the defensive. Only Calixto García was having some successes, capturing the town of Las Tunas, in August.[16] In New York, Tomás Estrada Palma resigned from the leadership of the Cuban Revolutionary Party. In Madrid, Prime Minister Cánovas del Castillo was convinced that victory in Cuba was at hand, although he was concerned about a new insurrection in the Philippines.

Additional assistance had been provided to Spanish authorities by McKinley's presidential address on March 4, 1897. McKinley indicated a careful and conservative foreign policy. He spoke against wars of conquest and stated that he opposed territorial aggression. In his closing remarks, McKinley said that Cubans could only expect moderate comfort from his administration.[17]

While the Cuban rebels were successfully battling Spanish forces a different sort of conflict, also about Cuban independence, was being waged in Washington. While McKinley continued to hold the line against Cuban intervention, or any move which could drag the United States into war, every congressional session after 1895 presented pro-Cuban resolutions in both houses. The Senate's Foreign Relations Committee was staffed by Republican and Democratic expansionists, always prepared to clash with McKinley on Cuba issues. In May 1897, the Senate passed a resolution favoring recognition of Cuban belligerency, but the House killed it. McKinley's key advisors on Cuba were the American consul-general in Havana (Fitzhugh Lee) and the American Minister in Madrid (Hannis Taylor). Both men were President Cleveland's appointees and both were jingoes.[18]

In the meantime, U.S. public opinion had turned belligerently anti-Spanish as a result of Weyler's repressive tactics against the Cuban population. It is indeed possible that Weyler was on his way to a costly military victory, which only a very unusual event could derail. The unusual event materialized in the form of three bullets shot by Italian anarchist Michele Angiolillo, which killed Spain's Prime Minister Antonio Cánovas del Castillo on August 8, 1897. Cánovas del Castillo had been vacationing with his family at the spa of Santa Águeda in Mondragón, Guipúzcoa, northeast Spain.

There is evidence that Angiolillo's original plan was to kill one or two young members of the Spanish royal family. Angiolillo met a Puerto-Rican revolutionary, Ramón Emeterio Betances, who apparently persuaded him to kill Cánovas del Castillo instead.[19] Betances was a good friend of Calixto García, and it is possible that Betances rightfully thought that the death of Cánovas del Castillo would put an end to the suffering of Cuban people.

The new Prime Minister was Práxedes Sagasta, a liberal leader, who was a firm believer in autonomous rule for Cuba. As soon as the news of Sagasta's appointment reached Havana, Weyler tendered his resignation. Sagasta appointed General Ramón Blanco as Cuba's Captain-General.

The war was not going well for the Cuban rebels. Havana Province was mostly under Spanish control. The remnants of Maceo's forces were conducting guerrilla warfare in the westernmost portion of Pinar del Río Province. Significant fighting was taking place in Matanzas Province, under Quintín Banderas. Máximo Gómez was active in central Cuba, and Calixto García was in control of most of the countryside in Oriente Province. The refurbished trocha from Júcaro to Morón had been made practically impassable by Spanish engineers. They had installed movable field artillery at Ciego de Avila in the center of the trocha. The three rebel groups were thus isolated from one another.[20]

There is no doubt that with both José Martí and Antonio Maceo dead, the rebels were in trouble. On the political side, Martí was the organizer, an indefatigable money raiser, and most importantly, a man trusted by Cubans living in Cuba, as well as Cubans living in exile. Further hindering the political angle, Juan Gualberto Gómez was either in prison, or closely watched under house arrest. Frustrated by the internal bickering of military and political leaders, Estrada Palma had resigned in mid-1897. The only active political leader was Salvador Cisneros Betancourt, but he was a tired elderly gentleman aged seventy-one at the time.

On the military side, Calixto García was in control of Oriente Province and the portion of Camagüey Province east of the trocha, other than the major population centers, which were under the control of Spanish troops. In Pinar del Río Province, west of the trocha, General Juan Rius Rivera had taken command of the Cuban rebels after Antonio Maceo's death, and was having a successful campaign harassing Spanish troops.

It was in central Cuba, in the provinces of Havana, Matanzas, and Las Villas, where the Cuban rebels were being punished. Máximo Gómez was in trouble, militarily as well as politically. Fearing the wrath of wealthy white planters, Salvador Cisneros Betancourt had instructed Máximo Gómez to sever relations with Antonio Maceo. With Maceo now dead, Cisneros' request was a moot point, but Gómez had sent for Maceo rather than obeying a direct order.

By mid-1897, Weyler's troops had gained the upper hand. Spain ruled the cities, while Cuban rebels occupied limited territories on the countryside. Weyler's policy of *reconcentración*, however cruel and inhumane to the civilian population, was producing the intended military success. Had Weyler remained as Cuba's Captain-General for another two years, the Cuban rebels would have been defeated. But Weyler had resigned after the assassination of Cánovas del Castillo and had been replaced by a much more humane General Ramón Blanco. The liberal Prime Minister, Práxedes Sagasta firmly in power in Madrid, was looking for a rapid solution to the conflict which Spanish historians call *La Guerra de Cuba*, or Cuba's War.

In the meantime, wanting to avoid war at any cost, McKinley tried his hand at diplomacy. McKinley demanded that Spain declare a unilateral cease fire and institute an autonomous Cuban government, run by Cubans. Spain's strategy was to delay. The U.S. Minister to Spain, Steward Woodford, went as far as to threaten María Teresa, Spain's Queen Regent with armed intervention of Cuba. The Queen asked for more time to define and implement a Cuban autonomy policy.

The offer of autonomy finally arrived. On November 6, 1897, General Ramón Blanco offered autonomy for Cuba and decreed an amnesty for all Cuban political prisoners. The offer of autonomy backfired on both Spain and the United States since it only convinced the Cubans that they were winning the war.

Gómez remembered well how Spain failed to comply with the terms of the Pact of Zanjón, and flatly refused Blanco's peace overtures. Bartolomé Masó proclaimed an alliance of Cubans and Americans against Spain.

Gómez announced an immediate court martial for any Cuban officer accepting Spain's amnesty offer and/or participating in Spain's autonomous government. In addition, Gómez stated that total Cuban independence was a necessary condition for them to lay down their arms. Meanwhile, public opinion in the United States had increasingly turned venomously anti-Spanish, and the U.S. press was having a field day exposing, and usually exaggerating, the situation in Cuba.

On January 20, 1898, Fitzhugh Lee reported to Washington the failure of Spain's offer of autonomy.[21]

Notes

1. Juan Gualberto Gómez, *Por Cuba Libre* [For a Free Cuba] (Municipio de La Habana: Oficina del Historiador de la Ciudad, 1954), 19–24.
2. Gott, *Cuba*, 83.
3. Thomas, *Cuba or the Pursuit of Freedom*, 293–99.
4. Jaime Suchlicki, *Cuba from Columbus to Castro* (Washington, DC: Brassey's, 1990), 75–77.
5. Gómez, *Por Cuba Libre*, 32–47.
6. Thomas, *Cuba or the Pursuit of Freedom*, 300–9.
7. Gott, *Cuba*, 88–89.
8. Thomas, *Cuba or the Pursuit of Freedom*, 316.
9. Ibid., 321.
10. Ibid., 328.
11. Gott, *Cuba*, 92–93.
12. Ibid., 94.
13. Philip S. Foner, *The Spanish-Cuban-American War and the Birth of American Imperialism* (New York: Monthly Review Press, 1972), 379.
14. Thomas, *Cuba or the Pursuit of Freedom*, 328–38.
15. Trumbull White, *United States in War with Spain and the History of Cuba* (Chicago, IL: International Publishing, 1898), 254–55.
16. Gott, *Cuba*, 96.

17. H. Wayne Morgan, *William McKinley and his America* (Syracuse, NY: Syracuse University Press, 1963), 273.
18. Ibid., 328–37.
19. Félix Ojeda Reyes, *El Desterrado de París: Biografía del Dr. Ramón Emeterio Betances (1827-1898)* (San Juan, Puerto Rico: Ediciones Puerto, 2001), 356–59.
20. Thomas, *Cuba or the Pursuit of Freedom*, 348–60.
21. Morgan, *William McKinley and his America*, 354.

Part 4

Cuban-Spanish-American War

13

USS *Maine*, Yellow Journalism, and War Preparations

While Cuban patriots were fighting Spain to attain Cuba's independence, two different wars were being fought in the United States, also ostensibly for Cuba's independence. One of these wars was being waged by newspapers for the purpose of increasing circulation. The other one was being fought between pro and antiexpansionism politicians. This last conflict, ultimately won by the expansionists, used Cuba's struggle for independence as an excuse to declare war on Spain, only to ultimately sacrifice Cuba's independence on the altar of greed.

It is difficult to explain the rationale used by the United States declared war on Spain on April 25, 1898. The U.S.' desire to own Cuba as foreseen in Manifest Destiny was an important reason. In the past, on several occasions, the United States had sufficient justification to declare war on Spain, but the difference is that in 1898 they knew they would win. They could take Spain's overseas colonies, and Spain would be out of the Americas. Also, the United States was actively planning the construction of a canal across Central America, and they could ill afford Spain's interference on this strategic project from nearby Cuba and Puerto Rico.

There were many Cuban exiles living in the United States at the time, and Tomás Estrada Palma, President of the Cuban Revolutionary Party in the United States did a good marketing job for Cuba's independence. With offices in Washington, DC and New York City, Estrada Palma's assistants lobbied politicians, journalists, and the public in general for support of Cuba's freedom.

Perhaps the most convenient reason for the timing of the U.S.' declaration of war was the journalistic war taking place in New York during the 1890s. Joseph Pulitzer, publisher of the *New York World*, used sensationalism and hyperbole to increase circulation. Pulitzer was taken head on by William Randolph Hearst, publisher of the *New York Journal*, and in the process of outdoing one another the term "yellow journalism" emerged.

The *World* had a popular color comic strip called "Hogan's Alley" which featured a character dressed in yellow named "the yellow kid." Hearst hired artist R. F. Outcault, the creator of "Hogan's Alley." Pulitzer hired another cartoonist and created a new "yellow kid." Thus the term Yellow Journalism was created.

There were many domestic and international fronts in the Pulitzer–Hearst war, but the main battleground appeared to have been the liberation of Cuba from Spain. Starting in late 1895, U.S. newspapers commenced a relentless campaign for the United States to take action against the atrocities being committed by Spanish authorities and volunteers against the Cuban people. As a result of this journalistic campaign, the majority of the American people became convinced that liberating Cuba was the right thing to do, even if it meant the start of the first armed conflict since the Civil War.

With the arrival of Captain-General Weyler in Cuba in early 1896, U.S. newspapers had a field day. The February 23, 1896 issue of the *Journal*, refers to Weyler as: "a fiendish despot...the devastator of haciendas...there is nothing to prevent his carnal, animal brain from running riot with itself in inventing tortures and infamies of bloody debauchery."[1]

One of the most widely quoted examples of yellow journalism pertains to an exchange of telegrams between Hearst and his ace cartoonist Frederic Remington, who had been sent to Cuba by the *Journal* along with freelance reporter Richard Davis. Weyler had prohibited journalists from traveling with the troops and thus Remington and Davis languished in Havana bars and hotels. Remington telegraphed to Hearst "Everything is quiet...there will be no war. I wish to return," to which Hearst answered "Please remain. You furnish the pictures and I'll furnish the war."[2] Slightly over a year later, Hearst made good on his promise. His inflammatory articles had such a significant effect on American public opinion that many believe he was a key reason why Congress declared war on Spain.

This exchange of telegrams is so well known that a respected Spanish journalist, Manuel Leguineche, entitled his book about Hearst and the final days of the Cuban-Spanish-American War "Yo Pondré la Guerra," or in translation, "I Will Furnish the War."[3]

Another example of Hearst's yellow journalism regarding the Cuba situation has to do with Evangelina Cossío Cisneros, a daring seventeen-year-old Cuban girl whose father was imprisoned for rebel activities. She was the niece of Salvador Cisneros Betancourt, but Hearst insisted to use her mother's maiden name, Cisneros, for the readers to think she was the daughter, and not the niece, of the well-known President of the Republic of Cuba-at-Arms.

Evangelina first secured her father's transfer from confinement in Spain's prison in Ceuta, a Spanish enclave in Morocco, to the secure Spanish prison at the Isle of Pines, Cuba. She then tried to arrange her father's escape by pretending to seduce and then kidnapping the Spanish military commander of the island. Evangelina was captured and sent to trial. The *Journal* enlisted the women of America to clamor for Evangelina's release. The *Journal* claimed that she was being mistreated, when in reality she was being well treated while awaiting trial.

Hearst, with a flair for the dramatic, sent a reporter, Karl Decker, to Cuba with the mission of rescuing Evangelina. Decker, apparently a quite resourceful person, rented a house next to the prison. He then bribed the prison guards, cut the bars in Evangelina's cell, took her to the roof of the house he had rented, and smuggled her out of Cuba dressed as a sailor on a steamer heading for New York. Hearst arranged a welcome reception for Evangelina at Madison Square and claimed that he could carry out in a couple of weeks what the best efforts of diplomacy failed to obtain after many months.[4]

In June 1896, President Grover Cleveland had appointed former Confederate General Fitzhugh Lee, a nephew of Robert E. Lee, to the post of U.S. Consul to Havana. In December 1897, Lee became concerned about the safety of Americans living on the island and requested that a warship be deployed to Key West and be prepared to sail to Havana in case anti-American violence erupted.

Fitzhugh Lee was born in Virginia, and attended the U.S. Military Academy at West Point. Upon graduation, Lee served as a cavalry officer in Texas and participated in combat against Indians, where he was seriously wounded. In May 1861, Lee resigned his commission in the U.S. Army and joined the Confederate army. In September 1864, he was wounded again and by the time he recovered from his wounds, the Confederate army had surrendered.

The battleship *Maine*, which had been launched in 1890 and was considered to contain the latest available technology, was ordered to Key West. The *Maine* was under the command of Captain Charles

Sigsbee. The *Journal* and the *World*, upon learning the whereabouts of the *Maine*, embarked on an incredible battle of yellow journalism. The headline of the *Journal* read: "Next Door to War with Spain."[5]

President McKinley and Navy Secretary John Long, reacting to the newspapers, rather than to any communication between Lee and Sigsbee, ordered the *Maine* to Havana. The *Maine* arrived in Havana on January 25, and it was well received by Spanish authorities. In fact, Lee and Sigsbee went to a bullfight in Havana as guests of the Spanish commander.[6]

On February 15, 1898, at 9:40 p.m. the *Maine* exploded and sank in Havana harbor. Out of a complement of 354 officers and men, 266 American sailors were killed by the explosion. War between Spain and the United States became inevitable.

As could be expected, the U.S. yellow press blamed Spain for the disaster. The exaggerated notion of Cuban desire for U.S. intervention inevitably implicated Cubans in the destruction of the *Maine*. After all, Cubans had motive and opportunity. Spain at first blamed Cuban rebels; later, the Spanish press blamed the Americans themselves by saying that the United States was looking for a pretext to declare war on Spain.

The U.S. Navy appointed a committee to investigate the *Maine* disaster consisting of Captain W. T. Sampson as chairman and Captain F. E. Chadwick and Lieutenant Commander William Potter to report on the explosion. Spain offered to participate in the investigation but the United States declined. Spain conducted a separate study.

Immediately after the sinking of the *Maine* "[Fitzhugh] Lee and Captain Sigsbee of the *Maine* both held that it was an accident and urged a suspension of popular feelings, and McKinley himself felt that an investigation would prove the consul right."[7]

The American court of inquiry reported that an external explosion had destroyed the *Maine*. The Spanish commission reported that the explosion had been internal.

In 1976, Admiral Hyman G. Rickover conducted his own investigation which was detailed in his revealing 1976 book *How the Battleship Maine was Destroyed*. The explosion experts commissioned by Rickover concluded that the explosion was internal. It was later determined that the ammunition storage hold was adjacent to the ship's engine room and that the wall separating these two compartments was most likely not insulated. It was speculated that the heat from the engines combined with the elevated tropical temperatures in Havana caused the spontaneous combustion of coal dust, followed by the explosion of ordnance.[8]

The sinking of the *Maine* and yellow journalism may not have been the direct cause for the U.S.' declaration of war against Spain, but they were certainly powerful catalysts. War with Spain had been a predictable event since the Adams-Onís Treaty was ratified in 1821. Perhaps the United States wanted to wait until they were sure they would win. In any event, "the Naval War College, that service's highest-level staff school, had begun studying strategy for a war with Spain as early as 1895."[9]

The U.S. public and the press were ready to go to war with Spain after the sinking of the *Maine*. Both the House and the Senate clamored for war, while McKinley refused to discuss the matter and leaked information that he would veto a war resolution.

The American public was ready to go to war; unfortunately, the U.S. military was not. Having fallen victim to a number of cost-reduction moves by Congress, the authorized strength of the U.S. Army in 1897 was 25,000 officers and men. A number of states had volunteer or National Guard units that even though full of patriotism, were ill equipped and had little or no military training. The War Department estimated these resources to be about 114,000 officers and men. Graham Cosmas, Chief Historian for the U.S. Army concluded "The nation in 1898 did not have an army in any operational sense of that word."[10]

In 1898, the Spanish forces in Cuba consisted of 150,000 regulars from the Iberian Peninsula and an estimated 80,000 volunteers. The Spanish forces were well equipped, but they suffered from poor training and the ravages of tropical diseases. Spanish records indicate that since 1895, more then 13,000 Spanish soldiers had died from yellow fever alone. The American Consul at Havana indicated that 25–30 percent of Spanish soldiers lay sick in hospitals.[11]

The Spanish military presence in Cuba was intended to defend the island against rebel attacks. The forces were scattered in small garrisons with few fortifications. When war with the United States became a possibility, Spain should have concentrated their forces in a few critical cities and been ready to act aggressively against the invading forces. But Spain still viewed their only enemy as Cuban rebels and failed miserably to prepare for a U.S. invasion.

At the time of the U.S.' entry into the Cuban War of Independence, it is estimated that Cuban rebel forces ranged between 25,000 and 40,000 troops, the number depending on changes in the military situation.

Cuban rebels had learned to live off the land, often cultivating small gardens, particularly since Weyler's policy of reconcentración. They operated in small detachments which were controlled by a hierarchy of regional commanders. Although Máximo Gómez was the military chief of the Cuban rebels, the strongest field force was that of General Calixto García, operating in Oriente Province. García's forces, strengthened by their fourteen field cannons operated by American volunteers, often successfully fought large Spanish contingents.[12]

While U.S. politicians reacted to the agitation of U.S. journalists, the U.S. armed forces were planning for a war which appeared to be quite different to the expectations of Capitol Hill. The uncommunicative President McKinley had yet a different concept, but he would only disclose small portions of his strategy at a time.

The Army and Navy of the United States, armed with the knowledge that rebels had devastated most crops in Cuba, were aware that the Spanish armed forces in Cuba depended on shipments from overseas for their food and even the feed for their horses. Therefore, U.S. military planners decided that a naval blockade of key Cuban ports would starve Spanish forces into surrender. The U.S. Army viewed the war in Cuba essentially as the Navy's war. They further assumed that the political objective of the war with Spain would be to assist the Cuban rebels in expelling the Spanish army and in establishing an independent nation. And the best way to accomplish this objective was to supply weapons and ammunition to the Cuban patriots. It must have come as a big surprise to the U.S. military when they found out that an important group of Washington politicians wanted to keep Cuba.[13]

Ever since the presidency of Thomas Jefferson, U.S. politicians have understood the strategic and economic value of the island of Cuba. President McKinley appointed Whitelaw Reid to negotiate in Madrid to purchase Cuba from Spain immediately before the United States declared war on Spain. The price offered was $300 million, and it was met by mild interest in the part of the Spanish crown and perhaps anger from the politicians. Spain firmly believed that they could crush the Cuban rebellion. The *Washington Post* published a crusty rebuttal to the United States offer from Spain's Prime Minister Antonio Cánovas del Castillo, "Spain is not a nation of merchants capable of selling its honor."[14]

Clearly, now that the United States was going to fight Spain to liberate Cuba, why not make it part of the territory of the United States? Although U.S. politicians might not yet have determined how to proceed to obtain ownership of Cuba, they were content to take the first step, the liberation of Cuba from Spanish domination.

After the McKinley administration determined that its efforts to purchase Cuba had failed, on March 27, 1898, the United States delivered an ultimatum to Spain demanding an armistice until October 5, 1898. Spain accepted, but Calixto García and Máximo Gómez refused to accept the armistice and ordered their troops to continue fighting. Spain had no choice but to resume operations.

As is often the case, politicians wanted to move faster than the armed forces were able to deliver. So many Republican congressmen clamored to drive Spanish forces out of Cuba that President McKinley was afraid of losing control of Congress. On April 11, 1898, McKinley asked Congress for "authority to use the armed forces of the United States to secure a full and final termination of hostilities between the Government of Spain and the people of Cuba."[15]

Conspicuously absent from McKinley's message to Congress were any references to Cuban independence or recognition of the Cuban provisional government. McKinley did mention that the United States would be a *neutral* third party. McKinley's refusal to recognize Cuban independence, even on the threshold of war, angered the more ultraist element of both Republicans and Democrats. Questions arise as to why McKinley tried to buy Cuba from Spain. Was he really concerned about the suffering of Cubans under Spain's oppressive regime? Was it a last-ditch effort to avoid war? Or did he perhaps just want for the United States to own Cuba?

Hidden between the lines in McKinley's message was the notion that the war would be directed against both Cubans and Spaniards. Intervention without recognition provoked a strong reaction from Máximo Gómez, Calixto García, and the Cuban Junta in New York.

Congress did not stand idle after McKinley's message was analyzed and understood. Senator David Turpie of Indiana, an advocate of Cuban independence and recognition of the Cuban Republic-at-Arms introduced a resolution in the Senate. "The Turpie resolution favoring Cuban independence passed by a vote of 67 to 21; some 24 Republicans joined the Democrats to humiliate the President and only [through the efforts of the close associate of Roosevelt and Lodge, Thomas] Reed squelched it in the House."[16]

Before declaring war on Spain, McKinley proposed to deliver an additional ultimatum to Spain demanding Spain's relinquishment of authority in Cuba. Senator Joseph Foraker from Ohio asked that the message include *immediate recognition* of Bartolomé Masó's Cuban Government-at-Arms. After careful manipulation by McKinley's supporters in the House, Foraker withdrew his request in exchange for the Teller Amendment and a more strongly worded ultimatum.

The well-publicized *Teller Amendment*, which was added to the April 20, 1898 ultimatum given to Spain and later to the formal declaration of war, was ratified by the U.S. Congress. The amendment, put forward by Colorado Senator Henry Teller, a former annexationist, under the pressure, and some believe personal financial incentive, of the lobby of Cuban exiles, categorically rejected any colonial intent. The Teller Amendment, as summarized by British historian Richard Gott, reads "The United States hereby disclaims any disposition or intention to exercise sovereignty, jurisdiction or control over said island except for the pacification thereof, and asserts its determination, when that is accomplished, to leave the government and control of the island to its people."[17]

The Teller Amendment is clearly an afterthought to mask the true intentions of the McKinley administration. Spain rejected the ultimatum on April 25, 1898, saying that the ultimatum was a disguised war declaration.

The Cuban patriots became the allies of the invading U.S. troops. Cuban rebel leaders welcomed the help offered by the United States and were not concerned that the United States would occupy the island permanently since they had read and understood the Teller Amendment.

Declaring that the United States was a neutral third party was beyond doubt against U.S. public opinion, which clamored for Cuban freedom from Spain and independence.

On April 19, 1898, Congress authorized armed American intervention, declared that Cuba should be free and independent, and further added that the United States had no desire to annex Cuba. Spain and the United States broke diplomatic relations on April 20, 1898. On April 21, McKinley ordered the Navy squadron at Key West to blockade Havana and other ports in northwest Cuba. The Cuban blockade started on April 22, 1898. On April 25, Congress formally declared war.

The first engagement of United States versus Spanish forces took place on April 27, 1898 at Matanzas, east of Havana on Cuba's north coast. Three ships of Admiral Sampson's fleet, the flagship *New York*, the monitor *Puritan*, and the cruiser *Cincinnati*, opened fire upon the fortifications protecting said city. The Spanish batteries were silenced in less than twenty minutes.[18]

The war with Spain is the only instance in U.S. history in which the legislative power took the initiative of war over the executive power. Was President McKinley undecided, or did he not want to go to war? Once the decision to declare war was taken by Congress, McKinley became concerned with what would happen to American property and investments under a Cuban government. McKinley's actions, before and after war was declared, point to a desire to keep Cuba as a U.S. possession, without regard to the Teller Amendment and with no intention of ever granting statehood to Cuba.[19]

The most significant unknown factor to U.S. military planners was the Spanish fleet, under the command of Admiral Pascual Cervera y Topete, which they considered powerful and dangerous.

Cervera, a graduate of the Spanish Royal Naval Academy and veteran of the 1859 Morocco war was appointed Naval Attaché to the Spanish Legation at Washington. During the Ten Year War against Cuban rebels, Cervera was charged with the responsibility of blockading Cuban ports to impede the flow of weapons and insurgents. He then served in the Spanish Navy Department. Two years after he retired in 1896, the Queen Regent requested that he take command of the Spanish Caribbean Squadron for the impending war with the United States. Cervera had pleaded for time to refit, reinforce, and repair the vessels, but he was immediately dispatched to Cuba.

Cervera's flotilla consisted of six vessels, two destroyers and four armored cruisers. The destroyers, *Plutón* and *Furor* were two of the most feared torpedo-armed warships of the time. The destroyers were under the command of Captain Fernando Villaamil, the designer of the destroyer concept. The four armored cruisers were *Infanta María Teresa*, Cervera's flagship, and *Vizcaya*, *Cristóbal Colón*, and *Almirante Oquendo*.

Cervera had concentrated his naval force, not in Havana, but in the Portuguese Cape Verde Islands. Long before the days of satellites and GPS systems, the U.S. armed forces had their freedom of action constrained until they could actually see and hopefully defeat the Spanish fleet.

The U.S. squadron based at Key West was under the command of Admiral William T. Sampson. Sampson was born in upstate New

York, entered the United States Naval Academy, and graduated first in his class. He became an instructor at the Academy, and during the Civil War was executive officer of the monitor *Patapsco*, sweeping torpedoes off the Carolinas' coast. He later became Superintendent of the Naval Academy, and commanded the cruiser *San Francisco* and the battleship *Iowa*. In February 1898, he was made President of the Board of Inquiry to investigate the destruction of the *Maine*.

In early April, Sampson had presented a plan to attack Havana and capture the capital city by naval action. Sampson's plan was based on sound military strategy. His battleships would silence the forts guarding the city and then the city would surrender under threat of naval bombardment. The army's regular troops would then occupy the city and the war would be essentially over. Secretary of War Russell Alger was in favor of Sampson's plan and ordered Regular Army infantry forces to Gulf ports to be prepared to take over Havana after Sampson's proposed attack. Secretary of the Navy John Long refused permission for the attack on Havana until Sampson had met and defeated Cervera's navy.

On May 4, 1898, Spanish Captain-General Blanco made a last-ditch effort to reach a peaceful solution with the Cuban patriots, by writing a letter to the Cuban military leader. The text of this letter follows in translation.

> General Máximo Gómez, Commander-in-Chief of the [Cuban] Revolutionary Forces: Sir-It cannot be concealed from you that the Cuban problem has radically changed. We Spaniards and Cubans find ourselves facing a foreign people of different race, of a naturally absorbent tendency, and with intentions not only to deprive Spain of her flag over the Cuban soil, but also to exterminate the Cuban people, due to its having Spanish blood.
>
> The supreme moment has, therefore, arrived in which we should forget our past misunderstandings, and in which, united by the interests of our own defense, we, Spaniards and Cubans, must repel the invader.
>
> General, due to these reasons, I propose to make alliance of both armies in the city of Santa Clara. The Cubans will receive the arms of the Spanish army, and with the cry of *Viva España!* And *Viva Cuba!* We shall repel the invader and free from a foreign yoke the descendants of the same people.
>
> Your obedient servant,
>
> Ramón Blanco.[20]

Gómez quickly prepared a reply to Blanco's letter. Gómez's reply reveals a man quite different to the one portrayed by many historians. Gómez is usually pictured as a coarse, semi-illiterate man, who cursed constantly and severely punished disobedience. Some of these traits may have been correct, but Gómez was a scholarly man capable of producing deeply philosophical prose. A translation of Gómez's reply follows.

> Sir-I wonder how you dare to write to me again about terms of peace when you know that Cubans and Spaniards can never be at peace on the soil of Cuba. You represent on this continent an old and discredited monarchy. We are fighting for an American principle, the same as that of Bolívar and Washington.
>
> You say we belong to the same race and invite me to fight against a foreign invader, but you are mistaken again, for there are no differences of races and blood. I only believe in one race, mankind, and for me there are but good and bad nations, Spain so far having been a bad one and the United States performing in these movements toward Cuba a duty of humanity and civilization.
>
> From the wild, tawny Indian to the refined, blond Englishman, a man for me is worthy of respect according to his honesty and feelings, no matter to what country or race he belongs or what religion he professes.
>
> So are nations for me, and up to the present I have had only reasons for admiring the United States. I have written to President McKinley and General Miles thanking them for American intervention in Cuba. I don't see the danger of our extermination by the United States, to which you refer in your letter. If it be so, history will judge. For the present I have to repeat that it is too late for any understanding between my army and yours.
>
> Your obedient servant,
>
> Máximo Gómez"[21]

Following the exchange of letters with Captain-General Blanco, General Máximo Gómez wrote a letter to President McKinley asking for U.S. intervention in Cuba. British historian Hugh Thomas writes that Gómez's letter to McKinley "…sealed the fate of Spain in the New World, and also that of Cuba. It was the decisive act of welcome to the U.S. which dictated Cuban history for the next sixty years."[22]

U.S. Army Chief Historian, Graham Cosmas described three elements which combined to render the War Department unprepared for war with Spain. First, diplomats thought they were close to a peaceful solution and strongly discouraged military measures. This had little effect on the Navy's preparedness, as the Navy was always in a state of alert. Second, the War Department's plan called for the Navy to be the main player and kept the Army's mobilization modest in scale. Third, continued pressure from the National Guard through Congress to dramatically increase the size of the Army created inefficiencies, such as shortages of supplies and trained men.[23]

On April 23, 1898, the Key West squadron established a blockade of Cárdenas, Havana, Mariel, and Matanzas, all ports on Cuba's north coast. Four days later, Admiral Sampson extended the naval blockade to the port of Cienfuegos, on Cuba's south central coast. Concurrent with these actions, War Secretary Alger ordered Army General William R. Shafter to assemble 6,000 regular infantry, cavalry, and field artillery at Tampa.

Several valuable Spanish cargo ships were captured by the American fleet during the blockade of Cuban ports. Some examples are the *Buena Ventura*, *Pedro de Bilbao*, and *Miguel Jover* with a combined cargo valued at $400 thousand. Another valuable vessel was the *Catalina* with cargo worth nearly $600 thousand. Keeping in mind that these are 1898 dollars, we are speaking of large sums of money.[24]

It must have come as a surprise to many Americans when General William Rufus Shafter was selected to be Army field commander during the Cuba campaign. Shafter was sixty-three, unimaginative, and immensely fat. He weighed more than 300 pounds and could only mount his horse aided by a complex system of ropes and pulleys. He had perennial attacks of gout, which kept him from wearing boots, and hampered his mobility. His men often had to carry him. But Shafter had powerful friends in the Metropolitan Club and was a well-known expansionist.

Shafter was born in Michigan, was a schoolmaster before the Civil War, and received the Medal of Honor for his action at the Battle of Fair Oaks. He also served in the Indian Wars in Texas. Shafter's last post before the Cuban-Spanish-American War was as commander of the Department of California. More importantly, Shafter was appointed as the Army commander to the Cuba invasion because he did not have political ambitions. McKinley did not want to create a war hero who would disrupt his political machinery.

General Shafter's forces were to be transported by the Navy to Cape Tunas, some 120 kilometers east of Cienfuegos. Shafter was to contact Máximo Gómez, obtain information on the military situation on the island, and deliver weapons, ammunition, and supplies to the Cuban rebels. Shafter was to avoid engaging Spanish forces in battle.

On April 29, 1898, U.S. spies communicated that Cervera's Spanish fleet had sailed west from the Cape Verdes. Admiral Sampson could not escort Shafter's expedition since on May 3, 1898, the U.S. fleet off Havana sailed toward San Juan to intercept Cervera in the event that he was heading to Puerto Rico instead of Cuba. Shafter's expedition never sailed.

During May, June, and July 1898, mixed Cuban–American forces coming from Tampa repeatedly invaded the island to run weapons, supplies, and recruits to the insurgents.

The news of Admiral Dewey's crushing victory over the Spanish Pacific Ocean Fleet at Manila reached Washington around May 5, 1898. The war's objective was supposed to be the liberation of Cuba. Assistant Navy Secretary Theodore Roosevelt had instructed Dewey to attack the Spanish fleet as soon as war was declared. On February 25, 1898, Roosevelt had sent the following cablegram to Admiral George Dewey, Hong Kong, "In the event of declaration of war Spain, your duty will be to see that the Spanish squadron does not leave the Asiatic coast, and then [prepare for] offensive operations in Philippine Islands."[25]

Many questions remain unanswered on this move. Was it politically motivated? Did the United States want to take Manila and/or annex the Philippines? Did Roosevelt have the authority to issue this order? After supplying the Manila expedition there was not enough ammunition for the 70,000-man Cuba invasion.

On the political front, "McKinley refused to recognize the [Cuban insurgents] as the legal government of Cuba."[26] Furthermore, McKinley also refused to accept that a state of belligerence existed between the Cuban rebels and the Spanish colonial government. Mexico's President Benito Juárez and other Latin American leaders had declared that a state of belligerence existed between the Cuban rebels and the Spanish government. McKinley's public excuse for not accepting that the state of belligerence existed in Cuba was that Cuba did not have a stable government. This is a circular argument because the state of belligerence existed because there was not a stable government. Congress allowed politics to trump logic.

As his future actions would disclose, McKinley's private reason for not recognizing the Cuban rebels was that he wanted Spain's colonies for the United States, particularly Cuba. His hands were temporarily tied by the Teller Amendment, but McKinley possibly thought that eventually he would find a way to annex Cuba or in the very least for the United States to play a dominant role in determining the political future of the island.

The expansion of the war to the Pacific theater, coupled with the shortage of ammunition and the poor training of the National Guard units, started to point to an attack on weaker eastern Cuba. Also, eastern Cuba was where the Cuban rebels, American allies, at least at the moment, were having the greatest measure of success.

On May 13, 1898, the U.S. Navy finally discovered Cervera's fleet in the Caribbean, west of Martinique. The War Department canceled the attack on Havana and asked commanders to continue to train troops and assemble ships and supplies. On May 25, General Shafter reported that he had 17,000 troops in his camps consisting of regular infantry, cavalry, and artillery, as well as eight volunteer regiments. Tampa became so overcrowded that Shafter opened camps in Lakeland and Jacksonville. The troops were suffering from the intense heat, for they had been supplied with woolen uniforms.

In order to understand the racial prejudice which white American soldiers exhibited against their Cuban allies, it may be helpful to understand the level of prejudice which existed against African-American soldiers. The African-American Tenth Cavalry, which would later distinguish itself in the assault of San Juan Hill, because of overcrowding conditions in Tampa was forced to find a campsite in Lakeland, Florida. Even though they were wearing their blue U.S. Army uniforms, some soldiers from the Tenth Cavalry went into a drug store and asked for some soda water. A white barber, Abe Collins, armed with pistols went into the adjoining drug store and told the soldiers that black men would not be served there. When Collins drew his weapon, the soldiers fired and killed him. Two African-American soldiers were arrested.[27]

The volunteer regiments distinguished themselves during the Cuba campaign. Perhaps the most publicized one was the First United States Volunteer Cavalry, known as the *Rough Riders* under the command of General Leonard Wood, who was President McKinley's family physician. Second in command was Colonel Theodore Roosevelt, who had resigned as Assistant Navy Secretary to participate in the war. Years later, the Rough Riders were described as: "millionaires, paupers, shyster lawyers, cowboys, quack doctors, farmers, college professors, miners, adventurers, preachers, prospectors, socialists, journalists, insurance agents, Jews, politicians, Gentiles, Mexicans, professed Christians, Indians, West Point graduates, Arkansan wild men, baseball players, sheriffs and horse-thieves."[28]

Leonard Wood was born in New Hampshire, graduated from Harvard Medical School, and accepted a medical position in the Army as a contract physician. His first posting was in Arizona, where he participated in the last campaign against Geronimo. He was awarded the Medal of Honor in 1898 for his service as a medical and line officer.

Theodore Roosevelt was born in New York, attended Harvard College, graduated and studied in Germany for a year, and then entered politics. He was elected to the New York State Assembly, where he served for three years and developed a reputation as a reformer. His wife died in 1884, and Roosevelt purchased a cattle ranch in the Badlands of the Dakota Territory, where he became a passionate big game hunter. In 1886, Roosevelt returned to New York, remarried and reentered politics. President Benjamin Harrison (1889–1893), appointed Roosevelt to the Civil Service Commission, of which he later became president. In 1897, he became Chief of New York's Police Department, and in 1897, President McKinley appointed Roosevelt Assistant Secretary of the Navy.

On May 15, 1898, the U.S. Consul at Curaçao, Netherland Antilles, reported the arrival of the Spanish fleet there. Then, the Navy scout vessels lost Cervera again. On May 19, Cervera's fleet slipped into Santiago harbor. Essentially out of coal, Cervera felt protected in this strongly defended port. But he had bottled himself up if the U.S. Navy could get there quickly enough. Santiago was blockaded on May 28 and Sampson's force arrived on June 1.

Cervera was trapped, but Sampson could not reach him. Entrance to the bay is narrow, there were forts with heavy artillery on either side, and the entry channel was mined. Sampson was content to seal the harbor and wait. With Army and Marines on the way to eastern Cuba, war action was about to commence. After much deliberation, President McKinley and War Secretary Alger decided to attack Santiago first followed by Puerto Rico.

Shafter's expedition of about 17,000 men set sail from Tampa on June 14. On June 20, Shafter's transports dropped anchor off Santiago.

Notes

1. Joseph E. Wisan, *The Cuban Crisis as Reflected in the New York Press (1895–1898)* (New York: Octagon Books Reprint Edition, 1965), 204.
2. James Creelman, *On the Great Highway: The Wanderings and Adventures of a Special Correspondent* (Boston, MA: Lothrop, 1901), 177–78.

3. Manuel Leguineche, *Yo Pondré la Guerra* (Madrid: Ediciones El País, 1988).
4. Thomas, *Cuba or the Pursuit of Freedom*, 351–52.
5. Wisan, *Cuban Crisis*, 324–25.
6. Thomas, *Cuba or the Pursuit of Freedom*, 358–59.
7. Morgan, *William McKinley and his America*, 362.
8. Hyman G. Rickover, *How the Battleship Maine was Destroyed* (Washington, DC: Department of the Navy, Naval History Division, 1976).
9. Graham A. Cosmas, *An Army for Empire: The United States Army in the Spanish-American War* (College Station: Texas A&M University Press, 1994), 67.
10. Ibid., 9.
11. Quoted from various sources by Cosmas, *Army for Empire*, 70–71.
12. Ibid., 71.
13. Adm. French E. Chadwick, *The Relations of the United States to Spain: The Spanish-American War*, vol. 1 (New York: Charles Scribner's, 1911), 51–54.
14. *Washington Post*, May 25, 1897, quoted by Morgan, *William McKinley and his America*, 340.
15. Quoted by Cosmas, *Army for Empire*, 90.
16. Morgan, *William McKinley and his America*, 378.
17. Gott, *Cuba*, 102.
18. Trumbull White, *United States in War with Spain and the History of Cuba* (Chicago, IL: International Publishing, 1898), 408.
19. George C. Herring, *From Colony to Superpower: U.S. Foreign Relations since 1776* (New York: Oxford University Press, 2008), 308–14.
20. White, *United States in War*, 411.
21. Ibid., 411–12.
22. Thomas, *Cuba or the Pursuit of Freedom*, 379.
23. Cosmas, *Army for Empire*, 101.
24. White, *United States in War*, 45–52.
25. H. W. Brands, ed., *The Selected Letters of Theodore Roosevelt* (New York, NY: Cooper Square Press, 2001), 170–71.
26. Ibid., 115.
27. Harvey Rosenfeld, *Diary of a Dirty Little War: The Spanish-American War of 1898* (Westport, CT: Praeger Publishers, 2000), 2–3.
28. Hermann Hagedorn, *Leonard Wood: A Biography*, vol. 1 (New York: Harper & Brothers, 1931), 147.

14

Battles in Cuban Territory

There is incontrovertible evidence that even though the McKinley administration refused to declare that a state of belligerence existed in Cuba, the U.S. Army needed and wanted to secure the support of Cuban rebels during America's upcoming military operations in the island. The best example of this is the so-called *Message to García*. Secretary of War Russell A. Alger and General Nelson A. Miles, commanding general of the U.S. Army, had decided that the assistance of the Cuban forces was a requirement for their upcoming campaign.

In late March 1898, President McKinley asked the Bureau of Military Intelligence for a suitable envoy to travel to Cuba to request the cooperation of Cuban patriots during the seemingly inevitable war. A lieutenant, Andrew Rowan, was proposed, his credentials being that he had recently done a topographical study of the island, and that he had a well-deserved reputation of being a resourceful young man, even though he did not speak of word of Spanish.

A myth, supported by falsehoods, about Rowan's trip has been created in American historiography and still lives after more than a century. According to Rowan's own aggrandized account, widely disseminated by the press and Elbert Hubbard's book,[1] after single-handedly overcoming a number of obstacles, Rowan indeed reached General García. Until his meeting with García, not a single Cuban appears in this manufactured epic.

Historian Philip Foner, one of the first researchers to recognize that American historians had progressively distorted the facts about Cuban's contribution to Cuba's liberation, went to many original documents regarding Rowan's trip. He spent time at the Cuban National Archives, the Library of the City Historian of Havana, and met with many distinguished Cuban historians. The results of Foner's investigation are presented in his revealing book *The Cuban-Spanish-American War and the Birth of American Imperialism*. A summary of Foner's findings regarding Rowan's trip follow.

On April 9, 1898, Secretary of War Alger and General Nelson A. Miles, commanding general of the U.S. Army, asked Lieutenant Andrew S. Rowan to travel to Cuba with their "Message to García." The true story is that Rowan's trip was arranged by the War Department with the Cuban Revolutionary Junta in New York. Rowan was instructed to travel to Jamaica, where he was to meet Cuban rebel Comandante Gervasio Savio, who on a regular basis delivered supplies, soldiers, and mail to Cuban rebels fighting east of the Júcaro to Morón trocha. In the meantime, following the advice of Horatio Rubens, attorney for the Junta, the War Department had been informed that Rowan's passage was to be paid. The War Department insisted on an oral message. Clearly, a written message addresses to a Cuban rebel general would imply some sort of recognition that a state of belligerence existed and that there was a Cuban Army. The War Department indeed paid the required amount and the receipt was kept to prove that the U.S. authorities acknowledged that a Cuban government existed. After Savio was informed that the payment had been made, Rowan's trip was allowed to continue.[2]

Rowan was turned over to a group of Cuban rebels on the south coast of Oriente Province. Rowan communicated by sign language, since Savio, an English speaker, had returned to Jamaica. Rowan was delivered to Cuban General Salvador Henández Ríos, who harassed Spanish troops in the Manzanillo area. During his stay at the camp of General Hernández Ríos, the word came that García had taken the city of Bayamo. Rowan was taken to Bayamo by Lieutenant Fernández Barrot, and on May 1, 1898, after identifying himself with a letter of introduction from the Cuban Revolutionary Junta in Jamaica, he was finally able to deliver the Message to García.

Even though García commanded about one half of the total Cuban rebel forces, he was reportedly embarrassed because he thought the contact should have been through Máximo Gómez, head of the Cuban rebel armed forces, or Bartolomé Masó, the President of the Republic of Cuba-at-Arms. Masó had replaced Salvador Cisneros Betancourt on October 30, 1897. In any event, García sent General Enrique Collazo, Colonel Charles Hernández, and Lieutenant-Colonel Dr. Gonzalo García Vieta back with Rowan to pledge to Commander-in-Chief of the U.S. Army, General Nelson A. Miles his unconditional support and full cooperation. A few days later, in early June, Colonel Hernández returned with a message from General Miles to General García, asking that García keep 5,000 Cuban rebel troops in the Santiago area.[3]

The Message to García took place on or about the time when the McKinley administration and the War Department were developing a strategy as to what to do with Cuba after the war. McKinley, Alger, and Miles were well aware of the arrangements made for Rowan's trip; yet, when Rowan reported to his superiors and intimated that he had accomplished his objective unaided and hardly any Cubans, other than General García, were encountered, his superiors chose not to correct Rowan's tale. Rowan's story was widely disseminated by the media, and McKinley, Alger, and Miles remained silent. Was this the starting point of the U.S.' strategy of denying the existence of a Cuban rebel army and convincing the American people that Cubans were not capable of self-government? If this question is answered affirmatively, it can then be stated that the Message to García myth was a watershed event in the relationship between the United States and the Cuban Revolutionary Government. Almost magically, the Cuban rebels transformed from heroes being compared to Minutemen during the U.S. Independence War to nonexisting bums. The defamation campaign was likely started by the McKinley administration, then it moved to senior officers in the U.S. military, and finally the yellow press took over in convincing the American people that Cubans were lazy, disorganized, and utterly incapable of self-government. The machinery for the United States taking over Spain's colonies was thus set in motion.

When General Shafter arrived in the southeast coast of Cuba, at the head of an American expeditionary army of 17,000 men, he lost no time in consulting with García and his staff. Shafter and Sampson went ashore on June 20, 1898, to discuss the best location for landing Shafter's army. García's temporary HQ was west of Santiago, high up on the hills overlooking Aserradero beach. General Shafter's 300-plus-pound frame, clad in a woolen uniform, had developed a painful gout attack and was unable to walk. The Cuban rebels could not find a horse capable of carrying the General. "After a frustrating, irritable delay, someone does find a white mule, and this superior animal manages to get the general to the top of the cliff."[4]

García's original plan proposed that the American troops disembark west of Santiago, near his camp at El Aserradero. Neither Sampson nor Shafter agreed with García, who then proposed an alternate location east of Santiago at Daiquirí and Siboney. This was a terrain that García knew well since his family owned property in that area. Thus, the actual landing was made in an area recommended by the Cubans. García promised to protect the American landings, and he was as good as his word. The U.S. forces went ashore on June 22, 1898 at the beach of Daiquirí, about 25 kilometers southeast of Santiago, covered by 1,500 Cuban insurgent troops, while other Cuban units impeded Spanish troop movements in the interior.[5]

García proposed that while Shafter's troops were disembarking east of Santiago, Sampson's Navy vessels should bombard the fortress of La Cabaña, west of Santiago. Simultaneously with the Navy's action, Cuban troops led by General Rabí would conduct fake attacks west of Santiago. The Spanish troops, thinking the landing would be west of Santiago, would be moved in that direction, thus allowing the Army to go ashore unmolested. Both Sampson and Shafter agreed with García's strategy.

García was an experienced military tactician and knew the territory like the palm of his hand. He further recommended a series of Cuban troop deployments near significant Spanish strongholds.

García was concerned with the fact that the Americans had changed their battle plans. The original plan which was previously communicated to the Cuban rebels included a continued American blockade of Cuban ports, followed by an attack on Puerto Rico and then a bombardment of Havana by the Navy. It was at the meeting with Sampson and Shafter that García learned that the combined Cuban–American attack would take place at Santiago. García stated that based on the plan originally communicated by the Americans, several thousand Cuban rebel soldiers had been sent to reinforce Máximo Gómez's troops in central Cuba. Gómez was expected to attack Havana by land after the American bombardment. Unfortunately, the troops sent to central Cuba were the ones that would have prevented Spanish Colonel Federico Escario's troops located at Holguín from joining Toral's forces in Santiago. García pleaded with Shafter that since the United States had not communicated the change in plans, he should be allowed to send General Rabí with approximately 1,500 troops to reinforce the Cuban rebel forces of General Francisco Estrada and prevent Escario's troops from joining the Santiago forces. Shafter disagreed with this element of García's plan and insisted that all Cuban troops must remain in the Santiago area. This decision by Shafter would have damaging consequences on the Cuban rebels and the future of Cuban independence, as this plan isolated Máximo Gómez and his troops in Santa Clara and prevented them from joining the important battlefields in Oriente Province.

As planned, prior to the landing, the selected place at Daiquirí was secured by a Cuban rebel division commanded by General Demetrio

Castillo Duany. Simultaneously with the landing of U.S. troops, Cuban General Jesús Rabí attacked Spanish forces at La Cabaña, west of Santiago bay, to prevent any interference with the American landing. The U.S. Navy also fulfilled its part of the bargain. In fact, 15,000 U.S. troops landed within a twenty-four hour period, and not a single enemy shot was fired.[6]

General Arsenio Linares, the Spanish Commanding Officer of Santiago de Cuba wrote "without the help of the Cubans, the Yankees never could have disembarked. The assistance of the *insurrectos* was extremely powerful."[7]

In early June 1898, looking for a place to seek refuge from hurricanes, for which the season was approaching, and to establish a coaling station, Admiral Sampson's lighter ships had entered the lower end of Guantánamo Bay. Guantánamo is approximately seventy-five kilometers due east of Santiago.

In order to secure this base, a Marine battalion of 600 men, commanded by Lieutenant-Colonel R. W. Huntington, landed from the transport *Panther* on the east shore of the bay on June 10, 1898. They camped at an abandoned telegraph cable station at the entrance of the outer harbor of Guantánamo. On this date, the first-ever U.S. Marine landing on foreign soil took place in Guantánamo, Cuba. American writer Stephen Crane stated that "...without the fire power of the Cuban patriots, the Marines would not have been able to land."[8]

The Marines and Cuban patriots established a camp and a coaling station and fought and defeated Spanish infantry troops in a number of encounters. "A thirteen hour battle raged from 3 pm June 10, 1898 to 4 am June 11. U.S. Marines and Cubans fought Spanish regulars. The number of Cubans in this battle was estimated from as few as 200 to as many as 1,000."[9] Another battle took place on June 13, 1898, with U.S. Marines and Cubans fighting Spanish troops. "Only one American was wounded, while 2 Cubans were killed and 4 wounded."[10]

The Marines thus claim the honor of having secured the first permanent American foothold in Cuba.[11] With the capture of Guantánamo Bay, the U.S. Navy fleet blockading the entrance to Santiago harbor had a place to refuel in safety.

The Navy started working with the Cuban rebels shortly after arriving in the waters off Santiago. Admiral Sampson had sent Lieutenant Victor Blue to the headquarters of Cuban General Jesús Rabí with the mission of scouting the defenses around Santiago. The Cuban general escorted Lieutenant Blue around the city and pointed out the batteries that should be silenced by the Navy. The bombardment took place on June 16, 1898, and the batteries were indeed taken out of commission. Sampson reported the Cuban's great assistance in this operation as well as in the capture of Guantánamo Bay by American marines and Cuban soldiers.[12]

It did not take long after the landing of Shafter's American troops for a bitter hostility to grow between the American and Cuban troops. With transportation provided by the U.S. Navy, García brought 4,000 men to the coast to operate with Shafter's American forces at the ports of Siboney, 15 kilometers southeast of Santiago, and Daiquirí. The Cubans were to be used as scouts and guides. Shafter considered the Cuban troops as laborers whose purpose was to carry supplies and dig trenches for the Americans. The dignified old Cuban General García bitterly complained to Shafter that his men were good fighters and not "pack-mules."[13]

The animosity of American troops against Cuban rebels was, to a large extent, based on racial prejudices. At the time, American military forces were segregated. In fact, even white troops from former Union and Confederacy states were competitive and impolite to one another during the Cuba campaign. Cuban rebels were at least 80 percent nonwhite, and as could be expected from people living off the land, they were dirty, usually barefooted, and smelled bad.

Figure 14.1 depicts a magnified area in the south-east coast of Cuba where U.S. Army and Navy battled Spanish forces. Arrows indicate the U.S. Army troop movements prior to taking the city of Santiago de Cuba.

General Shafter considered that taking the city of Santiago was his main objective. Admiral Sampson, on the other hand, considered the destruction of Cervera's fleet as the main objective of the campaign, and further considered the city of Santiago as having little military importance. The narrow entrance to Santiago Bay was guarded by two impressive forts with heavy artillery: El Morro to the east and Socapa to the west. Sampson insisted that Shafter's forces should advance along the coast and attack El Morro. Shafter, armed with reports from García's Cubans, knew that the Spaniards had concentrated most of their troops in the vicinity of El Morro. Further, Shafter believed that attacking the high ground north and east of Santiago would not only encircle the city, but would prevent reinforcements from Manzanillo, 150 kilometers away, and Holguín, 125 kilometers away, from reaching Santiago.[14]

Figure 14.1 Battles of the Cuban-Spanish-American War

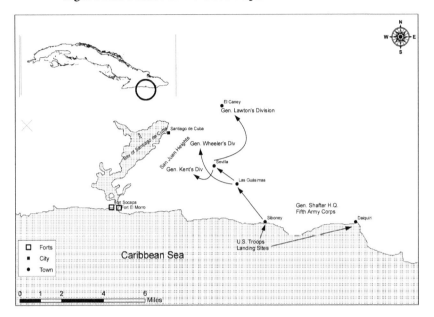

Therefore, Shafter and Sampson agreed to disagree, and Shafter prepared to march inland from Siboney and attack Spanish positions as his army advanced. The first such encounter occurred on June 24, 1898, at the village of Las Guásimas, some five kilometers north of Siboney. Roosevelt and the Rough Riders fought gallantly in this skirmish, which resulted in 16 Americans killed and 52 wounded, while the Spanish had 250 casualties. After Las Guásimas, no Spanish forces remained between Siboney and Santiago's outer defenses.[15]

The battle of Las Guásimas gave rise to one of the distortions of the truth of this war which has continued to be perpetuated by many American historians. Some writers state that Cubans did not fight during this engagement, while others go as far as to say that Cubans refused to fight. Historian Philip Foner consulted many original documents, from both American as well as Cuban participants, and a composite of the true events of this first land engagement of Spanish versus Cuban and American troops follow.

Shortly after the landing at Daiquirí, Shafter ordered General Henry W. Lawton to take a position on the road to Santiago beyond Siboney. The vanguard of Lawton's unit was Cuban rebel troops commanded by General Demetrio Castillo Duany and Colonel Carlos González Clavell. Covering the rear was the American dismounted (because of lack of horses) cavalry under the command of General Joseph Wheeler, a Confederate Army hero who had sixteen horses shot under him during the U.S. Civil War. The vanguard Cuban troops had been ordered by Lawton to continue firing against the 1,500 Spaniards inside the fortified Las Guásimas position, but not to advance against this heavily entrenched location. Cuban scouts had reported to Lawton that the Spaniards were preparing to abandon their position. As ordered, the Cubans continued firing all day on June 23, 1898. Wheeler, wanting to fight the first engagement of this war, under the cover of dark ordered the First U.S. Regular Cavalry under the command of General Samuel B. M. Young, to move in front of Lawton's men. The Tenth U.S. Regular Cavalry, consisting of African-American men (then called the Buffalo soldiers), and the Rough Riders, under the command of Colonels Leonard Wood and Theodore Roosevelt, were a part of Young's brigade. At first light on June 24, 1898, Young's brigade, with Wheeler at the front, followed by the Rough Riders, disobeyed Lawton's direct order and started their private war against Spain. Wheeler's men proceeded undetected, but Young's division came in contact with the Cubans who had been engaging the Spaniards for nearly twenty-four hours. Colonel González Clavell tried to explain to Young that this was an absurd move, but Young insisted on proceeding, at which point González Clavell provided him with scouts and information on the Spaniards position and weapons. Later, Young publicly criticized the Cubans for having abandoned him. American newspapers charged the Cubans with cowardice for not having joined the attack.[16]

It would be very difficult, perhaps bordering on the impossible, to prove that there was a concerted effort on the part of the McKinley administration and high-level military officers to prevent Cubans from being on the vanguard of the action against Spanish forces. Historiographer Louis A. Pérez Jr., in his revealing book *The War of 1898: The United States and Cuba in History and Historiography* states that "the absence of Cubans from frontline U.S. military operations was the result of decisions made at the highest official levels in Washington precisely as a means to reduce, if not preclude altogether, Cuban demands to participate in the negotiations of postwar settlements. Pérez also found a document from Colonel Arthur L. Wagner, a cavalry officer at Santiago de Cuba, who disclosed that he was 'enjoined to be extremely careful to avoid in every way anything that might be construed as a recognition by my superiors of the Cuban forces as the army of an independent power of belligerent nation."[17]

The Spaniards were indeed driven back at Las Guásimas, but they were retreating anyway. American and Cuban forces had sixteen dead and fifty-four wounded, while the Spanish had seven dead and twenty-four wounded. It is generally agreed by military historians that the Spaniards had already decided to abandon their positions because of the relentless firing of the Cubans during the previous twenty-four hours. Even though the engagement at Las Guásimas had no military significance, the Cubans were blamed for the heavy casualties sustained by the Americans. After his return to the United States in August 1898, General Wheeler praised the Cubans for their help and stated that the Cubans never refused to carry out orders when they understood the importance of this work. Wheeler added that owing to their physical condition Cuban soldiers could not persist too long doing physical work since they had been living on fruits and vegetables.

On June 27, 1898, Shafter was overjoyed when reinforcements arrived at Siboney, including half a brigade of Michigan Volunteers, from Shafter's home state. On June 29, 1898, Cuban scouts reported that 8,000 Spanish troops from Manzanillo had broken through rebel lines and were advancing toward Santiago, bringing cattle and other supplies. These Spanish reinforcements were due to arrive in Santiago in four or five days. Shafter decided to attack.

García's Cubans had scouted the terrain and determined that there were only two possible routes of advance into Santiago. One was by San Juan Heights and the other one was the road from Guantánamo, which went through the town of El Caney.[18]

General Henry Lawton had reconnoitered El Caney extensively and was convinced he could take it in about two hours. According to Shafter's plan, Lawton and his Second Infantry Division would take El Caney, and then they would be joined by General Joe Wheeler's dismounted cavalry division, and General Jacob Kent and his First Infantry Division and take San Juan Heights. There are two main elevations in San Juan Heights, and the American soldiers named one San Juan Hill and the other one Kettle Hill when they found a large sugarcane kettle at its top.

The datum that General Lawton had missed was that Spanish General Joaquín Vara del Rey commanded the defense of El Caney. Vara del Rey had approximately 540 men armed with 1893 model Mauser repetition rifles which used smokeless gunpowder and two

Plasencia-type field artillery pieces, and he had turned El Caney into a fortress protected by trenches, fortified buildings, and barbed wire entanglements. Vara del Rey had no intention of retreating.

The American force consisted of 7,000 men, armed with rifles and field artillery, under the command of Generals Lawton and Chaffee as well as 1,200 Cubans from González Clavell's unit. The attack commenced at daybreak on July 1, 1898. Cuban rebel scouts had been asked to reconnoiter the terrain and guide the Americans to their objective.

Instead of the two hours predicted by Lawton, the battle for El Caney lasted eleven hours. Spanish sharpshooters in the trees and behind rocks slowed the progress of the American units. The African-American Twenty-Fifth Infantry Regiment fought bravely in this encounter. The Spanish quit fighting only when they ran out of ammunition. For the final assault, General Lawton asked for reinforcements from General García, and a platoon of Cuban infantry joined the American servicemen in entering El Caney and driving the Spaniards out of the fortified houses. As Vara del Rey was ordering retreat, he was shot through both legs. He was loaded on a stretcher, but all four men carrying the stretcher as well as General Vara del Rey were killed. Two sons of Vara del Rey were also killed in this battle. Of the 540 Spanish defenders, only 80, most of them wounded, made it to the temporary safety of Santiago. The remaining 460 were killed in action, or captured by American forces. Americans forces had 81 dead and 370 wounded in the battle of El Caney. The Cubans also suffered serious losses.[19]

The American command circulated a report blaming the Cubans for the heavy casualties at El Caney. It is likely that this was an attempt at explaining why a quick victory was not achieved. After all, General Lawton stated that he would take El Caney in two hours, and the remaining battle plans were drawn based on this judgment.

General Kent's division, and General Wheeler's division, under the command of General Samuel S. Sumner since Wheeler had been taken ill, waited for Lawton for about three hours. The sound of heavy fighting could be heard from the direction of El Caney, and Kent and Sumner proceeded to attack San Juan Hill. The 3,000-man American force moved along a wooded, treacherous road where they could not see their objective. Fortunately, the Spanish could not see the Americans because of the same woods. The Spanish had artillery pieces both at San Juan Hill as well as at the nearby ridge which the Americans had named Kettle Hill. Additionally, the Spanish had in place a number of sharpshooters armed with smokeless powder rifles, hidden in trees along the road, and in carefully concealed places in front of Kettle Hill.

The Americans had no idea they were fighting only 250 Spaniards. As soon as the American field artillery had San Juan Hill in range, an artillery duel with the Spanish guns ensued. The noise of the artillery helped conceal the Spanish snipers who continued picking off American soldiers.

At around 11:00 a.m. a reconnaissance balloon flown by Colonel George Derby attempted to climb to obtain information on the Spanish position. As soon as the balloon appeared above the trees, both sides starting shooting at each other at once.

The balloon became tangled in the trees, revealing the Americans' position to the Spaniards. The balloonist did obtain one piece of useful information, and it was that there was another trail off the main road which would facilitate the deployment of Kent's division.[20]

It did not take long for Kent and Sumner to reach the erroneous conclusion that San Juan and Kettle Hills were heavily defended. Since they could hear the intense firing at El Caney, they also knew that they could not expect reinforcements from Lawton's unit. Shafter, aware of the situation, sent two reserve field artillery batteries which sank in the mud while moving to the front. By the time these batteries arrived, the final assault was underway.

A more significant help to the battle came in the form of four Gatling guns under the command of Captain John Parker. These rapid fire weapons were trained on the Spanish position in the south, which forced the Spaniards to keep their heads down. This allowed one infantry and two cavalry regiments, one white and one African-American, to charge the hill. Roosevelt and the Rough Riders followed close behind. Cuban troops under Colonel González Clavell were in the thick of battle and in the final assault on San Juan Hill, they scaled the heights together with American troops. The Spanish retreated to their next line of defense on the outskirts of Santiago. Other than for sporadic light weapon fire, the battle was over. Now the city of Santiago was in a state of siege by the debilitated American troops. Shafter was not sure that his forces were capable of assaulting Santiago; nevertheless, he ordered his troops to cut off the city's water supply.

U.S. Navy Admiral French Ensor Chadwick fought in the battle of San Juan Hill. He praised the contribution of an anonymous Cuban soldier. "A large, powerful man armed with a machete, showed perfect courage and was of greatest service in destroying with his heavy weapon the barbed-wire fencing which so impeded the advance toward the field in front of San Juan."[21]

American military paid a high price in the battles of El Caney and San Juan Hill. There were nearly 1,600 casualties, or roughly 10 percent of the total effective U.S. force. The Spanish had around 600 casualties. "None of the American commanders realized how few enemies they had fought on July 1 [1898]. Shafter, for example, thought that at least 12,000 Spaniards had opposed his troops at San Juan and El Caney."[22]

Theodore Roosevelt did an excellent marketing job of promoting himself as the architect of the American triumph at San Juan Hill. Newspapers hailed the defeat of a tired and decadent old nation by a young and energetic one. Roosevelt became an immensely popular war hero. He was elected Governor of New York and later Vice President for McKinley's second term, becoming president after McKinley's assassination.

British historian Hugh Thomas takes a radically different view of the battles of El Caney and San Juan Hill. Thomas believes that it would be more appropriate to "...recall the whole day [June 1, 1898] as an occasion when 700 Spaniards held up 6,000 North Americans and inflicted very heavy damages upon them."[23]

The weakened American Army was not in a position to pursue the fleeing Spanish forces into Santiago. The Spaniards had no intention of attempting to fight to regain El Caney and San Juan Hill. In fact, Shafter proposed abandoning this line of advance, but Wheeler strongly opposed Shafter's suggestion. Shafter was concerned about the Spanish reinforcement unit from Manzanillo, and being caught between the reinforcements and the Santiago defenders. Shafter telegraphed Washington that he was seriously considering retreating to Siboney. War Secretary Alger replied immediately that retreat would have a bad effect on the morale of the United States and promised to send reinforcements at once.[24]

The U.S. and Spanish navies took center stage for the next few days of the Cuban-Spanish-American War. Cervera had pleaded with the Spanish Admiralty to allow him to fight the American fleet near the Canary Islands, where his fleet could be repaired and refitted while they waited for the American Navy. His request had been rejected.

Cervera reluctantly obeyed his orders and sailed for various ports in the Caribbean in a failed effort to scatter the American fleet. He did manage to re-coal and took refuge in Santiago Bay.

Admiral Sampson's second in command was Admiral Winfield Schley, but animosity existed between these two officers. On May 18, 1898, Schley had been sent to Cienfuegos to pursue Cervera's squadron. Sampson, having learned that Cervera was at Santiago and not at Cienfuegos, had ordered Schley's squadron to Santiago. Schley had decided to disobey, but after learning from Cuban insurgents that Cervera was not at Cienfuegos, decided to obey Sampson's direct order three days later.

Sampson had another reason to distrust of Schley. Earlier, while at Santiago, Schley inexplicably decided to return to Key West to obtain coal for his ship. The Navy Department ordered Schley to stay at Santiago and he replied that he could not obey these orders. He did return to Santiago without re-coaling his ship on May 28, 1898, and learned that Cervera was indeed trapped inside the bay. Sampson arrived in Santiago on June 1, 1898 and assumed command.

Cervera's fleet could have escaped while Schley was on his aborted voyage to Key West, but Cervera's coal supplies were also running low. The vessel bringing coal to Cervera's fleet had been captured by the American cruiser *St. Paul* on May 25, 1898. Ironically, the commander of the cruiser *St. Paul* was Captain Sigsbee, formerly of the ill-fated *Maine*.

An impressive act of true heroism took place prior to the main naval engagement of Santiago. The U.S. Navy collier (coal supply vessel) *Merrimac* was a part of Admiral Schley's Flying Squadron and had been suffering a number of breakdowns. Assistant Naval Constructor Richmond Pearson Hobson suggested rigging the *Merrimac* with explosives and sinking her in the narrow part of the channel, thus blocking the channel and preventing the Spanish fleet from exiting. When Sampson asked for volunteers, every officer and man came forward.

In order to carry out his suicide mission, Hobson modified the *Merrimac* so that it could be operated by himself and a crew of seven men. The first attempt was on June 1, 1898, but it was called off when the crew determined that not all torpedoes could be fired. The second attempt was made on June 3, 1898. As the *Merrimac* entered the channel, a Spanish vessel fired, severely damaging the steering gear. Hobson chose to proceed, and the Spanish fleet opened fire, sinking the *Merrimac*, but not in a place that could block the channel. The crew attempted to escape, but the catamaran they were using to return to the U.S. fleet overturned. When they realized they could not rejoin the American fleet, they rowed straight toward the Spanish squadron. The whole crew was captured by Admiral Cervera and became prisoners of war. Cervera sent Captain Oviedo, under a flag of truce to Admiral Sampson to let him know his heroes were safe.

Cervera was instructed to deliver the American prisoners to General Arsenio Linares, who placed them in Morro Castle as human shields. Hobson was locked up in solitary confinement with little or no food. Sampson wrote to Cervera, holding him personally responsible for Hobson's well-being. Cervera spoke with Linares, who agreed to transfer Hobson and his men to barracks in the city of Santiago.[25]

After the assault on Santiago, Hobson and his men were exchanged for Spanish prisoners of war taken at the battles of El Caney and San Juan Hill. The prisoner exchange took place on July 6, 1898.

Hobson was born in Greensboro, Alabama, and graduated first in his class from the U.S. Naval Academy. Hobson was elevated to a hero by the American press while a prisoner of war in Cuba. After his release, the entire American camp stood in attention and cheered as he went by. Hobson later became a U.S. Representative from Alabama. In 1933, even though their mission had failed, Hobson and the entire volunteer crew of the *Merrimac* were awarded the Medal of Honor. In 1934, Hobson was awarded the rank of Rear Admiral and placed on the retired list.

Cervera could have stayed in Santiago for some time, for the fortresses of El Morro and Socapa, combined with the mined channel, would have prevented the American fleet from entering the bay. But Cervera was instructed that he and his fleet were under the command of Havana's Captain-General Ramón Blanco, and Blanco ordered Cervera to make a run out of the bay and attempt to escape the American fleet.

The American fleet consisted of eleven vessels. There were five battleships: *Massachusetts, Texas, Oregon, Iowa,* and *Indiana*; two armed yachts: *Vixen* and *Gloucester*; one torpedo boat: *Ericsson*; and three armored cruisers: *New York, Resolute* and *Brooklyn*.

The voyage of the USS *Oregon* from the U.S. west coast to waters off Florida had captured the imagination of the American public. The *Oregon* had arrived in San Francisco on March 9, 1898. On March 12, she was ordered to Cuba and departed on March 19. She arrived in Callao, Peru, on April 4 and departed on April 8 after coaling and provisioning. She entered the Strait of Magellan on April 16 and after fighting a vicious storm, arrived in Rio de Janeiro, Brazil, on April 30. The *Oregon* anchored at Jupiter Inlet, Florida, on May 24.

Captain Charles E. Clark had managed the 23,000-kilometer voyage in 66 days. This was the longest trip ever made by a battleship. The previous record was held by a British flagship which steamed from England to China. The perilous voyage of the *Oregon* convinced the American people that a canal across Central America was essential for American naval strategies.[26]

Spanish scouts indicated that three U.S. vessels had departed the blockage and Cervera decided that this was a good time to try to run for safety, although he thought that with or without the three missing American vessels, a Spanish defeat was imminent. Indeed, the *Massachusetts* had left early that morning for re-coaling. Admiral Sampson had a meeting at Siboney with Shafter, and had taken with him the *Ericsson* and his flagship the *New York*. Sampson had left Schley in charge of the U.S. fleet.

The Spanish fleet left the mouth of Santiago bay at approximately 10:00 a.m. on July 3, 1898. Cervera's flagship *Infanta María Teresa* was leading the way, followed by armored cruisers *Vizcaya*, *Cristóbal Colón*, and *Almirante Oquendo*, and finally torpedo boat destroyers *Furor* and *Plutón*. They headed south for the open sea, hoping to outrun the Americans since they knew they could not outgun the U.S. fleet.

Cervera decided to ram the *Brooklyn* with the *Infanta María Teresa* in the hope that his other vessels could get away. Schley tried to avoid colliding with Cervera's ship and caused his own fleet to tangle. The *Texas* had to come to a complete stop, to avoid ramming the *Brooklyn*.

Schley's *Brooklyn* opened fire on the wooden decked *Infanta María Teresa*, and soon she was on fire. The *Infanta María Teresa* ran aground in flames, and some sailors were able to swim to shore, including Admiral Cervera. Soon the *Almirante Oquendo* and the *Vizcaya* were also engulfed in flames. The two small torpedo boat destroyers, *Plutón* and *Furor* made a run in the opposite direction, but shelling by *Iowa* and *Indiana* forced them to try to ground their vessels. *Furor* sank, killing Captain Villaamil and many of his sailors. *Plutón* managed to ground herself, but immediately blew up.[27]

The fast *Cristóbal Colón* almost got away, but the faster *Oregon* gave chase. The *Oregon* opened fire with 330-mm shells, hitting just astern of the vessel. Captain Emilio Díaz Moreu turned his ship toward the coast, lowered the Spanish flag, and ordered the scuttle valves opened, thus saving the life of his crewmen. The demise of the *Cristóbal Colón* marked the end of European naval power in the Western Hemisphere.[28]

There were 350 Spanish seamen killed and 1,670 taken prisoners. The U.S. fleet had one sailor killed and two wounded. The Spanish prisoners, including Cervera, were taken to Seavey's Island in Kittery, Maine, by the *USS Resolute*. They were confined at Camp Long from July 11 until mid-September 1898.

Admiral Sampson, even though not present during the battle, attempted to take credit for destroying the Spanish fleet, partially by criticizing Schley for previous errors in judgment. A Court of Inquiry exonerated Schley and the press elevated him to the status of a national hero.[29]

Back to the ground war in Santiago, General Linares, the Spanish commander of Santiago, had been wounded in action and had turned his command over to General José Toral. Shafter sent a message to Toral asking him to surrender the city. In return, the United States would arrange for transportation to Spain for all Spanish military personnel. Shafter added that if Toral did not agree to surrender, he would give orders to shell the city. Toral replied that the city would not surrender. Instead, foreign consuls from Britain, Norway, China, and Portugal, stationed in Santiago, came to see Shafter to request that noncombatants be allowed to leave the city. Shafter agreed, and about 20,000 persons left the city for El Caney, where the U.S. armed forces struggled to supply them with food. A truce was agreed until July 5, 1898.[30]

It is difficult to ascertain if the Cuban rebels were perceived as a liability by the U.S. Army, or if political maneuvering in Washington was forcing the Army commanders to distance themselves from the Cubans. Many American historians claim that Cuban rebels did not participate in the battle of El Caney. They must have, to some extent, participated in the battle of San Juan Hill, for, according to Millis "in the battle of San Juan Hill Cuban forces had had only 10 casualties."[31]

It was known to General Shafter that on July 2, 1898, at dawn, a group of Cuban rebels, estimated to be 3,000 men, commanded by Cuban General Luis de Feria, had dislodged Spanish forces from Chabitas and Boniato, eventually covering the road from Holguín to Santiago. This action by the Cubans prevented the Spanish garrison of more than 10,000 men from Holguín from joining Toral's embattled forces in Santiago.[32] Also on the positive side, a group of approximately 3,000 Cubans under the command of General Pedro A. Pérez, helped American Marines bottle up 6,000 Spanish troops at Guantánamo, 65 kilometers east of Santiago.[33] A group of more than 1,000 Cuban soldiers commanded by Cuban General Salvador Ríos contained 6,000 Spanish soldiers in Manzanillo, west of Santiago. If all the Spanish troops in Oriente Province had been able to join forces at Santiago, it is likely that Shafter would have been defeated.

It is difficult to understand why many American journalists started to create an anti-Cuban sentiment for their readers. Ironically, the same reporters that had clamored for Cuban independence turned violently anti-Cuban. The Associated Press was particularly vicious in their attacks on Cuban Patriots. In fact, it was the Associated Press that reported that after the battle of El Caney, American soldiers entrusted forty Spanish prisoners to the Cuban rebels. When the Americans returned, they found that the Cubans had cut the prisoners' heads off. This report of unknown origin was widely disseminated in the United States.

The State, a South Carolina newspaper, asked General Shafter about the Associated Press report that Cubans were killing Spanish prisoners. General Shafter replied: "Dispatch as to killing prisoners by Cubans is absolutely false. No prisoners have been turned over to them, and they have shown no disposition to treat badly any Spaniards who have fallen into their hands."[34] Future actions would also confirm that the U.S. military, as well as U.S. journalists felt more drawn to the chivalrous, and white, Spanish enemy than to their Cuban allies.

An incident that appears to have driven the last nail in the coffin of the relationship between U.S. and Cuban troops occurred on July 3, 1898. Concerned about the feared 8,000 troop reinforcement force from Manzanillo under the command of Colonel Federico Escario, instead of agreeing to García's request to reinforce General Francisco Estrada's Manzanillo forces, Shafter had divided all possible land approaches to Santiago into sectors, and had assigned responsibility to protect these sectors to various commanders. There were two north sectors, one covered by General Lawton, and the other by García's Cubans.

Escario's troops had been harassed by Cuban rebels throughout their 150-kilometer march. In fact, only 3,500 troops arrived, and they were bringing neither food nor ammunition. It is known that the Spanish troops entered Santiago on a railroad approach, somewhere in between García's and Lawton's sectors. British historian Hugh Thomas indicated that the Spanish troops entered Santiago along El Cobre road "...without being prevented by Calixto García."[35] American historian David Healy, on the same subject wrote, "Spanish troops entered the city without opposition through the sector held by García."[36] American historian Walter Millis, in his 1931 book stated, "Colonel Escario's column...had slipped into the city. The Cubans who had been posted to intercept them had failed in their mission."[37] Millis, referring to Washington politicians, added "...the failure of García's insurgents to prevent the entrance of Colonel Escario's relieving column into Santiago had been severely commented upon."[38]

U.S. Army Chief Historian Graham Cosmas commented that Escario's troops "...entered Santiago that evening by slipping into town from the west through a gap between Shafter's right flank and the bay shore and brushing aside García's Cubans, who tried to block the way."[39]

Under normal conditions, Escario's march from Manzanillo to Santiago de Cuba should have taken six days. But due to the constant attacks by Cuban rebels, the journey took ten days. Escario and his remaining troops arrived on July 3, 1898, too late to assist in the battles of El Caney and San Juan Heights. It is also unlikely that Cervera would have sailed out of Santiago Bay if Escario had arrived sooner.

General Garcia's official report to his commanding officer, General Máximo Gómez may shed some light on this subject. This report was transcribed in 1946 by Cuban historian Aníbal Escalante from García's handwritten report. A translated version follows, with some words inserted to improve the readability and as replacement to missing words. "On the night of 03 (July), using the Cobre road, a column of 5,000 men, lead by Colonel Escario, entered Santiago de Cuba. Colonel Escario, who had left Manzanillo on 22 [June], was harassed from Manzanillo to Baire, by the [Cuban rebel] Manzanillo division. From Baire to Palma, this column was forced to fight hard against the [Cuban rebel] column of General Francisco Estrada. This caused the Spanish hundreds of losses, to the extent that all along the route [Spanish soldiers] bodies were found. This [Spanish] column also exchanged fire with Lieutenant Colonel Lora, [who commanded] part of the Bayamo Division cavalry, as well as my cavalry escort under the command of Lieutenant Colonel C. M. Poey. Colonel Escario recovered somewhat in Palma, where he abandoned his casualties. From Palma, by repeatedly changing routes, he reached [Santiago de] Cuba by the Cobre road along which he suffered some firefights. Perhaps the entry of this column could have been stopped if I had been able to use most of my forces for this purpose. However, to do this I would have had to abandon my positions to right flank of American Army."[40]

American journalists wanted to believe Shafter's continual blaming of the Cubans for his own military incompetence, and they shared Shafter's comments with the American people. Yet, these same journalists and many historians who later continued to cement the myth about Cuban disorganization and cowardice, failed to read the report from Shafter's commanding officer to the Secretary of War. On November 5, 1898, General Nelson A. Miles, Commanding General of the U.S. Army, wrote the following. "It will be observed that General García regarded my requests as his orders, and promptly took steps to execute the plan of operations. He sent 3,000 men to check any movement of the 12,000 Spaniards stationed at Holguín. A portion of the latter force started to the relief of the garrison at Santiago, but was successfully checked and turned back by the Cuban forces under Gen. Luis de Feria. General García also sent 2,000 men, under Pérez, to oppose the 6,000 Spaniards at Guantánamo, and they were successful in their object. He also sent 1,000 men, under General Ríos, against 6,000 men at Manzanillo. Of this garrison, 3,500 started to reinforce the garrison at Santiago, and were engaged in no less than 30 combats with the Cubans on their way before reaching Santiago, and would have been stopped had Gen. García's request of June 27 been granted..."[41]

The reader must decide what really happened on the night of July 3, 1898. In any event, Escario's troops did enter Santiago, but they were just an added burden to Toral's forces. They had brought no cattle or any other food, and no ammunition. They merely increased the number of hungry and thirsty Spanish soldiers trapped in Santiago.

Toral was receiving his negotiating instructions from Captain-General Blanco. It became clear that Blanco wanted Toral and his troops to leave Santiago with their weapons, to be able to fight another day. It also became clear that the word *surrender* was not to be used. Toral proposed leaving the city with his troops and going either to Holguín or to Manzanillo. Shafter denied his request even though he was not prepared for a full assault on the city. He simply continued to tighten his circle around the city.

Shafter ordered the Fifth Corps to close the last escape route, along the west side of the bay, to the Santiago Spanish garrison. The final battle of this campaign was fought on July 9–10, 1898, and it was mostly rifle and field artillery exchange from the trenches. The Fifth Corps had two killed in action and two wounded, while the Spaniards had seven killed and more than fifty wounded.[42]

In addition to negotiating with Toral, Shafter was negotiating with Sampson, as they held equal ranks. Sampson would not come any closer to El Morro and Socapa for fear of the mines, and Shafter knew that he did not have the firepower to bombard the city into submission. After the Escario affair, García was being completely ignored by Shafter.

The negotiations continued for a few more days. Shafter was concerned about his responsibility for feeding almost 40,000 people, which included 20,000 American troops, 16,000 civilians who had evacuated Santiago, and 4,000 Cuban rebels. But conditions in Santiago were significantly worse.

On July 11, 1898, General Nelson Miles arrived in Siboney with 1,500 fresh infantry troops and artillery. On July 14, Miles and Shafter met with Toral and informed him that they were prepared to attack the city if he did not surrender. Toral asked for a small delay to communicate with Madrid. Toral agreed to surrender all their weapons and the city and to be transported with all his troops to Spain. But he insisted that the word *capitulation* must be used instead of the word *surrender.* Once the word capitulation was accepted by the Americans, Toral surrendered not only Santiago, but the troops at Guantánamo and six other posts in eastern Cuba, all of which were under his command. These seven posts were being besieged by Cubans, and Toral was basically saving the lives of his soldiers.

At noon on July 17, 1898, the Spanish flag was lowered at the municipal palace and the American flag was raised. The Cuban-Spanish-American War lasted sixty days.

Historians have debated whether García was invited to participate in the negotiations. We now know that he was not, but neither was Sampson. Of course, the reasons were quite different. Shafter was under instructions from Washington to avoid the recognition of the Cuban Republic in any form, and that is why he did not invite García to participate in the negotiations.[43]

Admiral Sampson had informed Shafter that he expected to participate in any negotiations for the surrender of the city. Shafter agreed and promised the Admiral that he would be invited. A few minutes before the final ceremony, Shafter telegraphed: "Enemy has surrendered. Will you send someone to represent the Navy in the matter?"[44] When the Admiral's chief of staff arrived, the ceremonies were completed. The Navy had left the job to the Army, and the Army intended to take full credit.

General García was orally invited by Shafter to attend the transfer of power ceremony at the municipal palace. García had asked Shafter as to when the Cubans would be taking charge of Santiago's civil government. Shafter had replied that the Spanish civil authorities would remain in charge. An important reason why Cubans were fighting for independence from Spain was that people born in Cuba had not been allowed to occupy civil service jobs. These jobs were reserved for *Peninsulares*, or people born in Spain. This was perhaps the most grievous insult American forces did to Cuban patriots. Angrily, García took his forces to the interior, breaking off contact with Shafter.[45]

The Cuban-Spanish-American War actually ended on August 12, 1898, with the signing of a protocol by U.S. and Spanish representatives. Harvey Rosenfeld researched government archives and determined that there was a perceived administration's strategy as to the outcome of the peace treaty with Spain. "Most government officials were certain that McKinley would be content, they reasoned, with Spain's admission of Cuban independence; America acquiring Puerto Rico; the setting up a protectorate over the Philippines; and the payment of an indemnity by Spain."[46]

The peace treaty was signed in Paris on April 11, 1899. Spain relinquished all claims of sovereignty over Cuba and the Spanish military was to evacuate the island immediately. Spain also turned over to the United States, Puerto Rico, Guam, and the Philippines. General John Brooke had been appointed U.S. Military Governor of Cuba in January 1899.

The strong contempt of American soldiers toward Cubans was grossly unfair, for the help of the Cuban had been of great value. Cuban rebels had covered American landings and had been invaluable as scouts and guides. John Black Atkins, a British reporter from the *Manchester Guardian*, traveled with American and Cuban units and his description of the animosity of Americans against Cubans follows. "The fact is that the United States Army made the very old mistake of judging its allies by its own standards. The Cubans were excellent at quick concentrations and hit-and-run attacks, and at the kind of guerrilla warfare with which they had tied down over 200,000 Spanish regulars in Cuba, operating as irregulars in small, mobile bands. The Americans expected them to act like a formal, drilled army, and were disillusioned whenever they failed to do so. Their reaction was to use the Cubans as scapegoats for the errors and ills of the campaign."[47]

During and after the Cuban-Spanish-American War, U.S. newspapers had a change of heart regarding the Cuban patriots. Before the war started, Cuban rebels were heralded as modern Robin Hoods, stealing weapons from the Spanish troops to liberate their oppressed country. They were compared to the Continental Army of the 1770s in the United States.

War correspondent Trumbull White, in his 1898 book, wrote the following: "The parallels between the Cuban insurrection and that of the American colonies against Great Britain in 1776 are far more numerous than has been recognized. The Cuban army has been poorly clothed and scantily fed at times, and equipped with all sorts of obsolete weapons of offense. But these things are no disgrace, and indeed are the basis of much of the pride that Americans take in the splendid work which their ancestors did in that other insurrection, which, having resulted successfully is now known as the American Revolution."[48] It did not take very long for the opinion about Cuban patriots to change in the eyes of journalists and the American people. The greed of politicians and the desire to incorporate Cuba into the map of the United States certainly helped to obscure opinions along the way.

The opinions expressed by U.S. servicemen to journalists also had a significant effect on public opinion and on the mood of politicians. After all, who would know Cubans better than the men who were fighting alongside them?

History has shown that Cubans have not done a great job of ruling their own destiny, but interference from the United States during the first fifty-six years of the Republic of Cuba did not help matters either. An example of how the U.S. military felt about Cubans follows.

General William Rufus "Pecos Bill" Shafter was asked to assess if Cubans would be able to rule their own destiny. The December 19, 1898 issue of the New York Tribune, quoted a conversation between some reporters and General Shafter in Savannah, Georgia.

"How about self-government for the Cubans?" Shafter was asked.

"Self-government!" he replied. "Why, these people are no more fit for self-government than gun-powder is for hell."[49]

Shafter had clearly decided that the Cubans were the ideal scapegoat. He never missed an opportunity to blame them for anything that went wrong, and created opportunities to humiliate General García almost daily.

After the Battle of San Juan Hill, Stephen Crane reported that "both officers and privates have the most lively contempt for the Cubans. They despise them."[50]

Cubans were concerned about what appeared to be a defamatory campaign of the American Army against Cubans. Was it a conspiracy? If so, who was behind it? The Cuban Junta could get no answers as to what were the U.S. plans regarding Cuba. At the same time, U.S. military commanders were aware that Filipino patriots were fighting against American occupation forces and would not discuss the future of Cuba. Cubans began to get the impression that the United States planned to keep Cuba by right of honorable conquest.

Another distortion of the truth about the Cuban-Spanish-American War regarding the performance of the U.S. Navy has evolved over the years. The thesis of this myth is that the U.S. Navy routed the Spanish Armada in every encounter. This is true in the two main engagements, Manila Bay and Santiago de Cuba. However, there were other minor naval scrimmages in Cuban waters, where the Spanish Armada held their own against the U.S. Navy. Three such examples are the naval battles of Cárdenas, Cienfuegos, and Manzanillo.

On May 11, 1898, the torpedo boat *Winslow*, the gunboat *Wilmington*, and the Revenue Cutter *Hudson* were ordered to Cárdenas to destroy three Spanish gunboats which had been harassing the American squadron. The U.S. Revenue Cutter Service was a predecessor to today's Coast Guard. As soon as the *Winslow* entered the harbor, Spanish shore batteries fired, disabling her and killing or wounding many on board. The *Wilmington* and *Hudson* maintained a steady fire on the Spanish ships and shore batteries, while securing a tow line to the disabled *Winslow*, which was finally towed beyond the range of the Spanish batteries. On the American side, there were six killed, including Ensign Worth Bagley, the only naval officer lost during the war, and at least six wounded. The torpedo boat *Winslow* was taken out of service. On the Spanish side, two gunboats as well as a number of shore batteries were severely damaged, three Spanish soldiers were killed and one wounded.[51]

Also on May 11, 1898, U.S. Navy cruisers *Nashville* and *Marblehead* were ordered to the port of Cienfuegos to cut the communication cables that linked that important south-central Cuba port with Havana and Santiago. An all-volunteer force of fifty-two Marines armed with saws and axes approached the coast, while American battleships and Marines fired on Spanish positions. Two of the three cables were cut, but with high casualties for the Marines. Two Marines were killed and fifteen wounded. There is no record of any Spanish casualties.[52]

There were actually three battles of Manzanillo. The first engagement took place on June 30, 1898. Three U.S. Navy auxiliary cruisers, the *Hist, Hornet,* and *Wompatuck* spotted the Spanish gunboat *Centinela* and the *Hist* and *Hornet* moved in and commenced firing. The *Centinela* returned fire and Spanish shore batteries also began firing. After the *Centinela* ran aground, the three American vessels entered the port where they found several Spanish ships ready for action. The *Hist* and the *Hornet* were severely damaged and since the Americans were taking significant casualties, decided to withdraw. The second battle took place on July 1, 1898, when the U.S. Navy armed tugs *Osceola* and *Scorpion* arrived in Manzanillo unaware that the United States had lost the first battle. The *Scorpion* was hit twelve times and there were several American casualties. The American vessels withdrew. There is no data on Spanish casualties. The third and final naval engagement took place on July 18, 1898. The American force consisted of gunboats *Wilmington* and *Helena,* armed tugs *Scorpion* and *Osceola* and auxiliary cruisers *Hist, Hornet,* and *Wompatuck.* Americans had repaired their vessels, but so had the Spaniards. The American victory was decisive. The Spanish fleet lost four gunboats, three transports, and a pontoon. There were 200 Spaniards killed and an unknown number of wounded. There were no American casualties; however, the city of Manzanillo was not taken.[53]

Manzanillo held on to be the last city to be taken at the war's end. Even without a naval presence, the city only fell to American troops after a ferocious bombardment by the U.S. Navy combined with a land attack by Cuban rebels.

The Cubans soon became convinced that they had moved from one military occupation to another. General Leonard Wood had been appointed Governor of Oriente Province in early September 1898. On September 22, 1898, General Calixto García was allowed to enter Santiago as a *guest* of the United States.

As more and more American troops arrived in Cuba and Spanish civil servants continued running the Cuban public offices, the Cuban population became confused, and the Cuban Assembly was embittered and frustrated. The rest of the world already viewed Cuba as a part of the United States.

The Cuban rebel provisional government, which had been organized in 1895, had never been recognized by any foreign government. In October 1898, this shadow government was discarded and replaced by the Cuban Assembly, which in reality was composed of distinguished members of the Cuban rebel army.

In mid-November the Cuban Assembly asked to meet with President McKinley to explore the intentions of the United States toward Cuba, free trade, and the possibility of obtaining funds to pay off the Cuban rebel army. The Assembly appointed a committee headed by General Calixto García, José Antonio González Lanuza, Manuel Sanguily, José Miguel Gómez, and José Ramón Villalón. The Cubans in exile were represented by Gonzalo de Quesada, the Cuban *chargé d'affaires* in Washington, and Horatio Rubens, the attorney for the Cuban junta in the United States.

The McKinley administration was alarmed when the commission of the Cuban Assembly asked to come to Washington. The commission was received in Washington merely as citizens of the island, and not as representatives of a government. Initially, the committee was well treated with receptions, dinners, and the usual speeches. McKinley created a smokescreen on the future intentions of the United States regarding Cuba by highlighting the issue of the discharge of the Cuban rebel army. After all, it represented the only tangible threat to the American occupation of Cuba, and it was an easy problem to address, not requiring the explanation of a probably nonexistent, long-term, American strategy.

The committee's visit to Washington was going relatively well until they met with John Tyler Morgan, the powerful Alabama Senator and a member of the Foreign Relations Committee. Morgan was well prepared for his meeting with the Cubans, and started by pointing out that Congress had never recognized any government in Cuba other than Spain's, and he reminded the startled Cubans that during the war, all Spanish subjects were enemies of the United States, including Cubans. Morgan went on to say that the Teller Amendment was not an agreement with anyone, nor was it a decree or a law, and that it would be executed at such time and in such manner as the United States would provide. Morgan finalized his diatribe to the disheartened Cubans by informing them that the military occupation of Cuba was only a first step, and that the sovereignty of Cuba was in the hands of the United States and under the ultimate authority of the President. He ended with a clear threat, stating that there would be no peace in Cuba as long as there was any resistance to U.S. military authority.[54]

The Cuban commission disagreed with Morgan's analysis and provided a written rebuttal prepared by García. In their reply, the Cubans insisted that the Teller Amendment was a law like any other law, and that it was legally and morally binding upon actions of the

United States. The Cubans asked pointed questions about the limits, if any, of the American military power in Cuba, and short of declaring war, stated that if the U.S. military authorities violated accepted Cuban procedures or ideals, they would just stand to one side, refuse to cooperate, and hold the United States absolutely responsible for the results.[55]

The public statements by the Cuban commission grew increasingly threatening, and when it looked as if the situation could get no worse, General García took ill with pneumonia and died suddenly, on December 11, 1898. He was given an impressive funeral in Washington and his body temporarily interred in Arlington National Cemetery.

In addition to losing their beloved war hero, General Calixto García, the commission of the Cuban Assembly returned to Havana more embittered and frustrated than they were prior to departing for Washington.

The initial U.S. military occupation of Cuba would last for four years.

Notes

1.   Elbert Hubbard, *A Message to Garcia* (White Plains, NY: Peter Pauper Press, 1898), 6–7.
2.   Philip S. Foner, *The Spanish-Cuban-American War and the Birth of American Imperialism*, vol. II (New York: Monthly Review Press, 1972), 340.
3.   Thomas, *Cuba or the Pursuit of Freedom*, 386.
4.   John Tebbel, *America's Great Patriotic War with Spain: Mixed Motives, Lies and Racism in Cuba and the Philippines, 1898-1915* (Manchester Center, VT: Marshall Jones, 1996), 164–65.
5.   Chadwick, *Relations of the United States to Spain*, vol. 2, 23–26.
6.   Louis A. Pérez, *The War of 1898: The United States and Cuba in History and Historiography* (Chapel Hill: The University of North Carolina Press, 1998), 86.
7.   *Heraldo de Madrid*, September 9, 1898.
8.   Charles H. Brown, *The Correspondent's War* (New York: Charles Scribner's Sons, 1967), 279–89.
9.   Harvey Rosenfeld, *Diary of a Dirty Little War: The Spanish American War of 1898* (Westport, CT: Praeger Publishers, 2000), 109.
10.   Ibid., 111.
11.   Chadwick, *Relations of the United States to Spain*, vol. I, 236.
12.   Foner, *Spanish-Cuban-American War*, 348–49.
13.   David F. Healy, *The United States in Cuba (1898-1902): Generals, Politicians and the Search for Policy* (Madison: The University of Wisconsin Press, 1963), 32.
14.   Cosmas, *Army for Empire*, 204–5.
15.   Ibid., 209.
16.   Foner, *Spanish-Cuban-American War*, 357–61.

17. Pérez, *War of 1898*, 85–86.
18. Ibid., 210.
19. Archives of *The New York Times*, August 14, 1898.
20. Cosmas, *Army for Empire*, 216–17.
21. French Ensor Chadwick, *The Relations of the United States and Spain: The Spanish American War*, vol. II (New York: Charles Scribner's Sons, 1911), 95.
22. Ibid., 218.
23. Thomas, *Cuba or the Pursuit of Freedom*, 394.
24. Cosmas, *Army for Empire*, 218–19.
25. Turnbull White, *United States in War with Spain* (New York: International Publishing, 1898), 452–53.
26. Ibid., 452–55.
27. Thomas, *Cuba or the Pursuit of Freedom*, 396–97.
28. Walter Millis, *The Martial Spirit, A Study of Our War with Spain* (Cambridge, MA: The Riverside Press, 1931), 310–13.
29. Ibid., 368–71.
30. Thomas, *Cuba or the Pursuit of Freedom*, 397.
31. Millis, *Martial Spirit*, 398.
32. Ibid., 398.
33. Healy, *United States in Cuba (1898-1902)*, 35.
34. *The State*, July 8, 1898.
35. Ibid., 398.
36. Healy, *United States in Cuba (1898-1902)*, 32.
37. Millis, *Martial Spirit*, 320.
38. Ibid., 361–62.
39. Cosmas, *Army for Empire*, 226.
40. Aníbal Escalante Beatón, *Calixto García Su Campaña en el 95* (Havana: Arrow Press, 1946), 522–29.
41. Quoted by Foner, *Spanish-Cuban-American War*, 364–65, from *The State*, November 21, 1898.
42. Ibid., 227.
43. Healy, *United States in Cuba (1898-1902)*, 33.
44. Quoted by Millis, *Martial Spirit*, 327.
45. Healy, *United States in Cuba (1898-1902)*, 33.
46. Rosenfeld, *Diary of a Dirty Little War*, 164.
47. John Black Atkins, *The War in Cuba, The Experiences of an Englishman with the United States Army* (London: Smith, Elder, 1899), 288–89.
48. White, *United States in War with Spain*, 179.
49. Quoted by Healy, *United States in Cuba (1898-1902)*, 36.
50. *New York World*, July 14, 1898.
51. William H. Thiesen, *Combat Stories of the U.S. Coast Guard*, March 31, 2010.
52. Hermenegildo Franco Castañón, *1898: Los españoles que derrotaron a EE.UU* (Historia de Iberia Vieja), no. 7, 80–85.
53. Ibid., 80–85.
54. Healy, *United States in Cuba (1898-1902)*, 48–49.
55. Letter from García to Morgan, *Actas de las Asambleas de Representantes*, undated, vol. 5, 160–65.

15

American Military Occupation of Cuba

On January 1, 1899, U.S. Army General John R. Brooke became the first U.S. Military Governor of Cuba. The last Spanish Captain-General of Cuba, Adolfo Jiménez Castellanos, in a short and terse speech, transferred the sovereignty of Cuba to the custody of the United States. Even if the U.S. authorities had understood Spanish, they would not have been able to hear Jiménez's speech, on account of the noise made by an American regimental band playing patriotic tunes outside the building.

General Brooke, a Pennsylvania native, joined the Pennsylvania Infantry at the outbreak of the Civil War and fought bravely at the battles of Chancellorsville and Gettysburg. He later commanded the Seventh U.S. Cavalry at Wounded Knee. During the Cuban-Spanish-American War he fought in Puerto Rico and became military governor of Puerto Rico until his appointment to the same post in Cuba.

Did the McKinley administration have a strategy as to what the course of action on Cuba would be? They probably did not, particularly since both McKinley and War Secretary Alger were in favor of Cuba's annexation, but found their hands tied by the Teller Amendment. On the political side, McKinley had been careful not to make any moves that would appear that he was recognizing the Cuban Junta. Therefore, when a cease fire was negotiated with Spain, McKinley sent an agent, Charles E. Magoon, to New York to meet with Estrada Palma. McKinley wanted Estrada Palma to send a *personal* message to the Cuban rebel commanders informing them of the cease fire agreement. Horatio S. Rubens, the Junta's legal advisor, insisted that Estrada Palma's notification must be an *official* communiqué to the President of the Cuban Republic, and signed as Minister and Delegate Plenipotentiary to the United States. Magoon reluctantly agreed to the format proposed by Rubens.[1]

175

Cuba's Military Governor Brooke was faced with the nearly impossible task of rebuilding an economy that had been incredibly devastated by thirty years of war. To make matters worse, "General Brooke had, however, no specific instructions from McKinley."[2] Basically, all the guidance that Brooke had was the wording from the Teller Amendment, i.e., he was to pacify the island. To carry out the so-called pacification of the island, the United States sent a military force larger than the one that had fought against Spain. At the beginning of the occupation, there were 24,000 officers and men in Cuba. By March 1899, the number was approximately 45,000. All this time, the Cuban rebel army was functioning as an interim government, primarily maintaining law and order.

Brooke quickly moved to organize his government even though he had no idea as to how long the United States would hold on to Cuba, and under what terms. His appointments went generally to people familiar with Cuba. His chief of staff was his old friend, Colonel Adna R. Chaffee, who had commanded a brigade at the battle of El Caney; General Leonard Wood remained as military governor of Oriente, with Camagüey added; General Fitzhugh Lee, former Consul General in Havana, became military governor of the provinces of Havana and Pinar del Rio; General James Wilson was appointed military governor of the provinces of Las Villas (Santa Clara) and Matanzas; and General William Ludlow became military governor of the city of Havana.

General James H. Wilson, an Illinois native, was a West Point graduate and served as a topographical engineer at the start of the Civil War. He joined General Ulysses S. Grant at the Battle of Chattanooga and served under General William T. Sherman in the Battle of Nashville. Wilson later changed from engineering to cavalry, and his troops captured the city of Columbus, Georgia, as well as Confederate President Jefferson Davis as he fled through Georgia. After a fifteen-year retirement, Wilson returned to military service for the Cuban-Spanish-American War.

General William Ludlow was born in New York, graduated from West Point, and joined the staff of General William T. Sherman during the Civil War, in engineering and scientific duties. In 1898, he was appointed Chief Engineer of the armies in the field and commanded the First Brigade in General Henry Lawton's division during the battle of El Caney and the siege of Santiago.

Brooke left essentially the same civil government structure as the Spanish Autonomists had created, although he reduced the cabinet positions to four. Distinguished Cubans were appointed to the four posts: Domingo Méndez Capote as Secretary of the Interior; Pablo Desvernine became Secretary of Finance; José Antonio González Lanuza was appointed as Secretary of Justice and Education; and Adolfo Sáenz Yáñez became Secretary of Public Works, Agriculture, Industry, and Commerce.[3]

Brooke's military rule of Cuba did not have an auspicious beginning. There were two incidents that were considered major insults to the Cuban rebel army. The first incident was on the day of the inauguration of the official U.S. military rule in Cuba. The Cubans had planned a great victory celebration on the day of the termination of Spanish rule in Cuba. The rebel army committees in Havana had prepared a detailed program of events which was to last for five days, including a parade of Cuban troops while the Spanish would be boarding their vessels at the Havana water front. At the last minute, Brooke, through Ludlow, the military commander of Havana, notified the Cubans that no insurgent troops would be allowed in Havana at the time of transfer of government. The reason given by Brooke was that he was trying to avoid a confrontation between Spanish and Cuban troops. Historian Hugh Thomas disagrees with this rationale, as he uncovered evidence that Brooke was trying to avoid a confrontation between *American* and Cuban troops. Thomas reports some street fights in Havana, "...with U.S. troops being attacked and being exasperated waiting for a chance to sail into the Cubans. The ex-slave Montejo reports a similar incident in Cienfuegos...an attack on U.S. soldiers who were trying to seduce Creole girls, led by the ex-slave Claudio Sarriá."[4]

When the news of Brooke's decision to prevent a Cuban celebration reached the United States, Brooke was severely criticized. Even Senator Teller commented that Brooke's denial of a victory celebration had created a false impression of the future course of action of the United States in Cuba.[5]

The second insult to the Cuban rebel army occurred during the second funeral of General García on February 11, 1899. The U.S. military government authorized an impressive procession to honor a national hero. A number of Cuban leaders were to make farewell speeches at the gravesite. A prominent place in the parade had been assigned to the Cuban army and the Cuban Assembly. When the procession line formed, an American cavalry unit mistakenly took the place intended for the Cubans. The Cubans went to Brooke and Ludlow to complain, but since neither one spoke Spanish, they thought that the Cubans wanted to be in front of them, and angrily refused to do anything. As a result, the Cubans including troops, generals, and Assembly withdrew *en masse* from the procession. When the funeral parade arrived at the cemetery, not a single Cuban was present. The Americans had to conduct the entire ceremony themselves. This, coupled with the victory celebration blunder, confirmed the Cubans' belief that Americans were trying to humiliate the Cuban leaders.[6]

In Washington, McKinley and Congress were immediately facing two critical issues regarding Cuba. During the Paris Peace Conference, Spain had informed the United States that there was a Cuban external debt of approximately $400 million, which was secured against future Cuban revenues. Spain expected the United States to repay this debt, primarily held by French and German bondholders. Naturally, the United States claimed that this was Spain's debt, contracted to fight the insurrection in Cuba, and, moreover, that American authority over Cuba was to be merely a temporary trust. Eventually, the matter was settled by a U.S. payment to Spain of $20 million, on general principles.

Meanwhile, Brooke was facing the problem of the Cuban rebel army. Brooke wanted all 48,000 of them to lay down their arms and find jobs. The Cuban Assembly said that would be fine, except that the men must be paid their back wages, and since Cuba's customs revenue and taxes were going to the U.S. Army, the Assembly had no way to pay the men. Apparently, at a certain point, the Cuban Assembly had been promised that the United States would pay the rebel army's back wages. The Assembly was claiming $57 million and the McKinley administration had offered $3 million. This became a matter of concern to Brooke, since under similar circumstances the Filipino rebel army had rebelled and had decided to fight the Americans.

Brooke was a benevolent and pragmatic ruler, and commenced with the job of revamping the school system. He left the Spanish legal system in place, but felt free to amend specific laws that proved difficult to implement. Spanish taxes were retained with some minor revisions. Distinguished Cubans were appointed to municipal jobs. The country was giving signs that the wounds of war were slowly healing.

In Oriente Province, Leonard Wood was making significant progress. After all, he had been in charge there since August 1898 and had at least five months head start over Brooke. Wood, being a close personal friend of McKinley, was not waiting for guidance. He started an impressive sanitation program in Santiago and used customs and other revenues as he saw fit.

In Matanzas and Las Villas, Wilson wanted to revitalize farming by starting a program of farm loans. He also suggested appointing a group of highly regarded Cubans to draft a constitution. Brooke vetoed both of Wilson's pet projects. Wilson was also controlling his revenues and disbursing them on projects he considered worthy.

Both Wood and Wilson wanted Brooke's job and this became patently clear, not only among high-ranking U.S. military officers in Cuba, but also in Washington's political circles. Brooke tried to make Wood and Wilson look bad, but the problem was that both Wood and Wilson were better connected in Washington than Brooke.

Brooke centralized Cuban finances in Havana, mandating that all revenues be sent to a central office run by Brooke and Ludlow. This incensed both Wood and Wilson, but War Secretary Alger supported Brooke's position.

Unfortunately for Brooke, Alger was one of the most discredited members of the McKinley administration. Alger was blamed, and rightfully so, for the poor state of readiness of the Army at the start of the war with Spain. Pressure from the media and Congress to dismiss Alger was intense, and at McKinley's request, Alger resigned in July 1899.

To the surprise of most Washington insiders, McKinley appointed Elihu Root, a New York corporation lawyer, to the position of Secretary of War. Root took office on August 1, 1899, and spent several weeks carefully listening to opinions of politicians and military men as well. After Root gained an understanding of the Cuba situation, he ordered the following:

- A national census for Cuba
- Determination of the electorate from the census data. According to the treaty ending the war with Spain, residents were to choose Cuban or Spanish citizenship no later than April 11, 1900. Only then the number of electors could be determined
- Municipal elections
- Constitutional convention to frame a central government, to which the United States could surrender power
- Development of a tariff agreement between the United States and Cuba

The demise of Brooke was only slightly delayed by Root's appointment. The political heavyweights pushing for either Wood or Wilson had damaged Brooke's reputation as a leader. Brooke had, on two occasions at the start of his administration, insulted Cuban leaders, but otherwise he had had good ideas on how to improve living conditions in Cuba, and had been quick to put them into effect.

On December 13, 1899, the War Department published the order which assigned command of the Division of Cuba to Leonard Wood, replacing John Brooke.[7]

General Leonard Wood took over as Cuba's second U.S. Military Governor at noon on December 20, 1899. He immediately accepted the resignation of the four Cuban cabinet members, but left Brooke's military staff intact. During the first two weeks of his mandate, Wood reorganized the civil administration and then interviewed and hired candidates. With his Cuban Cabinet in place, he traveled to the major population centers on the island.

Wood split the duties of two of the former cabinet positions, thus creating two new positions, for a total of six cabinet positions. His appointments went to prominent veterans of the Cuban army and to Cuba's leading intellectuals. These were: Enrique José Varona (Finance), Cuba's leading economist and academic; José Ramón Villalón (Public Works), a rebel general; Juan Rius Rivera (Agriculture), Antonio Maceo's successor in command of the rebels in western Cuba; Luis Estévez Romero (Justice), a former associate judge of the Supreme Court; Juan Bautista Hernández Barreiro (Education), a leading Cuban jurist and educator; and Diego Tamayo Figueredo (Interior), a physician and former soldier.[8]

Following Root's orders, the Cuban census was carried out. The results were available in Washington in early April, and were published in U.S. and Cuban newspapers in early May 1900. The census showed a total population of 1.5 million, with two-thirds of all adults being illiterate and one-third of the population being nonwhite.[9]

Wood appointed a commission to draft an election law on February 16, 1900. This commission was headed by Diego Tamayo, Interior Secretary, and consisted of thirteen Cubans and two Americans. The electoral law was completed on April 18, 1900. The requirements to be eligible to vote were: male, more than twenty-one years of age, a citizen of Cuba according to the terms of the peace treaty with Spain, and either able to read and write, or own property worth at least $250 in U.S. gold, or have served in the Cuban Army prior to July 18, 1898 with an honorable discharge.[10]

The rules for voter eligibility were provided by War Secretary Elihu Root, the man who later drafted the Platt Amendment. This selective suffrage was clearly intended to eliminate from the voter's roles most individuals likely to be antiannexation. Universal suffrage would have insured that the U.S. occupation would have been of short duration.

Even though Wood was making progress in Cuba, and slowly gaining the trust of some segments of the population, Congress was becoming restive with the military occupation of Cuba. On January 17, 1900, the Senate passed a resolution demanding a detailed accounting from the War Department of all expenditures of Cuban revenues since the occupation began. Resolutions for withdrawing all U.S. forces from Cuba were introduced in the House by Alabama's Henry D. Clayton and in the Senate by Illinois' William E. Mason.[11]

Early in his tenure, just as his predecessor Brooke had done, Wood began having troubles with his immediate staff, with the exception of Fitzhugh Lee. Chaffee, who had been Brooke's ally against Wood, was promoted to a post in Washington. Secretary of Agriculture Juan Rius Rivera was fired for writing a letter to the newspapers calling for immediate Cuban independence. Ludlow got in trouble over a contract for the paving and sewerage of Havana's streets. Wood responded by eliminating Ludlow's position on May 1, 1900. The city of Havana was added to Lee's responsibilities as Military Governor of Havana and Pinar del Rio Provinces.[12]

The most serious political setback to American occupation was not military, but rather involved the embezzlement of Post Office funds by two well-connected American employees. Both the Brooke and Wood administrations had been careful not to appoint Cubans to positions involving the handling of money. In fact, President McKinley had insisted that the head of the Cuban Post Office report to the U.S. Postmaster General, and not to the Military Governor. Ohio Senator Marcus A. Hanna, a Republican Party boss, and McKinley's close personal friend, had recommended Estes Rathbone to head the Cuban Post Office.[13]

War Secretary Root was dissatisfied with the financial irresponsibility of the Cuban postal system. While Root negotiated with the Postmaster General for a better arrangement, Root asked Wood to conduct a routine Army audit of the postal books.

When military personnel appeared at the Havana Post Office, they discovered that Rathbone had assigned himself a salary equivalent to 10 percent of the revenues of his department. Rathbone initially refused to have his books examined, but finally relented.

On May 4, 1900, Wood telegraphed Root that a large-scale Post Office embezzlement had been discovered, and that it pointed to Charles Neely, head of the finance department. Wood added that the amount was at least $100,000 or perhaps more, and that records for the past year had disappeared. Neely and Rathbone had already left the country, but eventually, both were caught, tried, and sent to prison. Congress took the Post Office scandal seriously, and demanded an end to the military occupation of Cuba.

Cuban municipal elections were held on June 16, 1900. They were conducted quietly and peacefully, with wins for most proindependence candidates. Now that the Cubans were heavily involved in political matters, Root and Wood worked on a strategy that would give the Cubans a sense of self-rule, while retaining American control. Wood authorized flying the Cuban flag from all municipal and governmental buildings, and started conversing with his cabinet about proceeding with a constitutional convention. He wanted a Cuban constitution that would include a treaty defining the relations between Cuba and the United States.[14]

On July 25, 1900, the U.S. Military Government of Cuba issued a civil order calling for an election of delegates to a Cuban Constitutional Convention. The election was to be held on September 3, 1900, in accordance with the terms of the election law promulgated on April 18, 1900.[15]

Early in July 1900, when news of the Boxer Rebellion in China reached Cuba, Wood's attitude changed. Wood wanted to take part in this war, as his sister-in-law was trapped in one of the Beijing legations. Therefore, Wood commenced reporting that everything in Cuba was peaceful, and that an older man could now do his job. Also factoring into Wood's request was likely his concern about diminished probabilities of an early promotion.[16]

The Republican Convention was scheduled to commence on June 19, 1900 in Philadelphia. Intrigues and machinations had commenced during late 1899, with the futures of Cuba and the Philippines as significant campaign issues. Admiral Dewey of Manila Bay fame was opposing McKinley for the Republican presidential nomination. The party elders quickly convinced Dewey that his candidacy was neither welcome nor appropriate. McKinley was deeply concerned that Roosevelt would be nominated for the presidency by acclamation. Senator Marcus Hanna convinced McKinley that that would not happen. At any rate, McKinley did not want Roosevelt as his vice-presidential candidate, but he was not having much luck finding an alternate candidate.

McKinley's first choice was Elihu Root, but he declined. He then successively offered the vice-presidential candidacy to Senator William B. Allison, Cornelius Bliss, and Jonathan P. Dolliver. They all declined the opportunity. Finally, McKinley asked Roosevelt to be his running mate, before the Republican Convention could force his hand.

Back to the Cuba situation, it became clear to Wood that neither Root nor McKinley were inclined to allow him to serve in China. As his main staff was sent to the Boxer Rebellion or other posts, Wood could not ask for replacements since he had committed to the fact that all was quiet in the Cuban front.

When Wilson was assigned to China, Wood eliminated his position and assigned his territory to Lee. On July 23, 1900, Lee became Military Governor of Western Cuba which included the provinces of Pinar del Rio, Havana, Matanzas, and Las Villas. In October 1900, the Eastern and Western Cuba departments were combined into one under Lee. Soon Lee also left, and Wood was left in place to run the island government for the rest of the first occupation.

The Cuban Constitutional Convention opened at the Martí Theatre in Havana on November 5, 1900, exactly one day before the 1900 U.S. presidential election. McKinley did not want the Cuba issue to interfere with his re-election. During his campaign, McKinley said many times that most Cubans wanted the U.S. occupation to continue, but did not dare say so. The McKinley–Roosevelt ticket won with 53 percent of the votes cast. The Republicans also swept both houses of Congress.

The Cuban Constitutional Convention consisted of thirty-one delegates from the six provinces, on the basis of population. Wood tried to influence the selection of proannexation candidates to the Constitutional Convention, but he failed miserably, as most delegates were proindependence. When Wood opened the convention, he asked the delegates to frame a constitution for Cuba, and when "that had been done" to agree upon future relations with the United States.[17]

Wood and Root were prepared to allow the Cubans any constitution they desired. However, Root would not give independence to the Cubans without obtaining prior commitments vis-à-vis future relations and obligations to the United States. Wood reported to Root that the Cubans were making steady, though slow, progress in drafting a constitution, but that they were not spending any time on formatting future relations with the United States. After considering the state of affairs of the Cuban Constitutional Convention, Root decided that he would dictate to the Cubans about future relations with the United States.

In early February of 1901, Senator Orville Platt wrote to Root, "I think it is high time to give [to the Cuban Constitutional Delegates] as to what the United States is going to insist on."[18] This was an unnecessary request, since Root was already working on such a document. On February 9, 1901, Root wrote to Wood, providing the basic philosophy and outline of what would later on become the contentious Platt Amendment.[19]

The rationale behind Root's outline of the infamous document that would be known as the Platt Amendment was not neoteric. In his memoirs, Root admitted that his proposal for the Platt Amendment was inspired by England's relations with Egypt, which seemed to allow "England to retire and still maintain her moral control."[20]

On March 2, 1901, Wood invited a committee of members of the Cuban Constitutional Convention to a crocodile hunt on the edge of Zapata swamp, near where the ill-fated Bay of Pigs invasion would later land in 1961, and confronted them with Root's outline. Initial reaction was utter dismay. The committee strongly objected to the leasing of naval stations, the right of intervention by the United States, the omission of the Isle of Pines as Cuban territory, and the limitation on the capacity of the Cuban government to contract debts. In fact, the committee disagreed with the entire concept of the Platt Amendment. Wood replied to the committee that the principles could not be changed. In his report to Root, Wood stated that everything had gone well.[21]

The Cuban Constitutional Convention completed its work on the Cuban constitution, but failed to address its relations with the United States. Instead, Juan Gualberto Gómez replied in an eloquent and detailed report to Root the reasons why the Constitutional Convention could not agree with the concepts outlined by him. Excerpts from J. G. Gómez's reply follow: "The [Platt] Amendment alters the letter and the spirit of the Treaty of Paris and the Teller Amendment, since the Island of Cuba would be under the jurisdiction and sovereignty of the United States...the Cuban people become vassals of the United States...we have been asked to draft a constitution and now the United States are placing limits on the independence granted by our constitution...only weak governments would be able to rule Cuba...no country would ever take us seriously since the last word is in Washington...and we have been told that American troops would never leave the island if we do not approve verbatim the [Platt] Amendment and make it a part of our constitution."[22] Not all members of the Constitutional Conventional took a negative view. Manuel Sanguily stated that independence, with some restrictions, was better than a permanent military occupation. A few others supported the U.S. actions.

Meanwhile in Washington, the Platt Amendment was introduced to the Senate on February 24, 1901, as an amendment to the current Army appropriations bill. The Platt Amendment stated that the President was authorized to end the military occupation of Cuba as soon as this resolution (Platt Amendment) was a part of, and had been appended to the Cuban Constitution. The subcommittee that drafted Root's requests into a resolution consisted of Senators Hernando de Soto Money of Mississippi, Orville H. Platt of Connecticut, John C. Spooner of Wisconsin, and Henry M. Teller of Colorado.

It is curious that Teller formed a part of this subcommittee. McKinley probably imposed this penance on Teller for having authored the Teller Amendment of April 20, 1898. Debate in the Senate occurred on February 26 and 27, and strangely enough, the spokesman for the Democratic opposition was John Tyler Morgan of Alabama, the senator who had given the Cuban Commission such a hard time in December 1898. Morgan contended that the Platt Amendment was taking the place of diplomatic negotiations between two existing governments, and could not be imposed as a preexisting condition for creating a Cuban government. Final vote took place on February 27, 1901, strictly along party lines. The Amendment was passed by a forty-three to twenty margin. All forty-three yeas came from Republicans. Seventeen nays were cast by Democrats and Populists, with the remaining three by Republicans. Senator Teller, one of the authors of the bill, voted against it.[23]

The House adopted the Amendment on March 1, 1901, by a vote of 161 to 137, and it was signed by President McKinley on March 2, 1901, and thus became law.

The key terms of the seven clauses of the Platt Amendment follows.[24]

I.   Cuba will not allow any foreign power other than the United States to impair Cuba's independence or to operate military facilities in Cuba
II. Cuba will not enter into inadequate financing of its expenditures
III. Cuba consents to military intervention by the United States in order to protect U.S. interests in Cuba
IV. Cuba will consider any U.S. military intervention in Cuba as a lawful act

V. Cuba will provide sanitation in the island to avoid epidemics and thus protect the commerce of southern ports of the United States

VI. The Isle of Pines is not a part of Cuba until its title is properly adjusted

VII. In order to properly protect Cuba, Cuba shall lease to the United States appropriate land and bays for naval bases and coaling stations

Cuban newspapers took a very negative view of the Platt Amendment, particularly Article III. The members of the Constitutional Convention realized that they were facing a burden of incredible relevance. If they approved the Platt Amendment, in Juan Gualberto Gómez's words: "the independence and sovereignty of the Cuban republic would be reduced to a myth."[25] If, on the other hand, they rejected the Amendment, American military occupation would continue for the foreseeable future, perhaps indefinitely. The Convention appointed a commission, headed by Domingo Méndez Capote, to travel to Washington to explore the true meaning of the controversial clauses of the Amendment.

The commission arrived in Washington on April 24, 1901, accompanied by Wood. The main speaker for the Platt Amendment was War Secretary Root. He explained Article III by saying that the Amendment was just an extension of the Monroe Doctrine, and that it did not give the United States any rights it did not already have. Regarding the naval and coaling stations, they were for the defense of both countries, and would never be used to interfere in Cuba's internal affairs.

The commission returned to Cuba just as confused as they had been when they left, as they were unable to reconcile the Platt Amendment and the Teller Amendment. They argued about the word *pacification,* and they all agreed that Cuba had been properly pacified. The Cuban Constitutional Convention thus decided to debate the Platt Amendment.

On May 28, 1901, the Convention accepted the Platt Amendment by a vote of fifteen to fourteen, with two abstentions from Juan Rius Rivera and Antonio Bravo Correoso. A listing of the voting on this date follows.

Accepting the Amendment	*Against the Amendment*
José Miguel Gómez	José Luis Robau
Pedro González Llorente	José B. Alemán
Martín Morúa Delgado	José Lacret
J. J. Monteagudo	Rafael Portuondo

Gonzalo de Quesada
Leopoldo Berriel
Alejandro Rodríguez
Manuel Sanguily
Pedro Betancourt
Emilio Núñez
Diego Tamayo
Joaquín Quílez
Eliseo Giberga
Enrique Villuendas
Domingo Méndez Capote

Luis Fortún
Juan Gualberto Gómez
Rafael Menduley
Manuel R. Silva
José Fernández de Castro
José N. Ferrer
Eudaldo Tamayo
Alfredo Zayas Alfonso
Miguel Gener
Salvador Cisneros Betancourt

It was the smallest of victories for the United States, only a one vote difference. Unfortunately, the Cubans had made some very minor changes to the wording, and had added a section on trade. Wood was furious. He met with the Convention and told them that they could neither change nor add to nor delete from the exact wording of the Amendment, and if they failed to approve it in its exact format, the President would never withdraw the Army from Cuba.

On June 12, 1901, after renewed debate, the Convention again voted, but this time on the exact format of the Platt Amendment. The vote was sixteen in favor and eleven against. Juan Rius Rivera, Miguel Gener, José Luis Robau, and Antonio Bravo Correoso, all opposed to the Amendment absented themselves. Thus the Republic of Cuba agreed to be ruled by the Platt Amendment. A complete breakdown of the voting follows.

Accepting the Amendment
José Miguel Gómez
Pedro González Llorente
Martín Morúa Delgado
J. J. Monteagudo
Gonzalo de Quesada
Leopoldo Berriel
Alejandro Rodríguez
Manuel Sanguily
Pedro Betancourt
Emilio Núñez
Diego Tamayo
Joaquín Quílez
Eliseo Giberga
Enrique Villuendas
Domingo Méndez Capote
José N. Ferrer

Against the Amendment
Salvador Cisneros Betancourt
José B. Alemán
José Lacret
Rafael Portuondo
Luis Fortún
Juan Gualberto Gómez
Rafael Menduley
Manuel R. Silva
José Fernández de Castro
Alfredo Zayas Alfonso
Eudaldo Tamayo

Regarding Article VII of the Amendment, the United States took four bays for naval and coaling stations, including Guantánamo. The size of this land grant is 45 square miles and the rent is $2,000 per year, with no termination date and no price escalation clause.

Article VI, the ownership of the Isle of Pines, continued to be a source of irritation for many years. In 1907, the U.S. Supreme Court ruled that the Isle of Pines was Cuban territory, but it was only in 1925 that the U.S. Senate ratified Cuba's ownership of the Isle of Pines.

On September 14, 1901, McKinley died from an assassin's bullet and Roosevelt became President. The Cuban Constitutional Convention found Article III of the Platt Amendment to be the most offensive to Cuba's independence. Wood defended Article III by saying that it was intended to insure Cuba's independence. However, Wood was communicating just the opposite message to Washington. An example of the incredible level of deceit utilized by the McKinley administration to force the passage of the Platt Amendment by the Cuban Constitutional Convention is contained in an October 1901 private letter written by Leonard Wood to President Roosevelt. "There is, of course, little or no independence left [for] Cuba under the Platt Amendment."[26]

Edmund Morris, President Roosevelt's biographer, in his revealing book *Theodore Rex* states that Roosevelt was convinced that he personally had liberated Cuba from Spain. Roosevelt also intimated that he had a special love and responsibility for the island of Cuba. In this connection, during Roosevelt's first Cabinet meeting, on September 20, 1901, Roosevelt demanded "a timetable for the independence of Cuba."[27] It is difficult to understand why Roosevelt was pushing for a rapid resolution to the issue of Cuba's independence. In spite of rigging the electorate, pressuring the Cuban Constitutional Convention, and conducting a comprehensive marketing campaign in the Cuban media, the annexation of Cuba to the United States by popular demand had failed. It is possible that Roosevelt viewed the Platt Amendment as an instrument to control Cuba economically as well as politically. If that is the case, then it makes sense that Roosevelt wanted the Cuban *independence* to be formalized quickly so that American corporation could commence the economic takeover of the island.

President Roosevelt did not wait very long to implement his expansionist agenda. Within weeks of taking over following McKinley's assassination, "...he elicited charges of imperialist high-handedness by sponsoring a coup in Panama, guaranteeing the new government against Colombian intervention, and negotiating American control of a canal zone."[28]

With the Platt Amendment approved by the Cuban Constitutional Convention, having appended the amendment to the Cuban Constitution, Wood could now concentrate on being a good Cuba Military Governor, and he certainly did a lot for the Cuban people. He embarked on a program to reform Cuba with results of permanent importance such as improved sanitation, new roads, added telegraph wires, the creation of a public school system, overhaul of the judicial system, settlement of the claim by the Catholic Church for the land taken away from them by Spain, and perhaps most importantly, the attack on tropical diseases.

As improved sanitation bettered the health conditions of the island, yellow fever continued to kill. At the time, it was believed that yellow fever was a filth-generated disease. In 1901, at Wood's request, the Surgeon General of the Army authorized a Yellow Fever Commission to travel to Cuba.

This group's mission was to discover the causes of yellow fever. It was headed by Army Major Dr. Walter Reed, and included both Cuban and American doctors. A Cuban doctor of Scottish origin, Carlos Juan Finlay, was working with the group and explained his theory that the transmission of yellow fever required a vector. He further believed that the vector was the mosquito *Stegomyia fasciata* (later known as *Aedes aegypti*). After an exhaustive series of tests, Finlay's theory was found to be correct. The conquest of yellow fever was perhaps the most significant contribution of the American military occupation of Cuba. Finlay's discovery was called by Wood "worth the cost of the war."[29]

At Finlay's urgings, Dr. William C. Gorgas, U.S. health chief in Cuba, and an old friend of Wood's, began a program to exterminate the mosquito. This program was later extended to Panama, thus saving many lives during the construction of the Panama Canal. Historian Hugh Thomas adds, "Carlos Finlay (1833-1915) has never really been given the credit in North America for what was, all things considered, a major contribution in this field."[30]

On April 11, 1902, a report on the Philippines was published by the Anti-Imperialist League which included information on atrocities committed by the U.S. occupation forces, including the slaughter of Filipino boys. War Secretary Elihu Root immediately became the target of the U.S. media, which clamored for his resignation. Later, General Jacob H. Smith disclosed that the accusations were true. This made the situation unbearable for Root, who in order to get out of Washington traveled to Havana to negotiate the final details of Cuban independence. In spite of the relentless criticism, Root refused to resign.[31]

Cuba had been properly pacified and the United States could no longer find excuses for continuing the military occupation. The time had come to remove the troops from Cuban soil and attempt to run the affairs of the island nation from Washington and from the U.S. Embassy in Havana. Leonard Wood was to prepare the transfer of power.

Notes

1. Healy, *United States in Cuba (1898-1902)*, 39–40.
2. Thomas, *Cuba or the Pursuit of Freedom*, 420.
3. Ibid., 421–22.
4. Quoted by Thomas, *Cuba or the Pursuit of Freedom*, 437, from Edwin F. Atkins, *Sixty Years in Cuba* (Cambridge, MA: Riverside Press, 1926), 303.
5. Healy, *United States in Cuba (1898-1902)*, 54.
6. Quoted by Healy, *United States in Cuba (1898-1902)*, 70–71, from Letter from Domingo Méndez Capote to José Miguel Gómez and others, printed in *Actas de las Asambleas de Representantes*, vol. 5, Havana, February 14, 1899, 35.
7. Healy, *United States in Cuba (1898-1902)*, 124.
8. Thomas, *Cuba or the Pursuit of Freedom*, 444–45.
9. Healy, *United States in Cuba (1898-1902)*, 130–31.
10. Ibid., 132.
11. Quoted by Healy, *United States in Cuba (1898-1902)*, 133, from Records from the 56th Cong., 1st Sess., *Senate Document 177* and *Congressional Record*, 1287, 4696, Washington, DC.
12. Healy, *United States in Cuba (1898-1902)*, 135–37.
13. Thomas, *Cuba or the Pursuit of Freedom*, 421, 445–46.
14. Healy, *United States in Cuba (1898-1902)*, 143–46.
15. Thomas, *Cuba or the Pursuit of Freedom*, 448–50.
16. Healy, *United States in Cuba (1898-1902)*, 145.
17. Ibid., 150–51. Quotation in mid-paragraph from *Annual Reports of the Secretary of War*, 1899–1903, 109.
18. Platt to Root, February 5, 1901, *Leonard Wood Papers*, Library of Congress, Washington, DC.
19. Thomas, *Cuba or the Pursuit of Freedom*, 448–52.
20. Bacon, Robert, ed., *Elihu Root, Military and Colonial Policy of the United States* (Cambridge, MA: Harvard University Press, 1916), 172–73.
21. Healy, *United States in Cuba (1898-1902)*, 157–59.
22. Gómez, *Por Cuba Libre*, 105–11.
23. Healy, *United States in Cuba (1898-1902)*, 162–67.
24. Jaime Suchlicki, *Cuba from Columbus to Castro* (Washington, DC: Brassey's, 1990), 81–84.
25. Gómez, *Por Cuba Libre*, 108.

26. Letter from Wood to Roosevelt, October 28, 1901, copy in *Leonard Wood Papers*, Library of Congress, Washington, DC.
27. Edmund Morris, *Theodore Rex* (New York: Random House, 2001), 42.
28. Brands, *Selected Letters of Theodore Roosevelt*, 265.
29. Hagedorn, *Leonard Wood*, 324–28.
30. Thomas, *Cuba or the Pursuit of Freedom*, 461.
31. Morris, *Theodore Rex*, 99–104.

16

Cuba's Constrained Independence

Leonard Wood scheduled the Cuban presidential election for December 31, 1902. Máximo Gómez refused to run and said: "men of war for war, and those of peace for peace."[1] Gómez backed Tomás Estrada Palma, the candidate of the National Party, as did most members of the Cuban Constitutional Convention. Bartolomé Masó, the candidate for the Democratic Party, campaigned for the presidency, but a few weeks before the election withdrew his candidacy, even though he had strong popular support in eastern Cuba.

At around noon on May 20, 1902, at Havana's Palacio del Gobernador, Leonard Wood transferred the government and control of the island to President Tomás Estrada Palma who became the first constitutionally elected Cuban president. Estrada Palma served in the Ten Year War and had been appointed President of the Cuban Provisional Government in 1876. In May 1895, Estrada Palma had been named Minister Plenipotentiary of the Cuban Junta in New York. From this post, he carried negotiations with the United States, raised funds for the war effort, and promoted the cause of Cuban freedom. At the end of 1896, Estrada Palma resigned his position in the Junta, and began running a private Quaker school in upstate New York.[2]

Cuba had ceased to be a European colony, at least in name, in 1898. The Platt Amendment would insure U.S. domination of the Cuban economy for at least three decades. Cuba rapidly became a de facto U.S. colony as U.S. corporations gained control of most sectors of the Cuban economy and political life.[3]

The presidency of Tomás Estrada Palma (May 20, 1902–September 1906) was marked by honesty and fiscal conservativeness. Unfortunately, he was to head the first and last honest Cuban government. Under the Platt Amendment, four bays awarded to the U.S. Navy for coaling stations: Guantánamo, Bahía Honda, Nipe, and Cienfuegos. Estrada Palma managed to cut the United States back to only two: Guantánamo and Bahía Honda.

On January 8, 1903, President Roosevelt held the annual Diplomatic Reception. The presence of Gonzalo de Quesada, Minister of Cuba, reminded the President that the Cuban trade reciprocity treaty was still a draft protocol. On December 13, 1903, the Senate approved Cuban trade reciprocity by a vote of 57 to 8.[4]

The 1906 Cuba elections were conducted under tranquil conditions. The incumbent, Estrada Palma, identified as a moderate, was seeking a second term. The candidate for the liberals was General José Miguel Gómez. Estrada Palma won the elections by a landslide. Gómez, realizing that Estrada Palma was heading for a second term in office, claimed that the elections were rigged.

General José Miguel Gómez was born in 1858 in Sancti Spíritus, Province of Las Villas in central Cuba. He participated in the Ten Year War as well as in the Guerra Chiquita. He joined the Independence War in 1895 and rose to the rank of General. After the war, José Miguel Gómez became a member of the Cuban Assembly, was appointed governor of Santa Clara, and participated in the Constitutional Convention, which drafted Cuba's first constitution. During his tenure in the Constitutional Convention, he was the most vocal advocate for the approval of the Platt Amendment.

José Miguel Gómez was a very likeable individual, but also very crafty, Machiavellian, and did not like losing at anything. On or around August 17, 1906, he started a revolution called the *Guerrita de Agosto*, or August's Small War.

On September 3, 1906, while watching a display of the Navy's newest ships, Roosevelt faced the reality that because of August's Small War some of these ships might soon be required for active duty in Cuba.[5]

Since Cuba's army had been disbanded by the United States, Estrada Palma asked the United States for help in putting down the insurrection. Estrada Palma explained that having only a small cadre of Rural Guards scattered throughout the island, he had to choose between protecting American property and fighting against the José Miguel Gómez's rebels. While he waited for a reply from the United States, Estrada Palma instructed his scant military to concentrate on protecting American life and property. At the same time, José Miguel Gómez erroneously invoked the Platt Amendment and asked for immediate American intervention.

Cuba was neither being invaded by a foreign power (Article I of the Platt Amendment), nor were U.S. interests threatened (Article III) since Estrada Palma's army was protecting U.S. interests in Cuba. Therefore, the Platt Amendment could not be used as an excuse for intervention, unless Roosevelt believed that the Platt Amendment had made Cuba an American protectorate and that Cuba had become unable to govern itself.

On September 8, 1906, Roosevelt authorized the dispatch of two warships to Cuba. Upon learning of Roosevelt's action, Assistant Secretary of State Robert Bacon warned the President that "intervention should be considered a very serious thing and that he should be certain that the Cuban government was indeed helpless."[6]

The situation in Cuba was quite upsetting to the Roosevelt administration. The following paragraph is from a letter Roosevelt wrote to his friend Henry White on September 13, 1906. "Just at the moment I am so angry with that infernal little Cuban republic that I would like to wipe its people off the face of the earth."[7]

Contrary to Roosevelt's instructions, Secretary Bacon authorized the landing of a party of 5,600 Marines in Cuba. Furiously, Roosevelt cabled that U.S. forces were there only to protect American life and property. Roosevelt made a final appeal to both Cuban factions to end their differences and find a peaceful solution, thus avoiding foreign interference. Fighting continued, and on September 20, 1906, Roosevelt authorized Secretary of War William Taft to militarily intervene in Cuba.

Senator Joseph B. Foraker severely admonished President Roosevelt over having unilaterally taken action on Cuba. According to the Platt Amendment, if the United States was authorized to intervene in Cuba, this action was only within the province of Congress. Additionally, congressional approval was required before troops could be sent. Roosevelt ignored Foraker.[8]

It is generally believed that Estrada Palma asked for U.S. intervention. This is not correct, Estrada Palma asked the United States for help to end an insurrection, and instead he was threatened with U.S. intervention. José Miguel Gómez, who had little to lose and a great deal to gain, did ask for intervention. Estrada Palma insisted that he was the duly-elected President, and that he was willing to accept full American control, but refused any power-sharing with Gomez's faction. Taft issued a declaration of intervention by the United States. He added that Cuba would be governed in accordance to the Cuban Constitution and under the Cuban flag. José Miguel Gómez's forces agreed to cease insurrectionary activities only if a new free and legal election would be conducted. In fact, he was asking the United States to nullify the results of a Cuban election which had been lawfully conducted.

Estrada Palma was incensed. He asked the United States for help in putting down an insurrection. Instead, the United States sent Marines to Cuba and started a second intervention that would last for close to four years. This was not the type of help that Estrada Palma had in mind; therefore, he, along with his Vice President Méndez Capote and the entire Cabinet, resigned on September 29, 1906. President Roosevelt took back the reins of power in Cuba in October 1906, where he had left them in 1902.

William Howard Taft was temporary governor for a few days and then appointed the domineering Charles E. Magoon as Provisional Governor of Cuba. Roosevelt insisted that the *second Cuban independence* take place before he left office. Cuba was returned to self-government on January 29, 1909. The 1909 presidential election was won by General José Miguel Gómez, with Alfredo Zayas as his vice president. Roosevelt left office on March 4, 1909.

Magoon was uncouth, greedy, and authoritarian. Cubans who knew him disliked him. Since he was the absolute ruler, corruption could not be proven by Cubans, and was never investigated by U.S. authorities. Prior to his departure, he signed a number of lucrative Cuban contracts with U.S. firms. Kickbacks were suspected. Upon his return to the United States, Magoon was given a commendation by President Taft for his Cuba service.

The second American intervention is a watershed event in Cuban history and politics. The Platt Amendment was no longer a harmless long-forgotten footnote to the U.S.' declaration of war on Spain. It was a weapon of mass destruction which could be used at any time and under any pretext to keep Cuban governments in line. José Miguel Gómez played his hand well and he won the jackpot.

The presidency of General José Miguel Gómez (January 1909–1913) initiated a concatenation of organized graft administrations, ostensibly with the tacit approval of the United States. The situation during the José Miguel Gómez presidency can best be explained with a bit of Cuban folklore. The nickname given to José Miguel Gómez by the people was *Tiburón*, or Shark. In order to describe the subtleties of organized corruption, the Cuban people composed the expression: *Tiburón se baña pero salpica*. A translation without explanation would probably have no meaning, but it would be "Shark goes swimming, but makes a nice splash." Going swimming pertains to skimming funds, and the splashing has to do with sharing some of the ill-obtained funds with his friends and supporters.[9]

In 1912, Gómez negotiated with the United States and exchanged the Bahía Honda naval station for a larger track of land in Guantánamo. The first twenty-five or so years of the Republic of Cuba were marked by the constant fear of further U.S. interventions. Even though the second interventionist forces were withdrawn from the island on January 28, 1909, in conjunction with the inauguration of President José Miguel Gómez, the Platt Amendment gave the United States the right to militarily occupy the island to defend its independence, as well as any American property. This prompted University of Miami historian Jaime Suchlicki to refer to Cuba, during this timeframe, as *The Platt Amendment Republic*.[10]

The United States continued to pull strings to select presidential candidates who would protect U.S. business interests. The Platt Amendment became a source of suspicion for Cubans in particular and Latin Americans in general, about the true intentions of the United States in regards to Cuba.

The third President of the Republic of Cuba was General Mario García Menocal (1913–1921). His vice presidents were Enrique José Varona during the first term, and Emilio Núñez during the second term. García Menocal was born in Jagüey Grande, Matanzas Province in 1866, was educated in the United States from age thirteen and graduated from Cornell University in 1888 with an engineering degree. He worked for a French company on the study to construct the Nicaragua Canal, and in 1895 joined the forces of Máximo Gómez in the War of Independence. With his engineering knowledge, he organized and commanded a field artillery unit which, together with the forces of Calixto García, took Victoria de las Tunas. In 1898, during the first American intervention, he became Havana police chief and later built and managed the Chaparra Sugar Mill, owned by the Cuban-American Sugar Company. His first election was fraudulent, but his presidency was constructive. He regulated the Public Treasury, reorganized the Army and Navy, supported business and agriculture, and strengthened relations with the United States. In fact, he authorized Cuba's declaration of war against Germany on April 7, 1917, one day after the U.S.' war declaration. García Menocal was actually defeated in the election for his second term. Strangely enough, a month later he announced that he had won. His two-term presidency was noted for the escalation of corruption and graft.

Alfredo Zayas (1921–1925) followed Menocal as the fourth Cuban president. His vice president was Francisco Carrillo. Zayas was a lawyer and a poet, as opposed to most Cuban presidents, who were military men. He was born in Havana in 1861 and because of his open support of Cuban independence, was arrested and sent to prison in Ceuta, a Spanish enclave in Morocco. While in prison, he wrote some of his best poetry. During the first American occupation, Zayas became acting mayor of Havana. As a member of the Constitutional Convention, he was one of the most active opponents of the Platt Amendment. When he took office in 1921, Cuba was on its way to bankruptcy as sugar prices had crashed from twenty-two to three cents per pound. His government was not honest, but it was less corrupt than prior and succeeding administrations. He reduced expenses by lowering the salaries of all civilian and military government employees, obtained a $50 million loan from J. P. Morgan to tie the country over during the financial storm, and started the process to give the vote to Cuban women. The bright spot of Zayas' presidency was his ability to negotiate the ratification by the U.S. Senate of Cuban ownership of the Isle of Pines. The United States had been the de facto owner of this large Cuban island since the end of the 1898 Cuban-Spanish-American War.

General Gerardo Machado (1925–1933), a close friend of *Tiburón* Gómez, was born in 1871 in Santa Clara, central Cuba. A man of humble beginnings, Machado became a butcher in Camajuaní and as a consequence of his trade his left hand only had three fingers. Before the independence war, Machado and his father had been cattle thieves. He joined the War of Independence in central Cuba and became one of the youngest generals in the Cuban Liberation Army. During the first American occupation, Machado was appointed mayor of Santa Clara. Shortly after taking office, a mysterious fire destroyed the court house which contained his criminal records.[11]

With the support of outgoing President Zayas, Machado won the 1924 presidential election, thus becoming Cuba's fifth president, with Carlos de la Rosa as his vice president.

American corporations had been buying Cuban property and businesses and building factories in Cuba since the first American occupation in 1899. During the Machado presidency, Cuban legislators became concerned that soon the entire Cuban economy would be in foreign hands. In this connection, the Customs-Tariff Law of 1927 was enacted to promote Cuban-owned industry. The opposite occurred, as North American corporations started producing in Cuba the goods protected by the 1927 law. Some companies taking advantage of this law were: Armour, Colgate-Palmolive, Fleischmann, Mennen, Owens Illinois, and Procter & Gamble.

The United States expanded its control of Cuban property and production exponentially and thus controlled almost every segment of the Cuban economy. The mining industry, including the highly profitable nickel and manganese deposits, was mostly in U.S. hands. Basically all utilities, including electricity, telephone, and water, were controlled by U.S. companies. Most banking institutions were either American-owned or controlled. U.S. companies owned significant portions of the sugar and tobacco industries, and practically controlled the entire cattle business.

At the end of his first term as president (1929), Machado set out to amend the constitution by first abolishing the vice presidency, and then arranging his appointment to a new six-year term to run from May 20, 1929 until May 20, 1935, an action which gives Machado the dubious honor of becoming Cuba's first dictator. This abuse of power served to unite the opposition and bring about popular unrest, particularly from the students at Havana University. Machado responded by closing the University.

The revolutionary students were joined by the University faculty, intellectuals, and the professional middle class. Many student leaders and intellectuals were assassinated or forced into exile. In April 1933, President Franklin D. Roosevelt (1933–1945) sent his personal friend, Ambassador Benjamin Sumner Welles, to the island as special envoy to find a peaceful solution to the political situation in Cuba. Welles, from his position of immense power, negotiated with the Cuban army, who were staunch Machado supporters, with the surprising result that Welles convinced Machado to resign. Machado left the country on August 12, 1933.

Carlos Manuel de Céspedes (August 1933–September 1933), son of the Father of the Country, was designated by the Cuban army and Welles to succeed Machado, thus becoming, by appointment, Cuba's sixth president. He voided the Machado 1928 constitution and restored the 1901 constitution. But the students would not accept a leader appointed by the United States and the Cuban army, and the rebellion continued. On September 4, 1933, Fulgencio Batista Zaldívar, an army Sergeant, led a revolt against the officers, and took control of the Cuban armed forces.

Batista was born in 1901 in Banes, Oriente Province. Hailing from a poor farming family, Batista worked at a variety of jobs until he joined the army in 1921. He was a sergeant stenographer at army HQ, Camp Columbia near Havana. It is generally believed that Ambassador Welles invited Batista to rule.

The students met with the new strong man Batista and agreed that Céspedes would be replaced by a *Pentarquía* (a five-person civilian committee) composed of: Dr. Ramón Grau San Martín, Porfirio Franco, José Miguel Irisarri, Sergio Carbó, and Guillermo Portela. The Roosevelt administration refused to recognize the *Pentarquía* and rushed Navy vessels to Cuba. After ruling for less than two weeks, Batista and the students appointed Dr. Ramón Grau San Martín as Provisional President. Thus Grau became Cuba's seventh president, also by appointment.

By early January 1934, it became clear that the Grau administration did not have a chance to succeed. On January 16, 1934, now self-appointed Army Chief Fulgencio Batista Zaldívar, forced Grau to resign, who went into exile in Mexico, and appointed engineer Carlos Hevia to the Presidency. Hevia became the eighth in Cuba's revolving door presidency. After a two-day rule by Hevia, Batista appointed Colonel Carlos Mendieta (January 1934–May 1936) as Provisional President. Mendieta was Cuba's ninth president. The United States recognized the Mendieta government after five days. It became clear to all Cubans that after the Sergeant's revolt of 1933, Batista had become the strong man and that he was ruling the destiny of the island-nation.

During the Mendieta mandate, the detestable Platt Amendment was partially abrogated. In the May 28, 1934 Agreement between the United States and Cuba, the right to intervention was deleted, but the *permanent* lease of Guantánamo Bay was conspicuously retained.

The Cuban government, now openly ruled by the military, returned to its normal corrupt ways. On the positive side, after more than three years without classes, Havana University was reopened in early 1934.

Fulgencio Batista, with the support of the United States, maintained control of Cuba through a succession of puppet presidents: Miguel Mariano Gómez, the son of José Miguel Gómez (tenth president May 1936–December 1936); Jose Antonio Barnet (eleventh president December 12, 1936–December 24, 1936); and Federico Laredo Brú (twelfth president 1936–1940). In early 1940, President Laredo Brú allowed exiles to return and prepared the country to accept the newly drafted 1940 Constitution, as well as general elections. Grau was a strong candidate, but as the people appeared quite happy with the new constitution, Batista (1940–1944) was elected as Cuba's thirteenth president, and the first president under the 1940 Constitution.

Batista worked closely with the United States during World War II, having declared war on Germany in 1941. Batista's first government, other than condoning and participating in the normal Cuban corruption, was generally good. He worked closely with labor unions, then run by the Cuban Communist party, and promoted racial equality and civil rights for women. Batista worked all sides to his benefit, but he knew that his main job was to keep the United States happy.

Dr. Ramón Grau San Martín (1944–1948) was the winner in the next election, defeating Batista's appointed candidate Carlos Saladrigas Zayas. Grau was the fourteenth Cuban president in what would be a short-lived return to democracy. He was anticommunist, and expelled the left-leaning labor leaders who had been appointed by Batista to key government jobs and had also gained control of trade unions. Grau supported his *protégé* Dr. Carlos Prío Socarrás (1948–1952) who won the next general election, thus becoming Cuba's fifteenth president.

A new political, *Ortodoxo*, party had won the Cuban hearts, through the oratory of its leader Eduardo Chibás, who in his Sunday radio address tried to expose the corruption of the Prío administration. One of Chibás' admirers was a young law student by the name of Fidel Castro. In August 1951, at the end of one of his radio diatribes, Chibás shot himself. Chibás has promised to present evidence that one of Prío's key Cabinet members was a crook, but Chibás was unable to obtain the evidence and instead took his own life. This suicide, coupled with the fact that Batista knew he could not win the elections scheduled for June 1952, facilitated Batista's *coup d'etat* on March 10, 1952. Batista, constantly vowing that he was an anticommunist leader, won the full support of the U.S. government. He became Cuba's self-appointed sixteenth president and dictator for the second time.

March 10, 1952 was the last day that Cuba had a government freely elected by the Cuban people. Arthur M. Schlesinger quotes Carlos Prío, as having said, "They say that I was a terrible president of Cuba. That may be true. But I was the best president Cuba ever had."[12] Dr. Carlos Prío Socarrás may not have been the best president Cuba ever had, but was certainly the last democratically elected president.

While the United States looked the other way, Batista invited the U.S. Mafia to enter Cuba, and allowed them to run Cuba's gambling and prostitution rackets. Batista, wanting to make sure he outdid *Tiburón*, became a killer whale. The Cuban middle class was deeply disturbed by the direction in which Batista was leading Cuba. Conspiracies commenced immediately, and many students and intellectuals were killed or forced into exile.

Fidel Castro, incensed that anyone would take power without democratic elections, organized an attack on the Moncada military barracks in Santiago de Cuba, which took place on July 26, 1953. The attack and conspiracy were a failure. Many men were killed, and Castro was captured and sent to prison. Faced with mounting opposition, Batista nonetheless insisted on staying in power until his term expired in 1958.

Fidel Castro, his brother Raúl, and eighteen followers were released early from prison on May 15, 1955. Castro traveled to the United States to collect money from anti-Batista Cuban exiles for his *26 de Julio* revolutionary organization, named after the date of his ill-fated attack on Moncada. Castro then went to Mexico to prepare an expeditionary force to invade Cuba, with the support of José Antonio Echeverría, the well known and powerful president of the University of Havana students association.

Castro, his brother Raúl, a young Argentinian physician by the name of Ernesto "Che" Guevara, and some eighty other combatants, landed in Oriente Province on December 2, 1956. Batista suspended constitutional guarantees, and urged the army to battle the revolutionaries. Dictator Batista was too busy with his planning of the November 1958 elections to worry about the reality of the Cuban political situation.

The army refused to fight against the insurgents, and this paved the way for Castro's triumph. Batista and his closest supporters fled to the Dominican Republic at the end of the 1958 traditional New Year's Eve party, and Fidel Castro quickly moved in to fill the power vacuum. More than fifty-one years later, the Castro brothers still rule Cuba without democratic elections.

Castro used his knowledge of Cuban, American, and world history to highlight to the Cuban people what he considered to be imperialistic moves by the United States. This helped him to cement his power. It was easy to convince the Cuban people that the United States wanted to own Cuba, especially since for more then 150 years, they did. While consolidating his power, Castro pretended to be a moderate, and allowed his close aides, such as his brother Raúl and Che Guevara, to play the extremist role.

Back in 1901, when he was fighting against the Platt Amendment, Juan Gualberto Gómez predicted that because of this Amendment, forcibly imposed as an appendix to the Cuban Constitution, Cuban governments would be weak by design. He further predicted that the main function of Cuban governments under the Platt Amendment would be to please Washington, and as such, Cuba would be run by the President of the United States, the State Department, the U.S. Embassy in Havana, and American financial interests. The United States would also run the Cuban government through trusts, monopoly of public service companies, loans, land grants, and other U.S. interests.

Juan Gualberto Gómez, the clear-thinking patriot, predicted the future of Cuba with frightening accuracy. What he failed to predict was the effect that having weak governments and being controlled by foreign economic interests would have on the future of the island nation. Did these weak governments pave the way for a Fidel Castro to emerge as Cuba's ruler? Did the American control of Cuba's economy and politics create a propitious environment for a Fidel Castro to take over the Cuban government by professing to be anti-American?

In fact, even governments not wanted by the Cuban people were imposed on them by American interests. Three examples are the governments of Menocal, Machado, and Batista. It is unfair to imply that all of Cuba's problems were created by the United States. The United States was instrumental in the final and decisive defeat of Spain, and Cubans are grateful for that.

The problem started when the forces of U.S. expansionism, early twentieth-century Manifest Destiny, and worries about the Central America Canal centered against Cuban independence. Cubans were the architects of their own problems. Had Cuba had an opportunity to have democratically elected strong governments, it is unlikely that a Fidel Castro and a few other bandits would have taken over the government. Without Castro, the United States would not have had a Bay of Pigs, no Cuban Missile Crisis, no Congo, no Angola, and countless other U.S. operations to preserve democracy and order in the world.

In the early days of the Castro regime, Castro, while consolidating his power, spoke repeatedly about the Platt Amendment, the U.S.' stranglehold on the Cuban economy, and the imposition of undesirable Cuban governments by the United States. Castro managed to convince a large percentage of the population that the only way for Cuba to be truly free was to break the umbilical cord tying her to the United States. And to a large extent, he was successful. Castro used historical truths from the past to sell to the Cuban people his personal lies about the future.

In her insightful book *Cuba and Castro*, Cuban-American writer Teresa Casuso, a former supporter of the Castro regime, agonizes over the Cuban-Spanish-American War, the U.S. military interventions of Cuba, and the first sixty years of Cuba's *independence*. She comes close to stating that what the Americans had done in 1898 gave rise to conditions propitious for a Fidel Castro to seize and control the destinies of the island-nation.[13]

Can we blame all that on the Platt Amendment? Or should we instead blame a small group of aggressive American expansionists who encouraged territorial growth during the 1890–1910 timeframe to the detriment of Cuban independence? On the other hand, perhaps we should believe that Gen. William Shafter was correct when he affirmed that possibly due to some intractable genetic aberration (obviously black-bean-induced), Cubans are nor capable of self-government.

The arithmetic of Cuban independence is not complicated. Cuba was under Spanish domination for four centuries. This was followed by a half century of independence constrained by U.S. interests and another half century of enslavement by the Castro brothers. It is self-evident that independence constrained by the United States is better than domination by Spain and infinitely better than being under the communist yoke.

Nevertheless, Cubans living in Cuba as well as abroad still wait for the day that Cuba will be free and truly independent.

Notes

1. Thomas, *Cuba or the Pursuit of Freedom*, 459.
2. Ibid., 314.
3. Louis A. Pérez, *Cuba Under the Platt Amendment, 1902-1934* (Pittsburgh, PA: University of Pittsburgh Press, 1986), 336.
4. Morris, *Theodore Rex*, 197, 305.
5. Ibid., 456.
6. Ibid.
7. Theodore Roosevelt, *Letters*, vol. 5, 401.
8. Morris, *Theodore Rex*, 459.
9. Thomas, *Cuba or the Pursuit of Freedom*, 504.
10. Jaime Suchlicki, *Cuba from Columbus to Castro* (New York: Brassy's, 1990), 87.
11. Thomas, *Cuba or the Pursuit of Freedom*, 569.
12. Arthur M. Schlesinger, *A Thousand Days: John F. Kennedy in the White House* (New York: Houghton Mifflin, 2002), 216.
13. Teresa Casuso, *Cuba and Castro*, trans. Elmer Grossberg (New York: Random, 1961), 43–49.

Timetables

U.S. Attempts to Acquire Cuba—Chapter 1

Approximate Date	Event
1808	President Jefferson proposed to Cuba's Captain-General to purchase the island. Negotiations failed
1808	Cuba's *No transfer policy* of Cuba stated by Jefferson and later formalized by Monroe
December 2, 1823	Monroe asked John Quincy Adams to draft a message to Congress–Monroe Doctrine
July 6, 1847	John O'Sullivan wrote to S of S Buchanan that wealthy Cubans would contribute to the purchase of Cuba by the United States
May 30, 1848	President Polk offered Spain $100 million for Cuba. Negotiations failed
May 19, 1850	U.S.-sponsored annexationist invasion by Narciso López failed
April 3, 1854	President Pierce offered Spain $130 million for Cuba, negotiation failed
October 11, 1854	Ostend Manifesto is drafted
July 21, 1869	President Grant offered Spain $100 million to exit Cuba. Spain did not reply
August 1897	U.S. Bankers Samuel Janney and John McCook offered to purchase Cuba. Spain did not take this proposal seriously
February 1898	President McKinley offered to pay $300 million for Cuba. Regent Christina did not reply

Expanding the U.S. Nation—Chapters 2–6

Approximate Date	Event
July 4, 1776	Declaration of independence, thirteen original colonies
1783	Treaty of Paris: Britain recognized sovereignty of the United States, thirteen original states
March 4, 1791	Vermont joined Union, land from New York and New Hampshire
June 1, 1792	Kentucky joined with consent from Virginia
June 1, 1796	Tennessee joined from land donated by North Carolina
1801	President Jefferson's first attempt to purchase Louisiana fails
March 1, 1803	Ohio joined from land donated by Pennsylvania, New York, Virginia, and other states
May 2, 1803	Louisiana Purchase Agreement was executed
December 20, 1803	The United States took physical possession of Louisiana Territory
Summer 1804	Lewis & Clark expedition departed St. Louis
September 1806	Lewis & Clark expedition returned to St. Louis
September 23, 1810	West Florida settlers rebelled against Spanish rule
October 27, 1810	President Madison annexed West Florida by proclamation
April 30, 1812	Louisiana joined-land from Louisiana Purchase and annexation of West Florida
December 11, 1816	Indiana joined-land from Northwest Territory
December 10, 1817	Mississippi joined-land donated by Georgia
May 28, 1818	Spanish surrendered Fort Barrancas to Andrew Jackson
December 3, 1818	Illinois joined-land from Northwest Territory

February 22, 1819	Adams-Onís Treaty for the purchase of East and West Florida was proclaimed
December 14, 1819	Alabama joined-land from Mississippi Territory
March 15, 1820	Maine joined-land from Massachusetts
February 24, 1821	Pacto de Iguala established Mexico as a nation
August 10, 1821	Missouri joined-land from Louisiana Purchase
1823	Christian Doctrine of Discovery was incorporated into the U.S. legal system
March 6, 1836	Battle of The Alamo
June 15, 1836	Arkansas joined-land from Louisiana Purchase
January 26, 1837	Michigan joined-land from Northwest Territory
March 3, 1845	Florida joined-land from purchase of East Florida
July 1845	First known use of the term Manifest Destiny by John L. O'Sullivan
December 29, 1845	Texas joined-land partially from Louisiana Purchase and to be taken during U.S.-Mexico War
May 13, 1846	U.S. Congress declared war on Mexico
June 15, 1846	Great Britain accepted that Washington, Oregon, and Idaho are part of U.S. territory
December 28, 1846	Iowa joined-land from Louisiana Purchase
September 17, 1847	Mexico surrenders
February 2, 1848	Treaty of Guadalupe Hidalgo was signed
May 29, 1848	Wisconsin joined-land from Northwest Territory
September 9, 1850	California joined-land from U.S.-Mexico War
June 24, 1853	Gadsden Treaty was signed
May 11, 1858	Minnesota joined-land from Northwest Territory and Louisiana Purchase
February 14, 1859	Oregon joined-land from Florida Purchase and cession from Great Britain

January 29, 1861	Kansas joined-land from Louisiana Purchase
April 12, 1861	U.S. Civil War commenced
June 20, 1863	West Virginia joined-land from Virginia with questionable consent
October 31, 1864	Nevada joined-land from U.S.-Mexico War
April 9, 1865	U.S. Civil War ended
March 1, 1867	Nebraska joined-land from Louisiana Purchase
March 14, 1867	Alaska Purchase negotiations commenced
July 27, 1868	President Johnson signed Alaska Purchase into law
August 1, 1876	Colorado joined-land from Louisiana Purchase and U.S.-Mexico War
November 2, 1889	North Dakota-land from Louisiana Purchase, recognized by Spain after Florida Purchase
November 2, 1889	South Dakota-land from Louisiana Purchase, recognized by Spain after Florida Purchase
November 8, 1889	Montana-land from Louisiana Purchase, recognized by Spain after Florida Purchase
November 11, 1889	Washington-land from Louisiana Purchase, recognized by Spain after Florida Purchase and cession from Great Britain
July 3, 1890	Idaho-land from Florida Purchase and cession from Great Britain
July 10, 1890	Wyoming-land from Louisiana Purchase and U.S.- Mexico War
January 4, 1896	Utah-land from U.S.-Mexico War
July 7, 1898	President McKinley signed joint resolution to annex Hawaii
November 16, 1907	Oklahoma-land from Louisiana Purchase and U.S.-Mexico War
January 6, 1912	New Mexico-land from U.S.-Mexico War and Gadsden Purchase

February 14, 1912	Arizona-land from U.S.-Mexico War and Gadsden Purchase
January 3, 1959	Alaska-land purchase from Russia
August 21, 1959	Hawaii-was annexed by the United States

The Spanish Empire Disintegrates—Chapters 7–9

1806	Independence movement started in Venezuela
September 16, 1810	Mexico declared its independence
May 14, 1811	Paraguay proclaimed its independence
August 6, 1813	Bolívar took Caracas
1814	Chile declared its independence
June 1815	Bolívar defeated
July 9, 1816	Argentina, Paraguay, and Uruguay declared independence
1817	Bolívar took Ciudad Bolívar, Venezuela
February 12, 1818	Chile became independent
February 1819	Venezuela, Colombia (+Panamá), and Ecuador proclaimed independence
January 1, 1820	Ferdinand VII accepted 1812 Constitution
July 28, 1821	Peru proclaimed its independence
September 15, 1821	Costa Rica, El Salvador, Guatemala, Honduras, and Nicaragua declared independence
May 24, 1822	Ecuador was liberated from Spain
August 6, 1825	Bolivia became independent
1828	Uruguay became an independent country
1833	First Carlist War started
1839	First Carlist War ended
1840	General Baldomero Espartero became regent
1843	Espartero was overthrown by Ramón Narváez
1844	Isabella II was crowned
1846	Second Carlist War started
1849	Second Carlist War ended
March 3, 1865	Dominican Republic became independent

1868	Generals Serrano and Prim sent Isabella II into exile
1871	Prim was assassinated—Amadeus I was crowned
1872	Third Carlist War started
1874	Isabella's son was crowned Alfonso XII
1876	Third Carlist War ended
1885	Alfonso XII died and his widow Christina of Austria was crowned
1893	Práxedes Sagasta Escolar became Prime Minister
1895	Antonio Cánovas del Castillo became Prime Minister
1897	Cánovas del Castillo was murdered

Cubans Fight for Independence—Chapters 10–12

1795	Nicolás Morales conspiracy
1809	Román de la Luz and Joaquín Infante conspiracy
1810	Unnamed conspiracy of Afro-Cubans and Freemasons
1812	José Antonio Aponte conspiracy
1836	Dr. Richard Madden appointed British Consul
1840	David Turnbull replaced Madden
March 27, 1843	Insurrection of *La Escalera* started in Cárdenas
November 1843	*La Negra Carlota* uprising
October 10, 1868	Ten Year War started by Carlos Manuel de Cáspedes at Yara, Oriente Province
Early 1867	Captain-General Lersundi recruited *voluntarios*
August 14, 1867	Cuban National Anthem composed by Pedro Figueredo at Bayamo
First half 1869	Antonio Maceo and U.S. General Thomas Jordan joined rebels
February 1870	Jordan resigned and returned to the United States
May 11, 1873	Ignacio Agramonte killed at Jimaguayú
March 1874	Carlos Manuel de Céspedes killed

November 27, 1871	Eight medical students executed by *voluntarios*
October 31, 1873	*USS Virginius* was captured
Mid-1877	Tomás Estrada Palma captured and exiled
February 1878	Pact of Zanjón was concluded
March 1878	Maceo and Martínez Campos met at Baraguá
August 1879	The *Guerra Chiquita* (Small War) broke out
August 4, 1880	Calixto García captured in Bayamo
February 24, 1895	War of Independence started
March 25, 1895	Manifiesto de Montecristi signed by José Martí and Máximo Gómez
May 19, 1895	Martí killed at Dos Ríos
Christmas 1896	Maceo and Gómez outside Coliseo, Matanzas Province
Early January 1897	Antonio Maceo entered Pinar del Río Province
July 5, 1896	José Maceo killed in Oriente Province
October 1896	Gómez asked Maceo to join him in Las Villas
October 8, 1896	Weyler ordered *reconcentración* in Pinar del Río
December 7, 1896	Maceo and Panchito Gómez killed near Havana
August 8, 1897	P.M. Cánovas del Castillo assassinated
November 6, 1897	Captain-General Blanco offered Cuba's autonomy

Cuban Spanish American War—Chapters 13–16

Early 1896	Valeriano Weyler arrived in Cuba
June 1896	President Cleveland appointed Fitzhugh Lee as U.S. Consul to Cuba
December 1897	Lee requested a warship be deployed to Key West
January 25, 1898	*USS Maine* arrived in Havana harbor
February 15, 1898	The *Maine* exploded and sank
March 27, 1898	The United States delivered an ultimatum to Spain

April 21, 1898	President McKinley ordered blockade of Cuba's northern ports
April 23, 1898	U.S. Navy blockaded Cuba's ports
April 25, 1898	U.S. Congress declared war on Spain
May 1, 1898	Lt. Rowan delivered McKinley's message to García
May 4, 1898	Cuba's Captain-General Blanco attempted to get rebels to join him against Americans
May 19, 1898	Spanish fleet under Cervera entered Santiago
May 28, 1898	U.S. Navy blockaded Santiago Bay
June 3, 1898	*Merrimac* attempted to block Santiago harbor
June 14, 1898	Shafter's Army expedition sailed from Tampa
June 10, 1898	U.S. Marines and Cubans secure beachhead for coaling station at Guantánamo
June 20, 1898	Shafter and Sampson met at García's camp
June 22, 1898	U.S. forces landed at Daiquirí
June 24, 1898	Battle of Las Guásimas
July 1, 1898	Battles of El Caney and San Juan Hill
July 3, 1898	U.S. Navy destroys Spanish fleet
July 3, 1898	Escario's troops entered Santiago
July 6, 1898	U.S. prisoners from the Merrimac traded for Spanish taken at El Caney and San Juan Hill
July 14, 1898	Toral surrendered Santiago to Shafter
July 17, 1898	U.S. flag replaced Spanish flag at Santiago
August 12, 1898	War officially ended
April 11, 1899	Treaty of Paris was signed
Early September 1898	Leonard Wood became Governor of Oriente
September 22, 1898	General García allowed to enter Santiago as a *guest* of the United States
Late November 1898	Cuban Assembly travelled to Washington

December 11, 1898	Gen. García died in Washington
January 1, 1899	Gen. John Brooke became first U.S. Military Governor of Cuba
February 11, 1899	Gen. García's Cuban funeral
July 1899	Alger resigned and McKinley appointed Elihu Root as War Secretary
December 20, 1899	Gen. Leonard Wood became Cuba's second U.S. Military Governor
February 16, 1900	Wood appointed a commission to draft election law
June 16, 1900	Cuban municipal elections were held
July 25, 1900	Wood called for an election of delegates to a Cuban Constitutional Convention
November 5, 1900	Cuban Constitutional Convention First Meeting
February 9, 1901	Root sent to Wood outline of Platt Amendment
March 2, 1901	Wood presented concept of Platt Amendment to Cuban Constitutional Convention
April 24, 1901	Cuban commission discussed Platt Amendment with Root in Washington
May 28, 1901	Convention accepted Amendment with changes
June 12, 1901	Convention accepted Amendment w/o changes
September 14, 1901	McKinley assassinated—Roosevelt now President
December 31, 1902	First Cuban presidential election
May 20, 1902	Wood transferred government to newly elected President Tomás Estrada Palma
1903	Estrada Palma negotiated number of bays down to two (Bahía Honda and Guantánamo)
August 17, 1906	José Miguel Gómez started *Guerrita de Agosto* after losing to Estrada Palma
September 20, 1906	Roosevelt instructed Secretary of War Taft to militarily intervene in Cuba
September 29, 1906	Estrada Palma and entire Cabinet resigned

January 29, 1909	José Miguel Gómez became Cuba's second President
1912	Gómez exchanged Bahía Honda for a larger track at Guantánamo Bay
1913	Mario García Menocal elected Cuba's third President
April 7, 1917	Cuba declared war against Germany
1921	Alfredo Zayas became Cuba's fourth President
1925	Gerardo Machado became Cuba's fifth President and first dictator
August 12, 1933	Machado resigned and left the country
September 4, 1933	Sgt. Fulgencio Batista Zaldívar took control of armed forces (Sergeant's Revolt) and became Cuba's second dictator
October 1933	Dr. Ramón Grau San Martín appointed President by Batista and University students
January 16, 1934	Batista forced Grau to resign and appointed Carlos Mendieta as Provisional President
May 28, 1934	Partial abrogation of Platt Amendment with the lease on Guantánamo becoming permanent
1941	Cuba declared war on Germany
1944	Dr. Ramón Grau San Martín elected President
1948	Dr. Carlos Prío Socarrás elected President
March 10, 1952	Batista took over government, becoming dictator for the second time
July 26, 1953	Fidel Castro and allies failed attack in Santiago
May 15, 1955	Castro released early from prison
December 2, 1956	Castro and eighty followers landed in Oriente
December 31, 1958	Batista and closest allies left Cuba
January 1, 1959	The Castro family became permanent dictators of Cuba

Bibliography

Books on the Louisiana Purchase

Adams, Henry. *History of the United States of America during the Administrations of Thomas Jefferson.* New York: The Library of America, 1986.

De Conde, Alexander. *This Affair of Louisiana.* New York: Charles Scribner's, 1976.

Duke, Marc. *The du Ponts: Portrait of a Dynasty.* Saturday Review Press, 1976.

Gaines, Ann Graham. *The Louisiana Purchase in American History.* Berkeley Heights, NJ: Enslow Publishers, 2000.

Gold, Susan Dudley. *Land Pacts.* New York: Twenty-First Century Books, 1997.

Michael P. Malone, Richard B. Roeder, and William L. Lang. *Montana – A History of Two Centuries.* Seattle: University of Washington Press, 1991.

Books on the Florida Purchase and Manifest Destiny

Gannon, Michael, ed. *The New History of Florida.* Gainesville: University Press of Florida, 1996.

McMichael, Francis Andrew. *Reluctant Revolutionaries: The West Florida Border-lands, 1785-1810.* Unpublished Ph.D. diss., Vanderbilt University, Nashville, TN, 2000.

Russell, Francis. *The American Heritage History of the Making of the Nation.* New York: American Heritage, 1968.

Books on the U.S.-Mexican War

Cantor, Carrie Nichols. *The Mexican War: How the United States Gained Its Western Lands.* Chanhassen, NM: The Child's World, 2003.

Leckie, Robert. *From Sea to Shining Sea: From the War of 1812 to the Mexican War, the Saga of America's Expansion.* New York: HarperCollins Publishers, 1993.

Long, Jeffery. *Duel of Eagles: The Mexican and U.S. Fight for the Alamo.* New York: William Morrow, 1990.

Books on the Alaska Purchase

Fremon, David K. *The Alaska Purchase in American History.* Berkeley Heights, NJ: Enslow Publishers, 1999.

Naske, Claus M., and Herman E. Slotnik. *Alaska: A History of the 49th State.* Norman: The University of Oklahoma Press, 1987.

Sherwood, Morgan B., ed. *Alaska and Its History.* Seattle: University of Washington Press, 1967.

Wheeler, Keith, ed. *The Alaskans.* Alexandria, VA: Time-Life Books, 1977.

Books on the Annexation of Hawaii and Expansionism

Beale, Howard K. *Theodore Roosevelt and the Rise of America to World Power.* Paperback ed. New York, NY: Collier Books, 1962.

Beisner, Robert L. *Twelve against Empire: The Anti-Imperialists, 1898-1900.* New York: McGraw-Hill Book Company, 1968.

Brands, H. W., ed. *The Selected Letters of Theodore Roosevelt.* New York, NY: Cooper Square Press, 2001.

Graves, William. *Hawaii.* Washington, DC: National Geographic Society, 1970.

Herring, George C. *From Colony to Superpower: U.S. Foreign Relations Since 1776.* New York: Oxford University Press, 2008.

Meining, D.W. *The Shaping of America.* Vol. 3. New Heaven, CT: Yale University Press, 1998.

Musicant, Ivan. *Empire by Default.* New York, NY: Henry Holt, 1998.

Okihiro, Gary Y. *Island World: A History of Hawaii and the United States.* Berkeley: The University of California Press, 2008.

Pringle, Henry F. *Theodore Roosevelt.* New York, NY: Harcourt, 1931.

Sforza, Teri. *Hawaii's Annexation, a Story of Betrayal.* Santa Ana, CA: The Orange County Register, November 9, 1996.

Times Editions. Hawaii, Les Editions du Pacifique, Singapore, 1986.

Books on the History of Spain and Spanish America

Carr, Raymond, ed. *Spain: A History.* Oxford: Oxford University Press, 2000.

Esdaile, Charles J. *Spain in the Liberal Age: From Constitution to Civil War, 1808-1939.* Oxford: Blackwell Publishers, 2000.

Harvey, Robert. *Liberators: Latin America's Struggle for Independence.* New York: The Overlook Press, 2000.

Lynch, John. *The Spanish American Revolutions, 1808-1826.* New York: W. W. Norton, 1973.

Pierson, Peter. *The History of Spain.* Westport, CT: Greenwood Press, 1999.

Scheina, Robert L. *Latin America's Wars, Volume 1: The Age of the Caudillo, 1791-1899.* Washington, DC: Brassey's, 2003.

Books on Cuban Wars of Independence

Barquín, Coronel Ramón M. *Las Luchas Guerrilleras en Cuba de la Colonia a la Sierra Maestra.* Vols. 1 and 2. Madrid: Editorial Playor, 1975.

Foner, Philip S. *A History of Cuba and its Relations with the United States.* Vols. I and II. New York: International Publishers, 1962.

Gómez, Juan Gualberto. *Por Cuba Libre* [For a Free Cuba]. Municipio de La Habana: Oficina del Historiador de la Ciudad, 1954.

Gott, Richard. *Cuba A New History.* New Haven, CT: Yale University Press, 2004.

Suchlicki, Jaime. *Cuba from Columbus to Castro.* Washington, DC: Brassey's (US), 1990.

Thomas, Hugh. *Cuba, or, the Pursuit of Freedom.* New York: Da Capo Press, 1998.

Books on the Cuban-Spanish-American War, the Military Occupation of Cuba and Cuban History Beyond 1902

Atkins, John Black. *The War in Cuba, The Experiences of an Englishman with the United States Army*. London: Smith, Elder, 1899.

Chadwick, French E. *The Relations of the United States and Spain, The Spanish American War*. Vols. 1 and 2. New York: Charles Scribner's, 1911.

Cosmas, Graham A. *An Army for Empire: The United States Army in the Spanish-American War*. College Station: Texas A&M University Press, 1994.

Foner, Philip Sheldon. *The Spanish-Cuban-American War and the Birth of American Imperialism, v. II, 1895-1902*. New York: Monthly Review Press, 1972.

Hagedorn, Hermann. *Leonard Wood*. Vols. 1 and 2. New York: Harper & Brothers, 1931.

Healy, David F. *The United States in Cuba 1898-1902*. Madison: The University of Wisconsin Press, 1963.

Millis, Walter. *The Martial Spirit, A Study of Our War with Spain*. Cambridge, MA: The Riverside Press, 1931.

Morgan, H. Wayne. *William McKinley and his America*. Syracuse, NY: Syracuse University Press, 1963.

Morris, Edmund. *Theodore Rex*. New York: Random House, 2001.

Pérez, Louis A., Jr. *Cuba and the United States: Ties of Singular Intimacy*. Athens: The University of Georgia Press, 1990.

_____. *Cuba under the Platt Amendment, 1902-1934*. Pittsburgh, PA: University of Pittsburgh Press, 1986.

_____. *The War of 1898: The United States and Cuba in History and Historiography*. Chapel Hill: The University of North Carolina Press, 1998.

Rickover, Hyman G. *How the Battleship Maine was Destroyed*. Washington, DC: Department of the Navy, Naval History Division, 1976.

Rosenfeld, Harvey. *Diary of a Dirty Little War: The Spanish-American War of 1898*. Westport, CT: Praeger Publishers, 2000.

Suchlicki, Jaime. *Cuba from Columbus to Castro*. New York: Brassy's (US), 1990.

Tebbel, John. *America's Great Patriotic War with Spain: Mixed Motives, Lies and Racism in Cuba and the Philippines, 1898-1915*. Manchester Center, VT: Marshall Jones, 1996.

Traxel, David. *1898, The Birth of the American Century*. New York: Alfred A. Knopf, 1998.

White, Trumbull. *United States in War with Spain and the History of Cuba*. Chicago, IL: International Publishing, 1898.

Index